IMAGES
of America

GENOA AND KINGSTON

I0900943

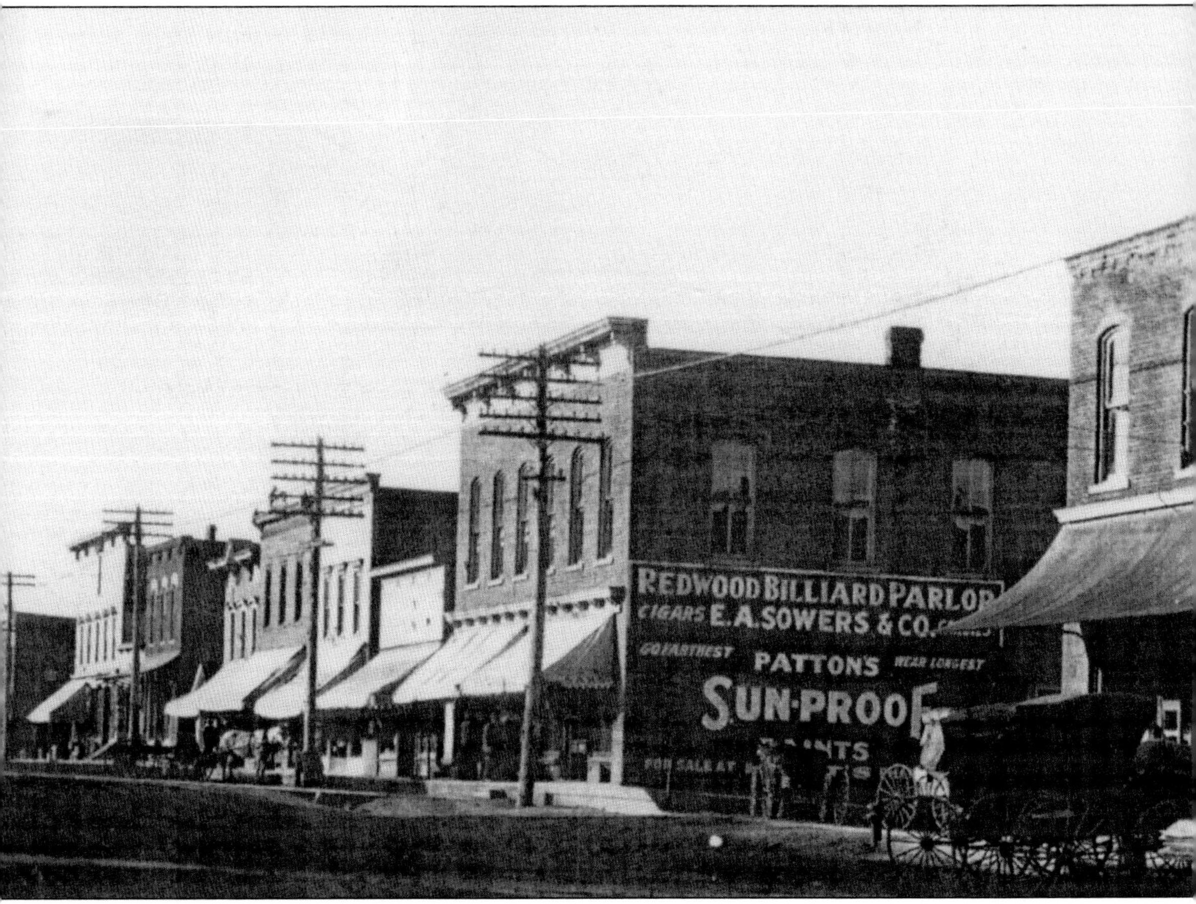

Horse-drawn buggies wait outside the different shops and businesses along Main Street in Genoa in 1906. The Crawford Building at 301 West Main Street once housed a first-class restaurant that served oysters in season. Billiard tables were added in 1903. Tobinson's Hardware moved to the building in 1974. Today Tobinson's Ace Hardware is located at 361 Sycamore Road in Genoa.

On the Cover: Genoa gentlemen gather at the Eureka Hotel at 240 West Main Street. Dr. A. M. Hill, standing, chats with car passengers Will Snow and "Sunny" Jim O'Brien, while Charles Saul leans on the hood. Hill, born in 1845, served in the Union Army during the Civil War in 1865. He was a local surgeon for the I. C. Railway and served two terms as Genoa's mayor.

IMAGES
of America

GENOA AND KINGSTON

Denise Moran

ARCADIA
PUBLISHING

Copyright © 2010 by Denise Moran
ISBN 978-0-7385-8447-8

Published by Arcadia Publishing
Charleston SC, Chicago IL, Portsmouth NH, San Francisco CA

Printed in the United States of America

Library of Congress Control Number: 2010921319

For all general information contact Arcadia Publishing at:
Telephone 843-853-2070
Fax 843-853-0044
E-mail sales@arcadiapublishing.com
For customer service and orders:
Toll-Free 1-888-313-2665

Visit us on the Internet at www.arcadiapublishing.com

To my husband, Brian; my sons, Erik and Sean; and my family members, Deborah, Dan, Rita, Dawn, Jim, nieces and nephews, and especially Gene and Flo.

Contents

ACKNOWLEDGMENTS

I would like to acknowledge the City of Genoa, the Village of Kingston, Joiner Room at the Sycamore Library, the Genoa Public Library, Genoa-Kingston High School, the Genoa Veterans Home, the Ellwood House Association, Genoa resident Marilyn Greenawalt, Molly Holbrook of Derby Line Farm in Genoa, the many business owners in Genoa and Kingston, Natural Resource Center at Russell Woods, the DeKalb County Forest Preserve, and especially the Kishwaukee Valley Heritage Society Museum for their help with this book. The majority of the photographs came from the Kishwaukee Valley Heritage Society Museum and are provided courtesy of them unless otherwise noted. While the different organizations mentioned above were sources for the images, the captions were written by the author of this book.

I am grateful to Kishwaukee Valley Heritage Society Museum president John Lyon, vice president Orrin Merritt III, Sandy Lyon, Bonnie Justis, and other museum volunteers for their time and effort in providing both the images I needed and the answers to my questions. I thank Don Billington, principal of Genoa-Kingston High School, for allowing me to look through the school's yearbooks. I appreciate Mim Evans, Gordon Jones, and David Glaum of Genoa Main Street, Inc. and Genoa couple Roger and JoAnn Watson for sharing their knowledge of Genoa. Roger was one of the founders of the museum, and JoAnn once served as the museum president. JoAnn also has served as an alderwoman on the Genoa City Council.

In addition, I would also like to extend my gratitude to DeKalb County historian Phyllis Kelley and Huntley Area Public Library local history coordinator Nancy Bacheller. They are both authors for Arcadia Publishing's Images of America series. Phyllis wrote a book about Sycamore, while Nancy wrote a book about Huntley. Their books inspired me to write this book about Genoa and Kingston.

Lastly, I want to thank my family and friends for their support. They were always ready to listen or offer a word of encouragement whenever one was needed.

INTRODUCTION

In 1949, some 13 country schools in rural northern Illinois were consolidated into Community Unit School District No. 424. These schools were started in the late 1800s and early 1900s and were known as Genoa School, Derby Line School, New Lebanon School, Hickory Grove School, Ney School, South Riley School, Genoa Center School, Olmstead School, North Kingston School, Arbuckle School, Oak Glen School, Henrietta School, and Pleasant Hill School.

Today the Genoa-Kingston area is known as the "Home of the Cogs." The acronym COGS comes from the phrase "Community of Genoa Schools." A cog is defined as "one of a series of teeth, as on the rim of a wheel or gear, whose engagement transmits successive motive force to a corresponding wheel or gear." The Genoa-Kingston High School Cogs mascot evokes a feeling of teamwork.

The high school's motto is "Small town school, big time pride." This motto can also be applied to the city of Genoa and the village of Kingston. These two communities have always displayed pride in the growth and achievements they have earned since being founded during the 1830s.

While there is little to no variation on how to pronounce Kingston, local residents would never pronounce Genoa in the same way that they would state the name of the Italian city. On Senior Skip Day in 1943, a group of Genoa Township High School seniors traveled to Chicago to attend the *Don McNeil Breakfast Club* radio show at the Merchandise Mart. One high school student said, "Everyone sat in terror as Don McNeil passed through the crowd with that menacing little microphone. McNeil pronounced the name of our school as it would be pronounced in Italy, which was most annoying to some of the seniors."

One of Genoa's most colorful characters was Ebenezer P. Gleason. According to the *History of DeKalb County, Illinois*, written by Henry L. Boies in 1868, Gleason was "a man of fine appearance, agreeable manners, fair in his dealing with his neighbors, and generally liked." He improved his community's landscape by planting a row of maples along Main Street in 1838 that were considered "a conspicuous ornament of the village."

Gleason "never passed bad money in his ordinary business transactions but had it manufactured and wholesaled it to his confederates." Deputies were commissioned to arrest Gleason. They reached his home at midnight and waited until dawn before Gleason showed up. While they were prepared to arrest him right away, Gleason insisted that they should first have breakfast in his home. Gleason took the deputies "into his garden to show them his fine crop of corn, of which he was justly proud. In an instant, he had disappeared in the tall corn, and for several years was not seen in this country."

When the evidence against him became unattainable, Gleason returned to Genoa. He owned and operated a store, a sawmill, and a farm. He also decided to marry a "respectable young woman of the neighborhood." A few years later, Gleason became ill. A traveling doctor named Smitch, who was a boarder in the Gleason home, became Gleason's physician. Gleason "grew worse without any evident cause. After eating one day of some porridge, prepared by his wife and the doctor, he complained that it did not taste quite right, but ate heartily, and soon after died in convulsions and delirium."

The doctor and Gleason's widow were arrested on a charge of murder by poison. Gleason's body was exhumed and the contents of his stomach were examined. Since there was not enough evidence to convict them, the doctor and the widow were released. The couple married soon after the trial and moved to La Salle County. The doctor "died under circumstances that led to the suspicion that he, too, had been poisoned. His wife soon after died very suddenly." Boies concluded that Gleason "escaped the punishment of his crimes against the law only to meet a more terrible fate."

While Dr. Smitch was a physician of questionable character, Dr. J. H. Fellows of Kingston was a doctor who was well respected in his community. He was born in 1851 in Jamestown, New York, and moved with his family to Boone County, Illinois, when he was still a child. He graduated from Chicago Medical College on March 5, 1878. In that same year, he married Florence Palmer of McHenry County. The couple had one daughter. A few years after his first wife died, Fellows married Kingston resident Allie Taylor.

One of the doctor's medical bills from that time showed how much patients paid for his services. From February 12 to March 14, 1879, Fellows paid 17 visits to a patient who had suffered a bullet wound through one of his lungs, charging $1.50 per visit. Fellows charged $5 for the last visit, when he finally extracted the bullet from the man's back.

Fellows died at the age of 37 in 1888. The cause of death was listed as "abscess and inflammation of the bowels." Funeral services at the Methodist Church drew an estimated crowd of 1,000 mourners. More than 70 carriages formed a procession to the cemetery. The doctor was a member of the Freemasons, and delegations of Masons came to his funeral from Belvidere, Hampshire, Genoa, Kirkland, Fielding, and Monroe. According to the obituary, "The streets were literally filled with people and vehicles. It is safe to say that never before were as many congregated at one time in that village. Only a portion could gain a seat in the church, but the day was pleasant and those outside suffered no discomfort."

The residents of Genoa and Kingston support each other through good times and bad. A variety of clubs and organizations have offered residents a chance to form friendships and help others. Chapter BG of the PEO Sisterhood was organized in Genoa in 1920. It was responsible for starting a library in the city in 1922, and members served as librarians for three-month periods. They also raised funds for the library through bake sales, card parties, roasted peanut sales, and rummage sales.

The Genoa Community Woman's Club was started in 1947 and has helped the local Girl Scout troop and given scholarships to area students. In 1954, the club participated in the national campaign known as Operation Santa Claus, to collect and send clothing to Korea. The Genoa club's president received a citation from the Korean ambassador for the club's efforts.

One

Founding Fathers

Traces of the settlers who came to the northern Illinois area during the 1830s can still be found in Genoa and Kingston. Wagon ruts from the stagecoaches are still visible. The natural spring where stagecoach drivers once watered their horses is still flowing. The Kishwaukee River often thwarted man's efforts to span it. When the river flooded and went around the original bridge, determined residents built a new one. During the Depression, the river overflowed again and rendered the second bridge useless. The remnants of the sister bridges offer testament that man cannot always beat Mother Nature. A number of descendants of the early settlers still call Genoa and Kingston home. Genoa resident Bonnie Justis can trace her ancestry to Jonathan Fairbanks Moore, the grandson of Genoa's first settler, Thomas Matteson. Genoa library clerk Jim Kline works in the building that was once run by his grandfather Bill Cooper as a furniture store and undertaking business. There have been three generations bearing the name of Orrin Merritt in Genoa. Orrin Merritt III once taught biology at Genoa-Kingston High School. He is now the vice president of the Kishwaukee Valley Heritage Society Museum.

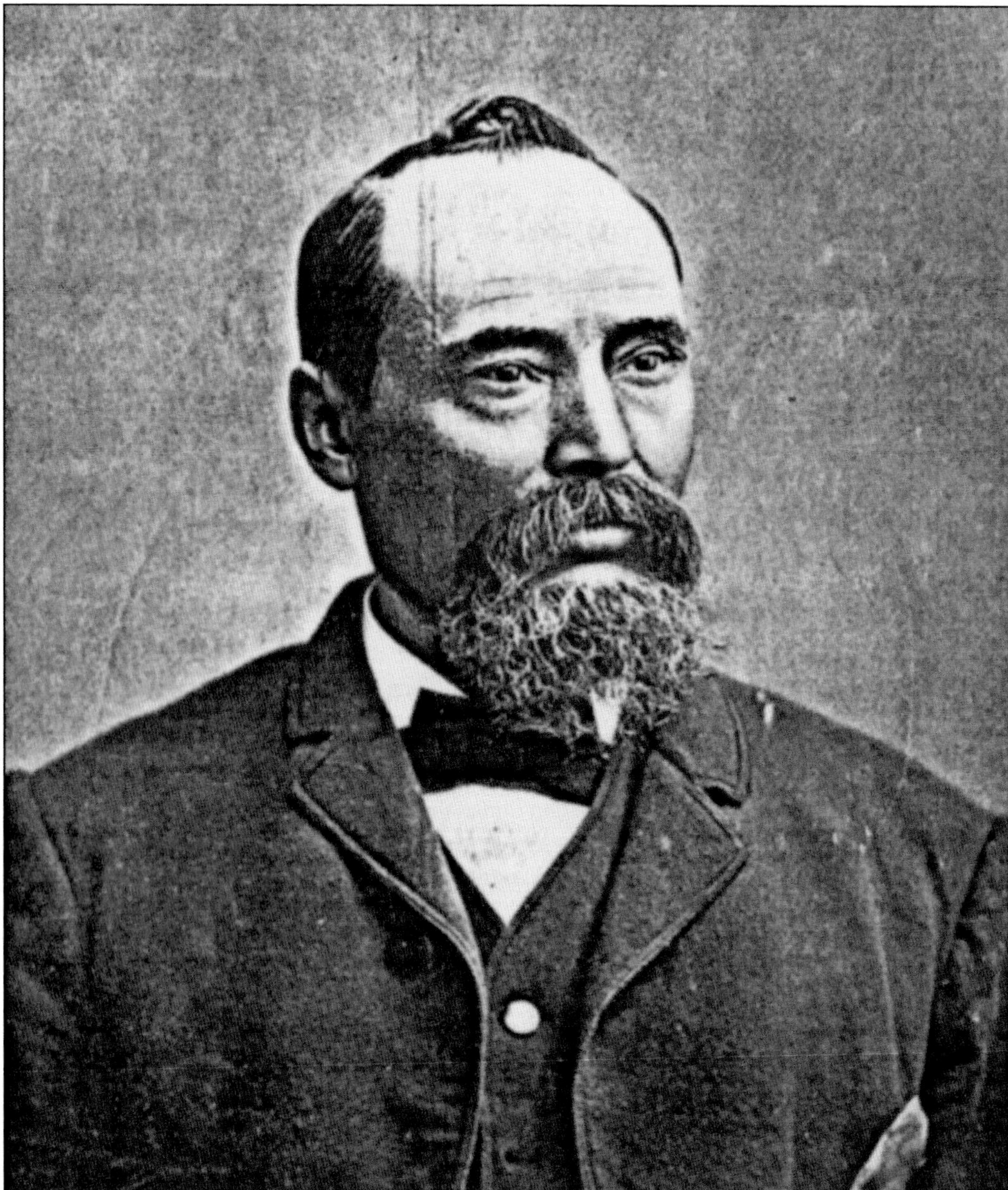

The first settlers of what is now Genoa arrived in three covered wagons from Ohio on May 18, 1835. Thomas and Sally (Sarah) Matteson arrived with their five children: William Perry, Celestia, Esther Susan, Thomas III, and Sylvia, who was married to Voranus Emory Moore. The Moores came with their daughter Clarissa. Their second child, James Harrington Moore (pictured), was the first white child born in Genoa, on December 29, 1835. Thomas named Genoa after a town in the state of New York where he had once lived, since he learned that two other northern Illinois settlements, Geneva and Batavia, had been named after towns in New York. The settlers lived in and around the covered wagons until they built a double log house to accommodate both families. Thomas, his wife, and some of their children left Genoa after only a few years and moved to Nacogdoches County, Texas. Thomas, born on August 24, 1789, died on December 8, 1841, shortly after he arrived in Texas. (Courtesy of Bonnie Justis.)

Jonathan Fairbanks Moore was a son of Voranus Emory and Sylvia (Matteson) Moore. He was also a grandson of Genoa's first settler, Thomas Matteson, and a brother to James Harrington Moore. Jonathan was born on September 12, 1840. Jonathan and Elizabeth Fothergill (pictured) were married in 1875. One of their daughters, Sylvia Mary, married Edwin Listy in 1907. Sylvia Mary was the grandmother of Genoa resident Bonnie (Justis). (Courtesy of Bonnie Justis.)

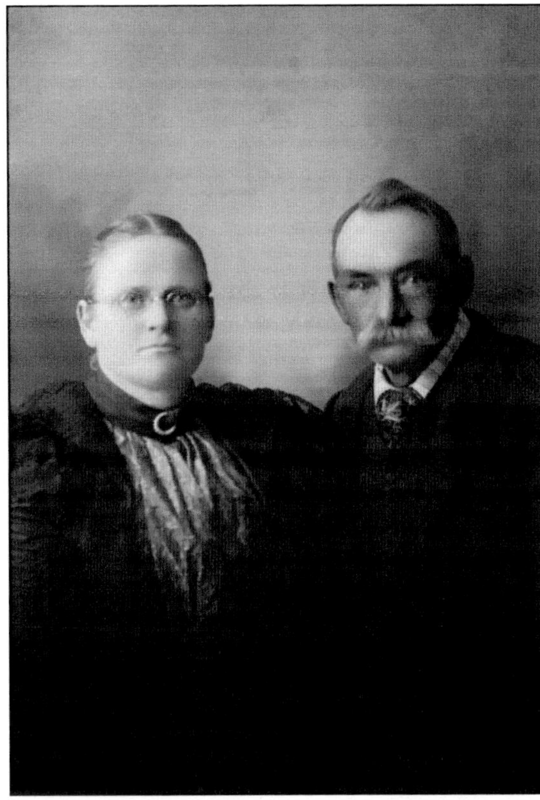

Voranus Emory Moore built a farm on his claim in the late 1830s at the northeast corner of Sycamore Street and Walnut Road. His son, James Harrington Moore, said they raised cows, sheep, hogs, geese, and chickens. James also said they enjoyed his mother's full cream sage cheese. Ben Awe and his family later owned the farm.

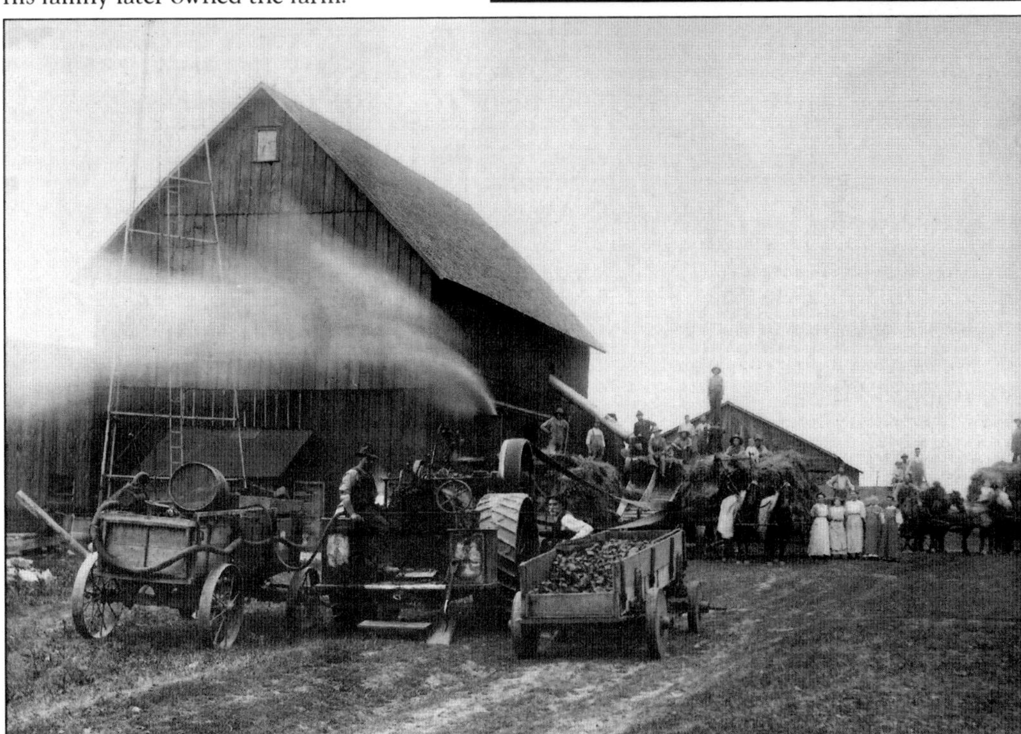

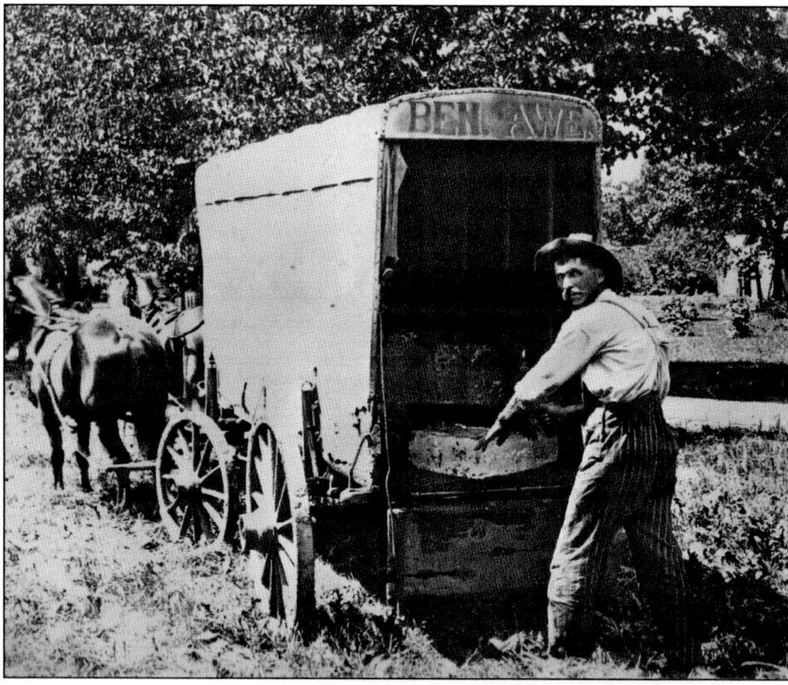

In addition to running a farm, Genoa resident Ben Awe owned and operated three icehouses during the early 1900s. He is shown here preparing to deliver ice from the back of his horse-drawn wagon. Ice was harvested from the Kishwaukee River during the winter and stored in icehouses. Awe would wrestle anyone who challenged him, and he seldom lost a fight.

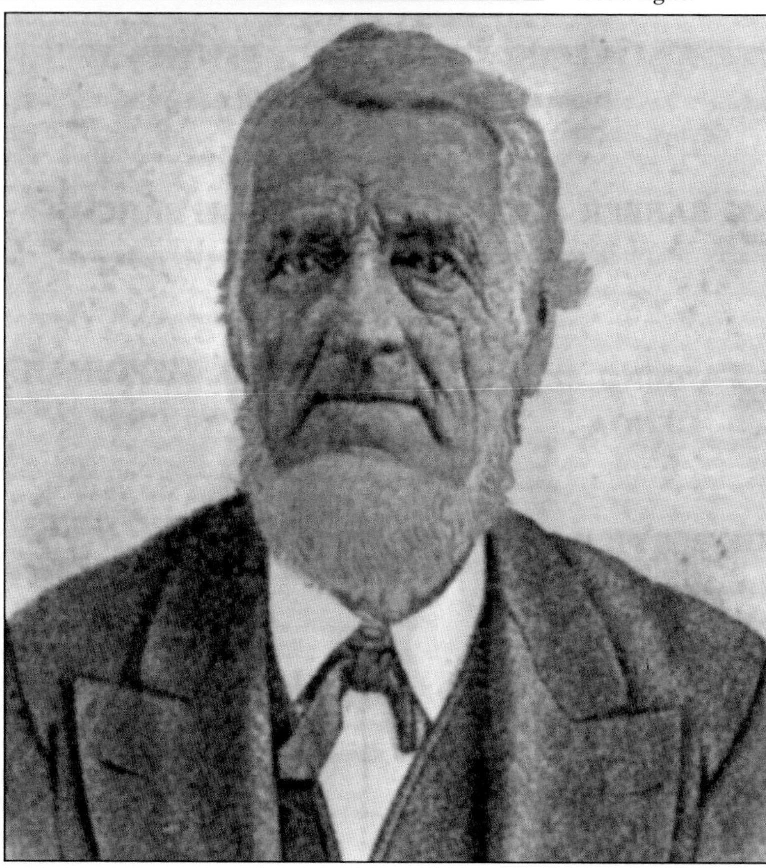

Horatio N. Perkins (pictured), Samuel Corey, Henry Durham, and Thomas Monahan bought out Thomas Matteson's claim in 1837. Perkins moved into Matteson's log cabin, raised it another story, and used it as a hotel and stagecoach stop. He later built the Pacific Hotel on the site in 1843. The hotel was used for balls, parties, and many other notable events.

Hardware store owner Henry Perkins (left) and Dr. A. M. Hill chat inside the store at 313 West Main Street in Genoa during the late 1800s. The store sold hardware, tinware, building materials, stoves, and ranges. Employees also installed furnaces and heating equipment. Perkins gave permission for the Independent Order of Odd Fellows Lodge No. 768 to add a second story above the hardware store for their meeting hall.

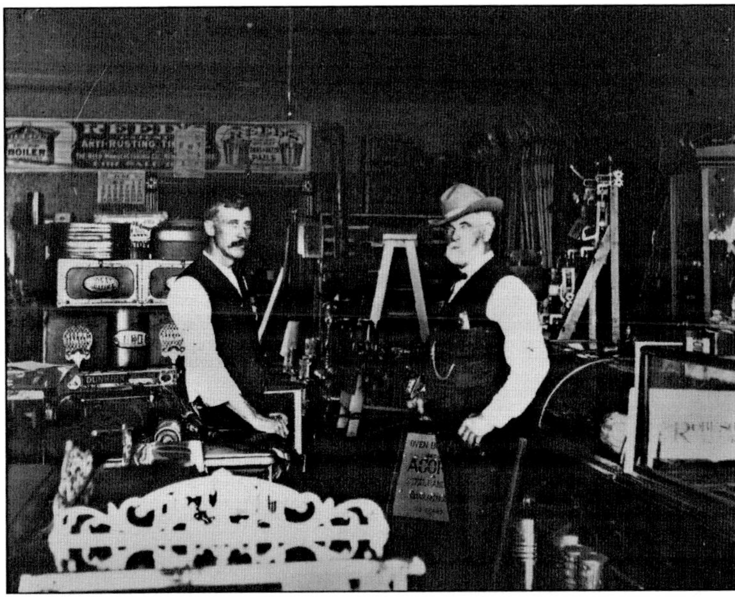

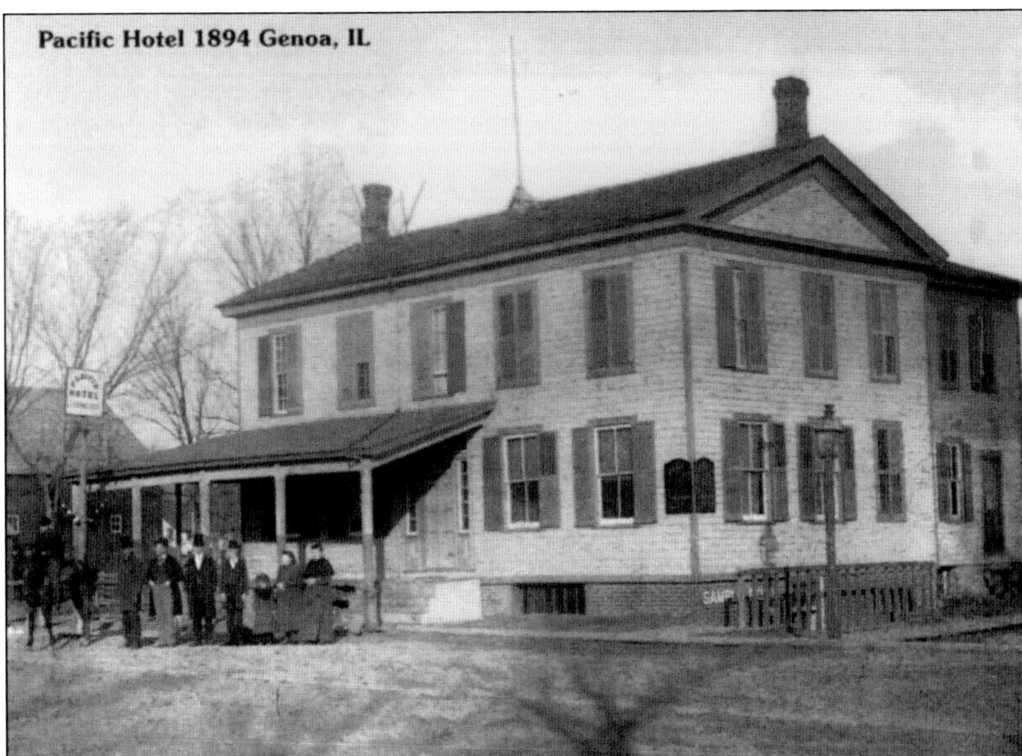

The Pacific Hotel, built in 1843, is Genoa's oldest building. It is located along what was once the stagecoach route that ran from Chicago to Galena. Horatio N. Perkins, Genoa's first mayor, ran the hotel from 1843 to 1854, long before his death in 1888 at age 79. The Pacific Hotel building, which once hosted grand balls, today houses the Illinois Community Credit Union.

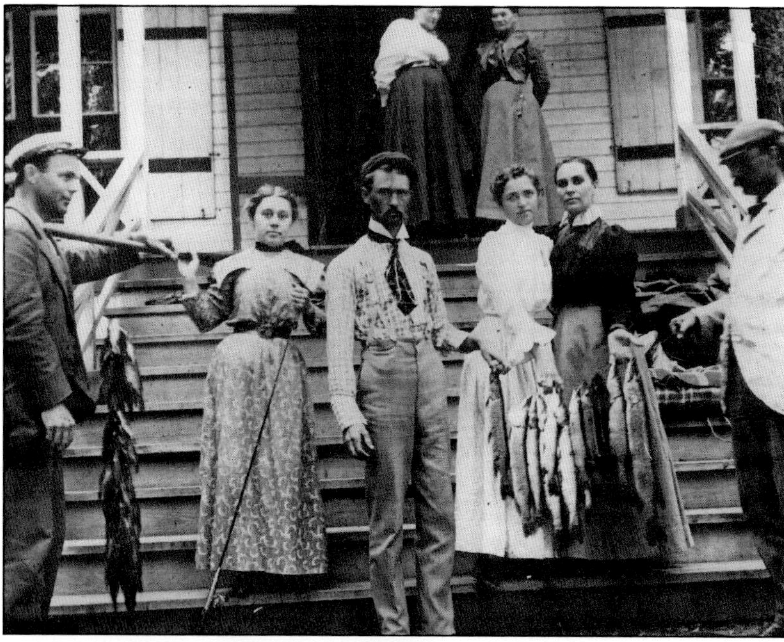

Mrs. George DePue and Lizzie Slater Hoffman stand in the front doorway of the Pacific Hotel. George and Gertrude Sisley (left) stand on the porch next to four hotel visitors and display fish caught from the Kishwaukee River. Fish were once plentiful in the region and often stored in barrels for future use.

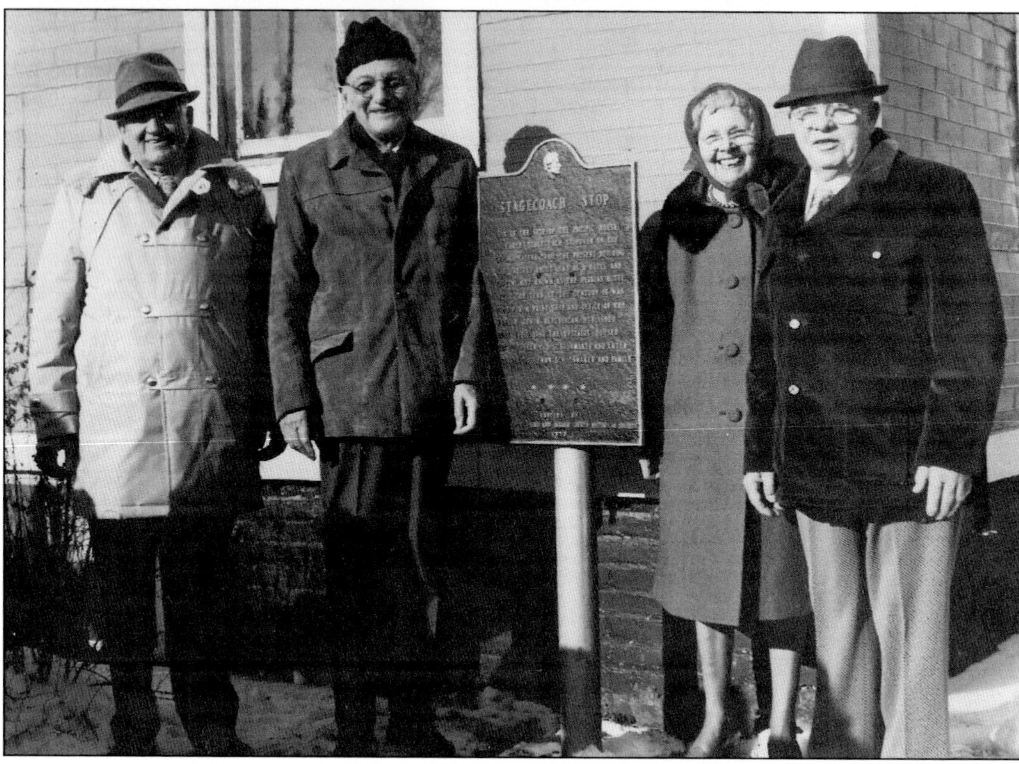

From left to right, Robert Hoover (founder of the Kishwaukee Valley Heritage Society Museum), Charles Hunt, and Anita and Charles Schoonmaker stand by the plaque erected in 1972 to dedicate the Pacific Hotel in Genoa. The plaque was erected by the DeKalb County Board and the DeKalb County Historical Society to honor the site as an early stagecoach stopover on the Chicago-Galena Trail.

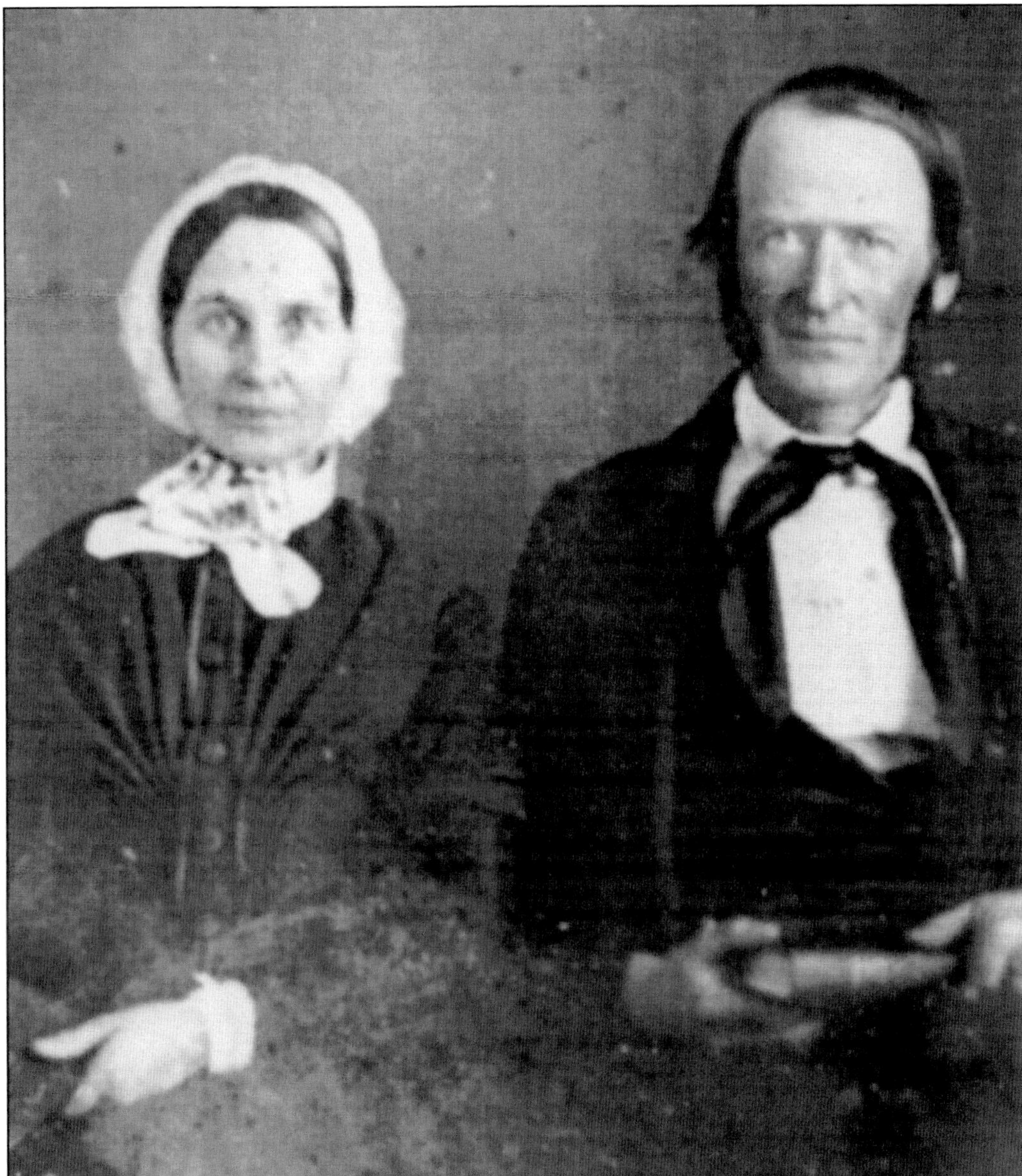

William and Patience (Allen) Miller, pictured here, were married in 1835 and owned a farm in Kingston. They had two children, William and Harriet, and were among the first settlers of DeKalb County. Isaac Ellwood worked on the Miller farm in Kingston in 1855 and married Harriet in 1859. The newlyweds moved to DeKalb, where Isaac purchased a half-interest in DeKalb farmer Joseph Glidden's patent for a new invention called barbed wire. The two men established the world's first barbed wire factory. The Ellwoods had a mansion built at 509 North First Street in DeKalb. Today the mansion is open to the public and operated by the non-profit Ellwood House Association in conjunction with the DeKalb Park District. When the Miller family decided they wanted a frame farmhouse instead of a log cabin, they did not demolish the cabin and instead built their farmhouse around it. In 2009, the farmhouse walls were torn down while the cabin within was dismantled. The cabin will be moved to a site near Russell Woods in Genoa. (Courtesy of the Ellwood House Association.)

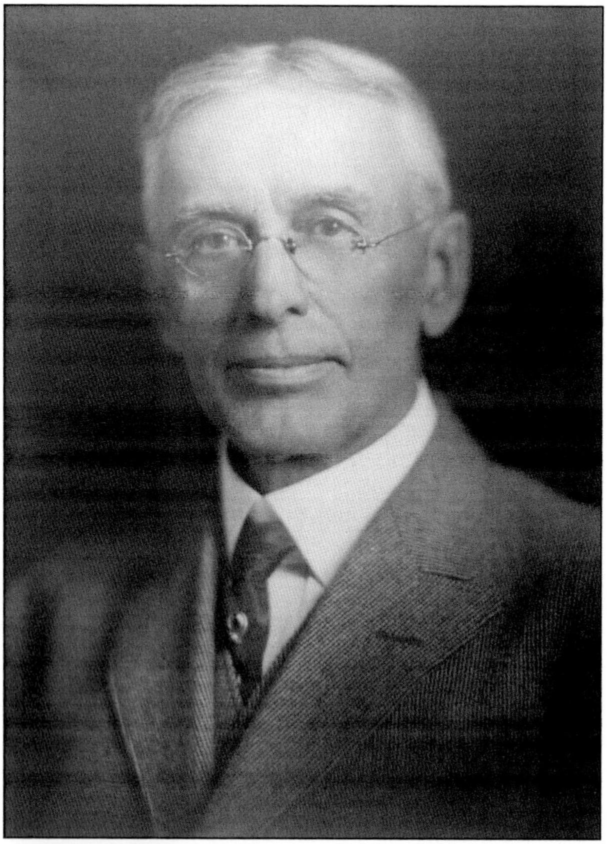

In 1912, the DeKalb County Soil Improvement Association was created. An executive committee included Genoa residents Dillon Brown (president, pictured), Henry Parke, and C. D. Schoonmaker. In 1926, the association became the DeKalb County Farm Bureau. DeKalb was the first county in the United States to establish a formal farm organization to carry local responsibility for extension work in agriculture.

Brothers Lyman and James Stuart platted the village of Kingston in 1876. Lyman was a lumberyard owner and grain buyer. One of his customers was Charles A. Pillsbury and Company. James owned a grocery outlet, steam sawmill, planning mill, and feed mill. The brothers built brick homes that are still standing. Lyman's home (pictured) is located at 300 South Main Street.

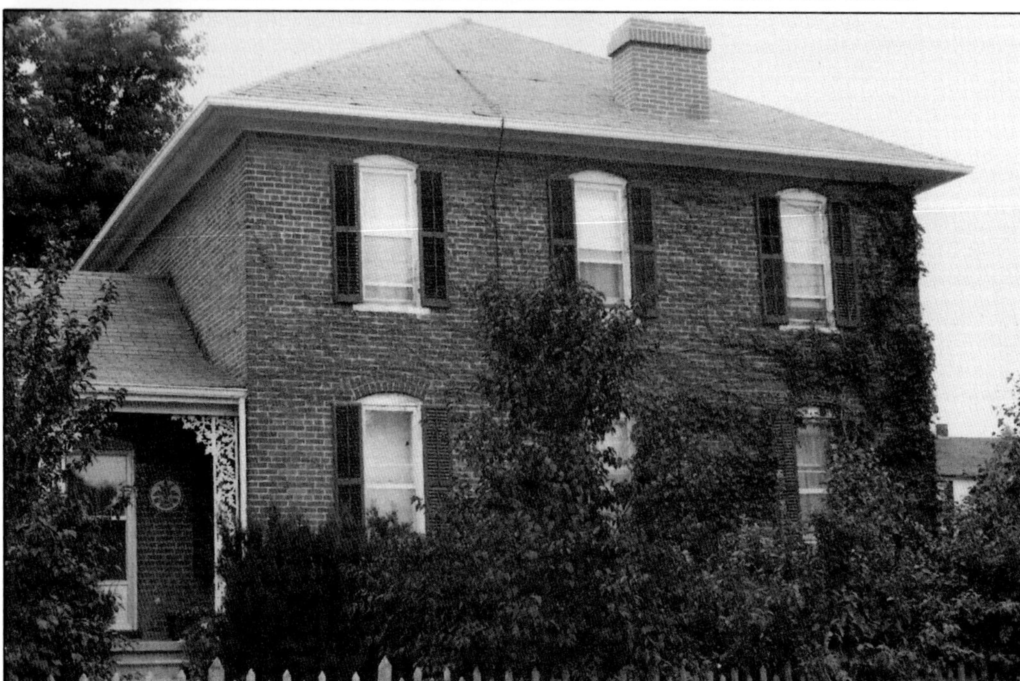

Two

Iron Horses and Horseless Carriages

The train and the automobile were once respectively called the "iron horse" and the "horseless carriage." These nicknames are a nod of acknowledgment to the mode of transportation they replaced. Horses were invaluable to the settlers of Genoa and Kingston. They pulled plows and wagons on the farm, as well as buggies so farmers could travel into town and buy supplies. Horses were often stolen during pioneer days. James Harrington Moore, Thomas Matteson's grandson, noted, "In running down the band of horse thieves in Genoa in the early days, Mr. Furness, Jerry Madison, and Mr. Riley assisted and were at the hanging of the rascals." In another account, Moore recalled a horse thief pursuit in Genoa. He said that the thief "gave them the slip at the edge of Pigeon Woods. The two lead horses were deserted by the thief and brought back to Genoa by the posse. The horses were kept in B. J. Brown's barn under guard until the owners came for them from LaSalle." The Genoa Horse Thief Detective Club was organized around 1854. The club drafted its constitution and bylaws on February 20, 1875, and lasted into the early 1900s.

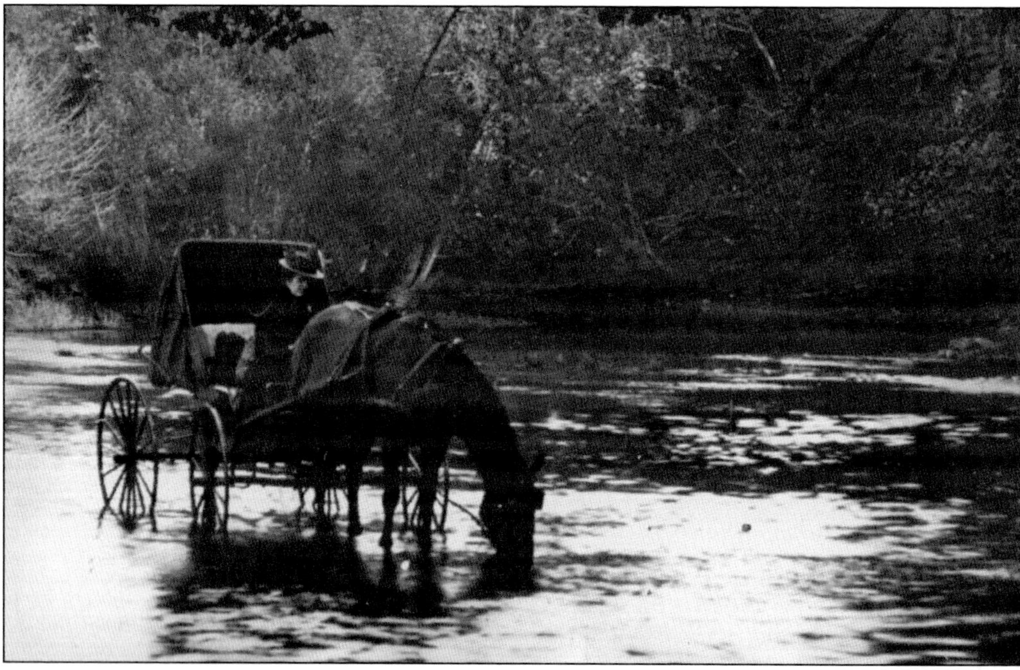

In this *c.* 1900 photograph, a bookseller from Aurora (above) relaxes while her horse takes a drink from the Kishwaukee River west of Genoa. She is driving a rig rented from W. W. Cooper Livery and Hitch Barn on South Emmett Street in Genoa. Native Americans once traveled by canoe along the Kishwaukee River. The name *Kishwaukee* comes from the Potawatomi word that means "river of the sycamore." The Potawatomi used sycamore trees for making dugout canoes. People today enjoy spending time by the river. A bridge across the street from the Natural Resource Center in Russell Woods in Genoa (below) spans the "Mighty Kish" and allows visitors the chance to explore both sides of the river.

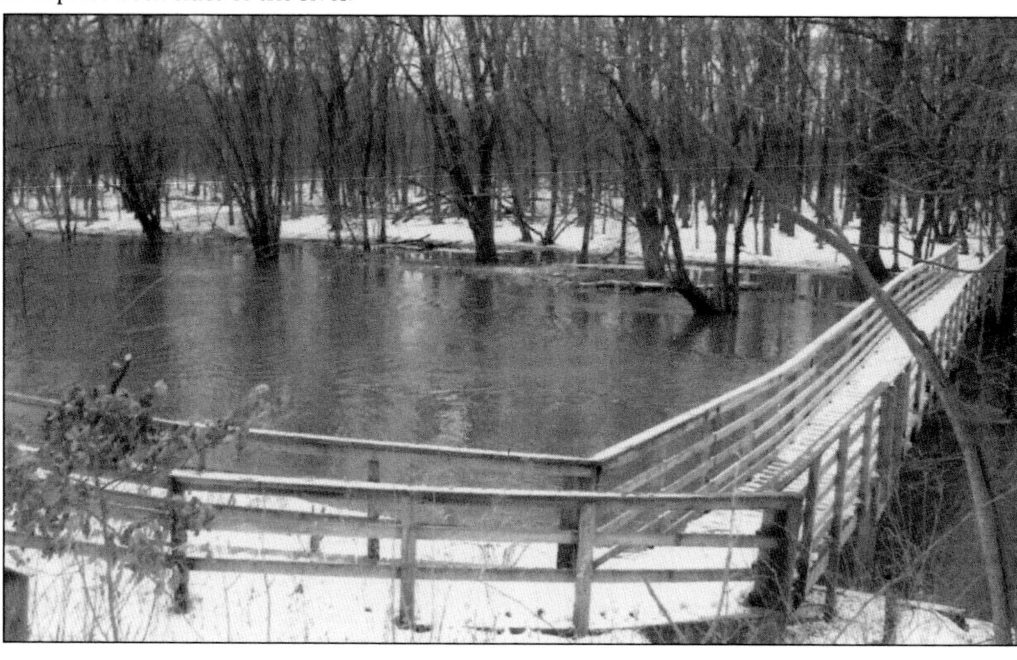

Genoa police chief Bill Heed drives the meat market delivery cart on Main Street in Genoa around 1900. The meat is stored in the wooden box in front of him to keep it safe from flies and dust rising from the dirt roads. Customers could order their meat fresh, salted, smoked, or pickled.

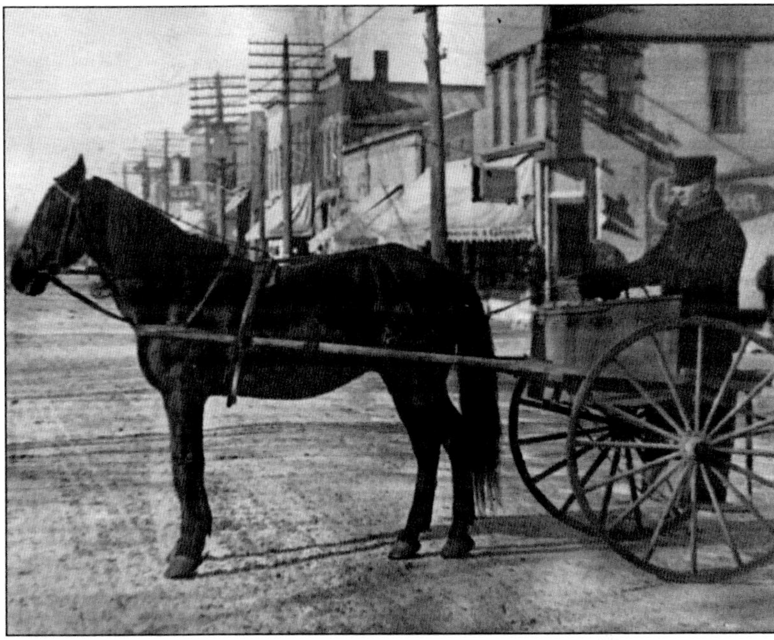

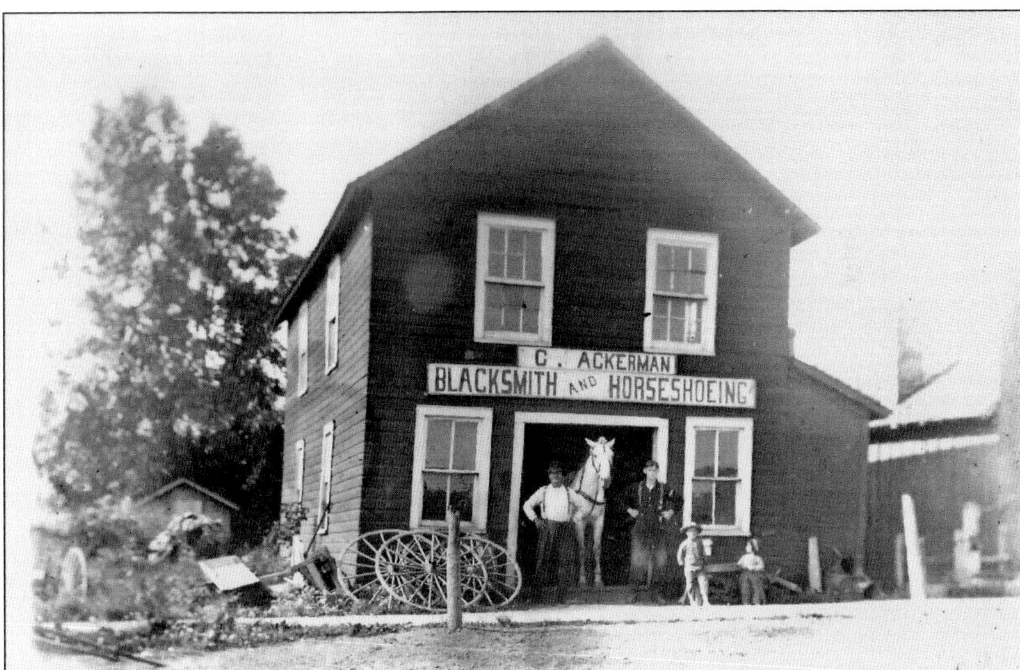

C. Ackerman was one of the many blacksmiths who set up shop in the Genoa area. The first blacksmith in Genoa Township was Joseph Maltby, who died in 1855. Other local blacksmith shops were Hoag, William Schmidt and Son, James A. Risdon, Frank Tischler, John Downing, and Corson Blacksmithing. The Corson blacksmithing building was torn down in 1922.

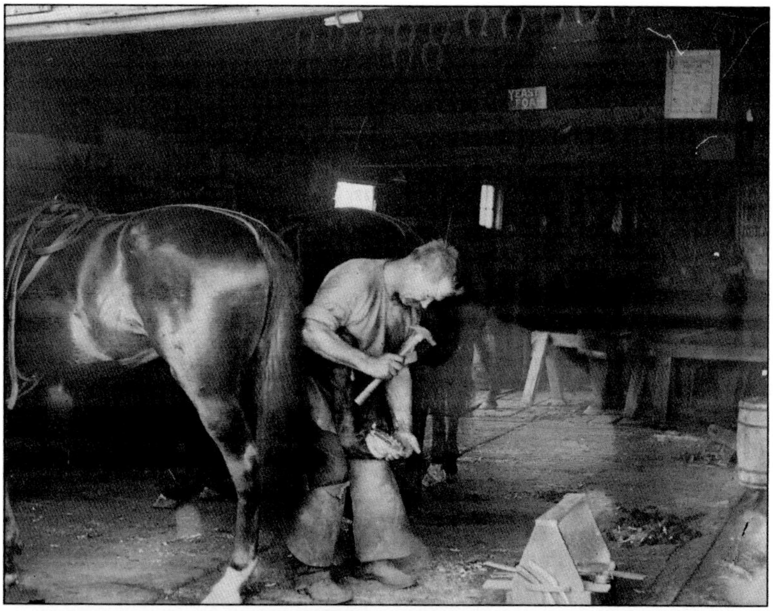

Seen here around 1900, John Downing shoes Dr. T. N. Austin's team of horses at Downing's Blacksmith in Genoa. Dr. Austin once had an accident in his Ford Coupe, turning the car over and injuring his shoulder. He gave the car to his brother and went back to traveling by horse.

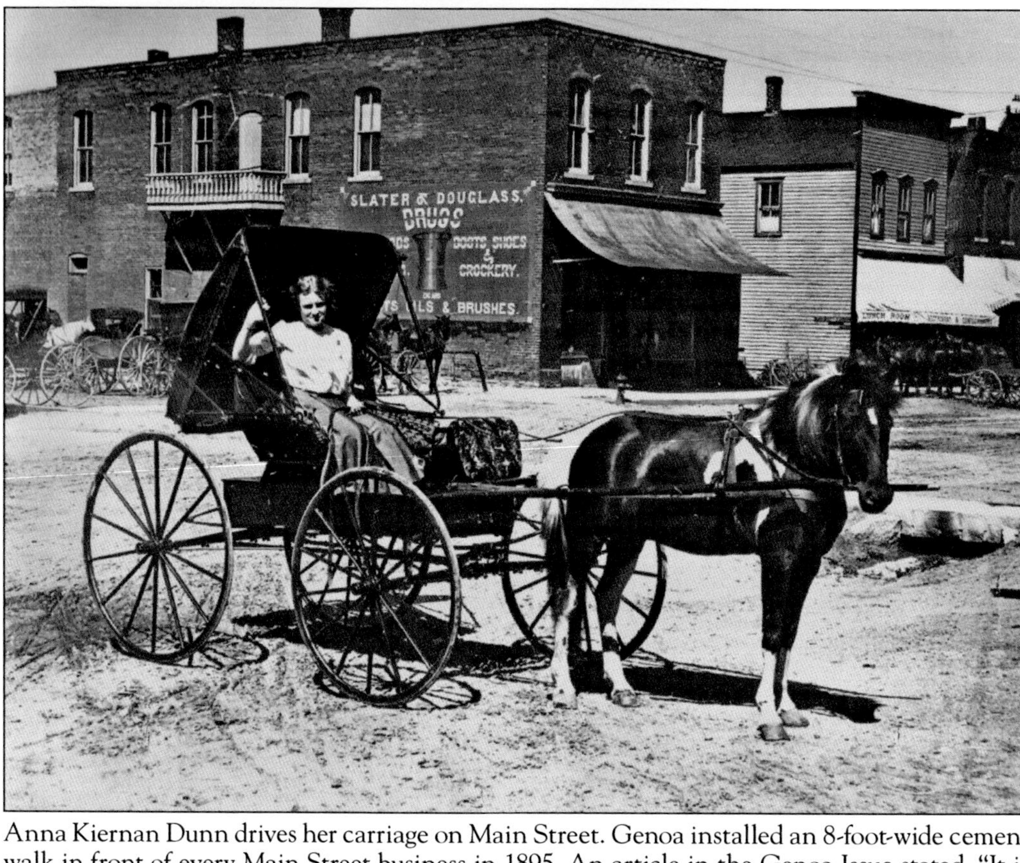

Anna Kiernan Dunn drives her carriage on Main Street. Genoa installed an 8-foot-wide cement walk in front of every Main Street business in 1895. An article in the Genoa Issue stated, "It is a source of great pride to our people. A number of cement walks have been laid in the residence section also. We have the best side-walked town in the state for its size."

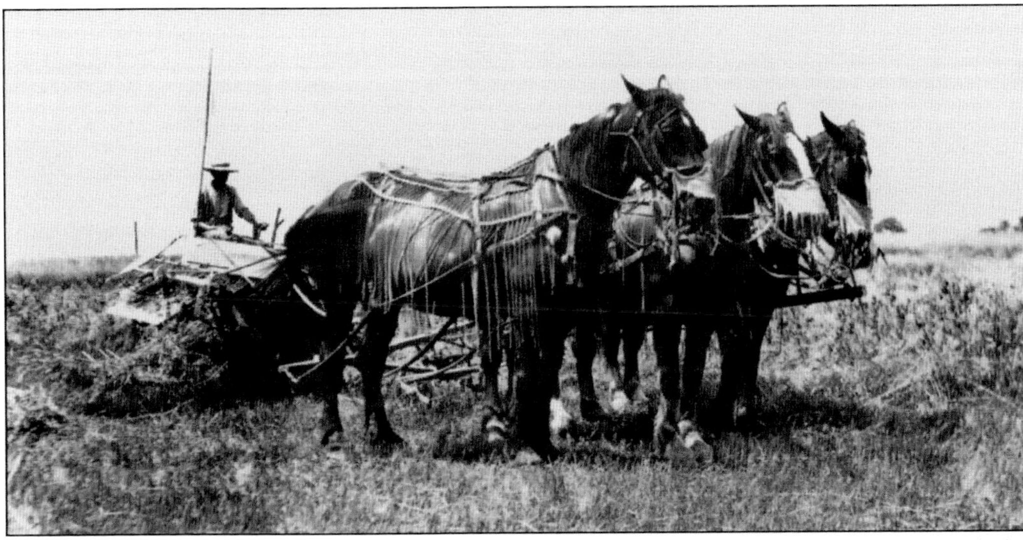

Horses were used for both transportation and working on the farm. Farming implements included the grain binder, which was pulled by the horse and used in harvesting grain. Grain binders were common in the Midwest, where the humid weather meant grain needed more drying time before it could be threshed. Grain bundles produced by the binder would be placed together into shocks.

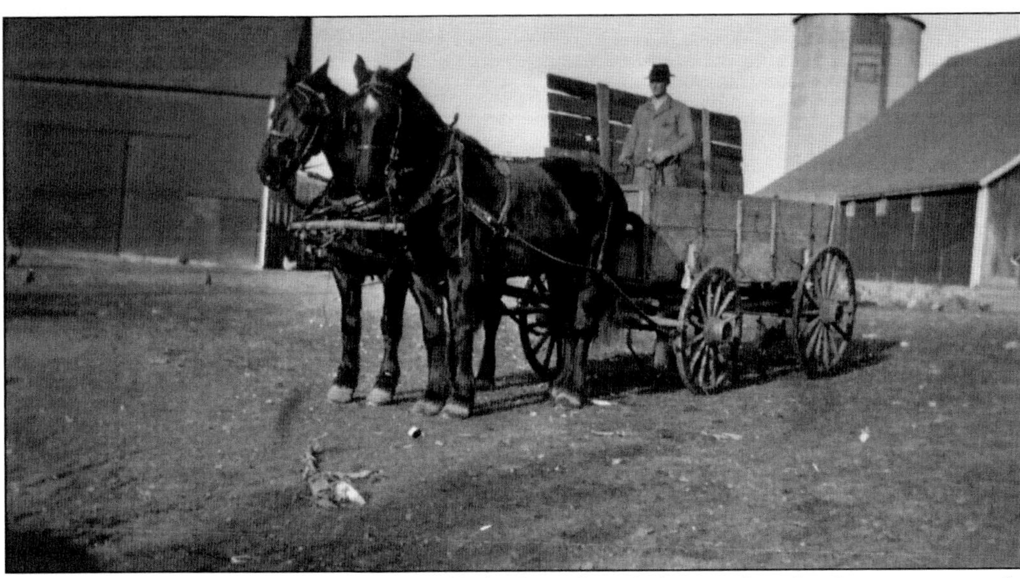

The high side of this farm wagon was called a bang board; farmworkers loading corn onto the wagon would hear a bang as each ear of corn hit the board. The bang board allowed workers to concentrate on picking the corn instead of continually checking if the corn was landing inside the wagon.

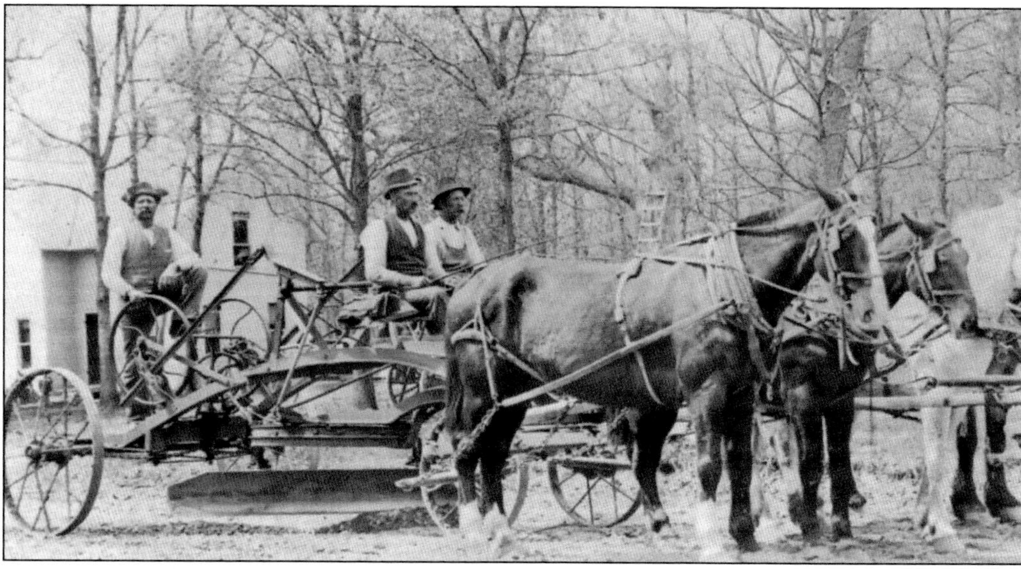

Road graders in the early 1900s were pulled by a team of horses and used to build and maintain dirt roads. Some horse-drawn graders were later converted by welding a hitch onto the grader so it could be pulled by a tractor. Graders today are still used for dirt and gravel roads, but they have three axles with a cab and engine.

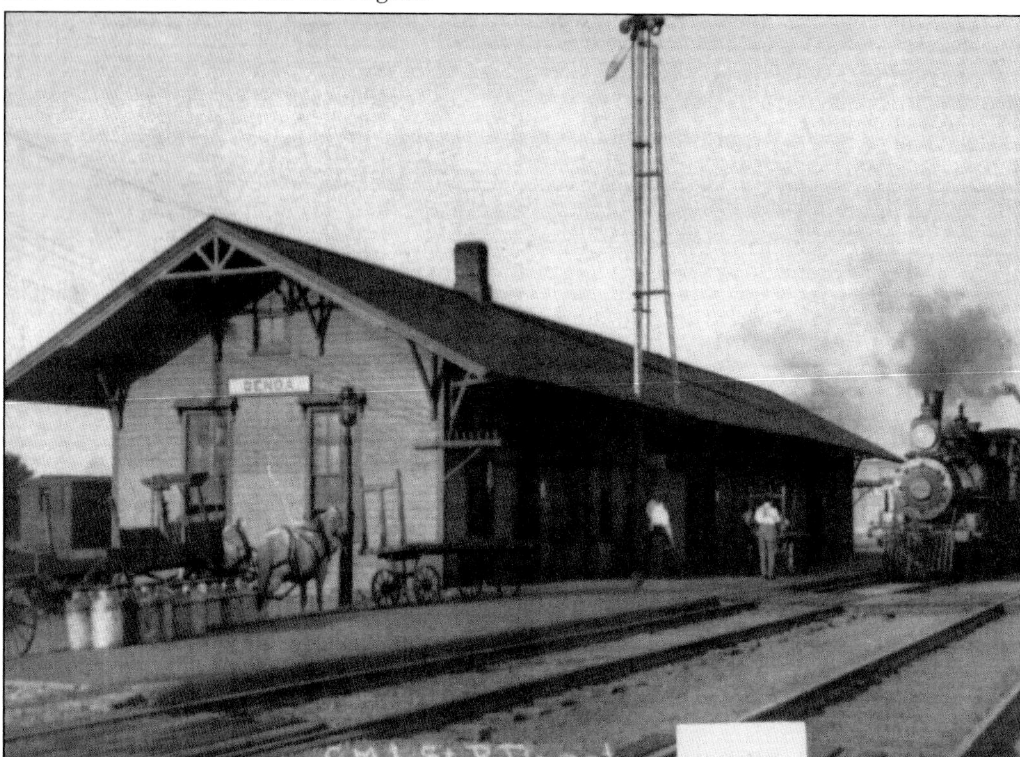

A train chugs into the Genoa train station in 1908. A train order semaphore signal is attached to the roof of the station. The extended arm of the signal indicates whether or not the train should stop or proceed. Milk cans lined up on the platform are ready for shipment by rail.

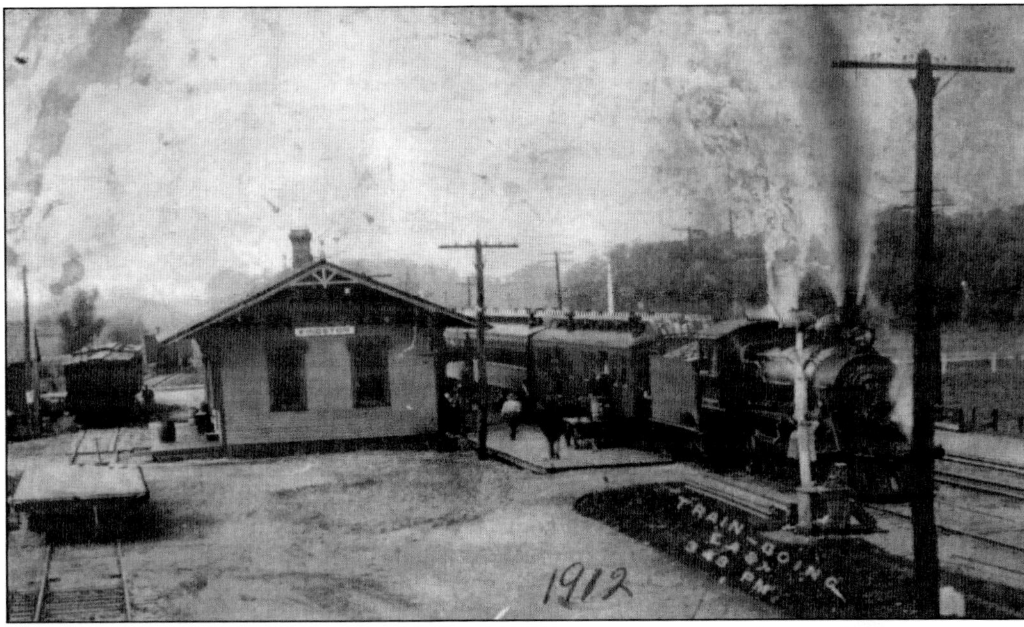

A burst of steam and the familiar "chuff" sound fill the air as the train pulls into the Kingston station in 1912. The Milwaukee Railroad first arrived in Kingston in 1875. The Chicago Northwestern was completed in 1885, with Henrietta serving as its depot and shipping warehouse. Kingston became the hub for these two railroads. (Courtesy of Joiner Room.)

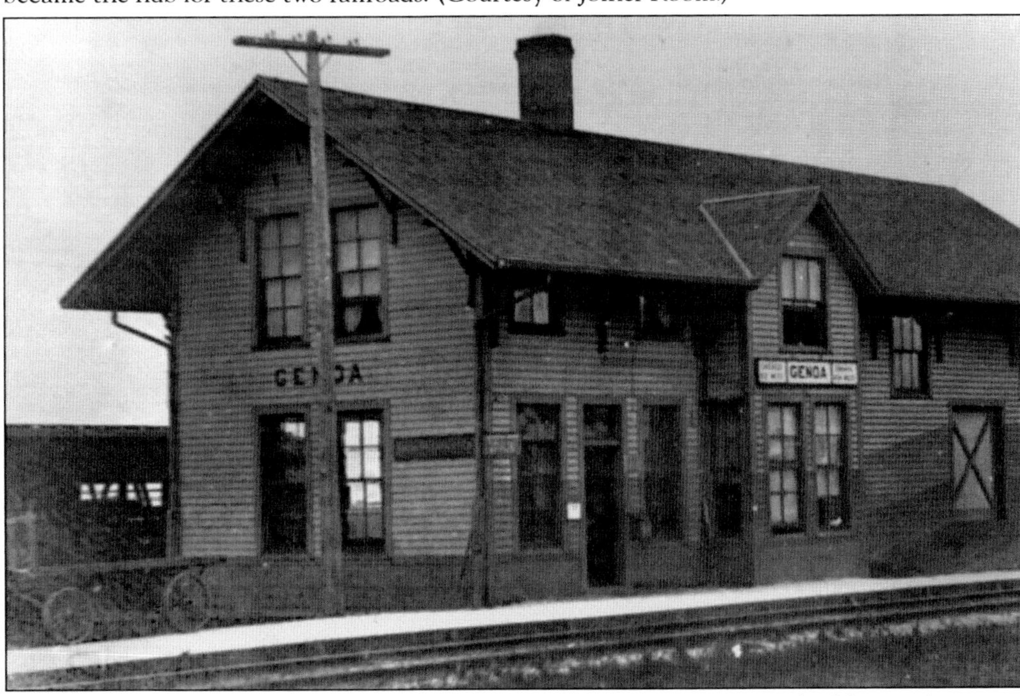

The Illinois Central Depot in Genoa, shown here in 1941, was a two-story building with quarters for the station agent and his family on the upper level. Henry Lein was the last station agent to live at the depot with his family. When the depot burned down, a smaller, one-story depot was built on the site. (Courtesy of Joiner Room.)

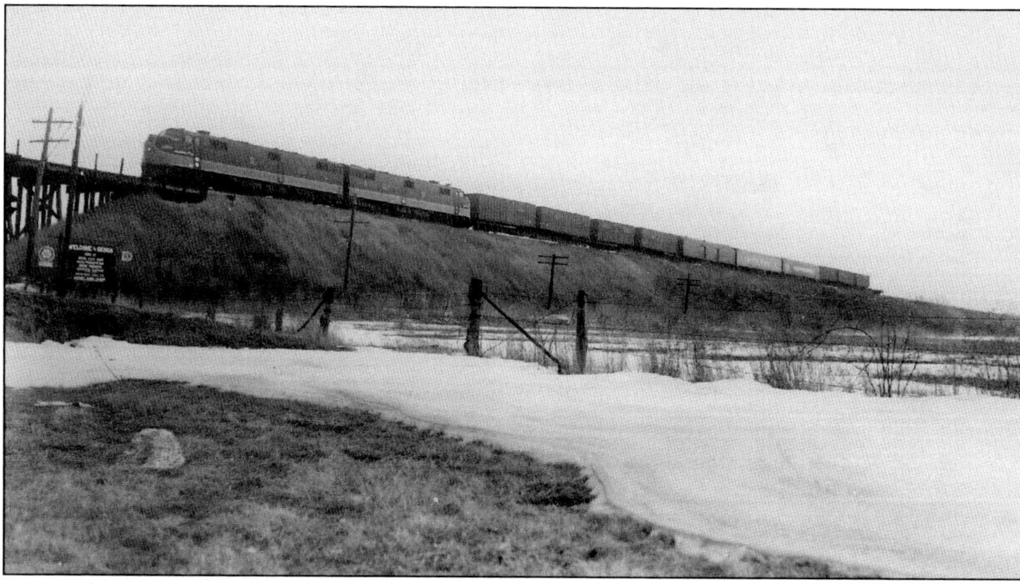

A train begins to cross the trestle as it approaches Genoa on a snowy winter day. A sign below the tracks reads, "Welcome to Genoa, Home of Genoa State Bank, Falls Products Inc., Argos Products Co., Greenlee Tool Co., and Automatic Electric." There is also a Genoa Lions Club sign. Argos Products Company moved to Genoa from Argos, Indiana, in 1950. (Courtesy of Joiner Room.)

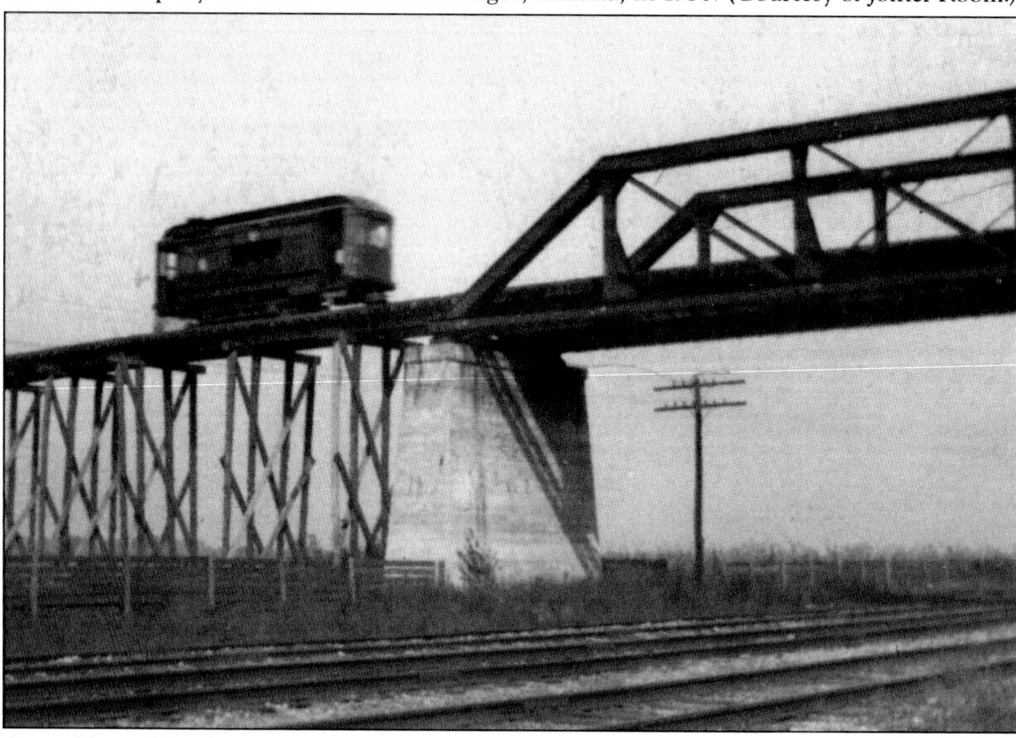

A southbound Fairbanks-Morse car passes over the Chicago, Milwaukee, and St. Paul railroad tracks east of Genoa in 1914. Passengers who were uneasy about the safety of crossing the bridge often disembarked and went the distance on foot. The Fairbanks-Morse car was nicknamed the "Gasoline Wagon," "Oilcan," "Creeping Peter," "Sycamore Pet," and "Woodpecker Special."

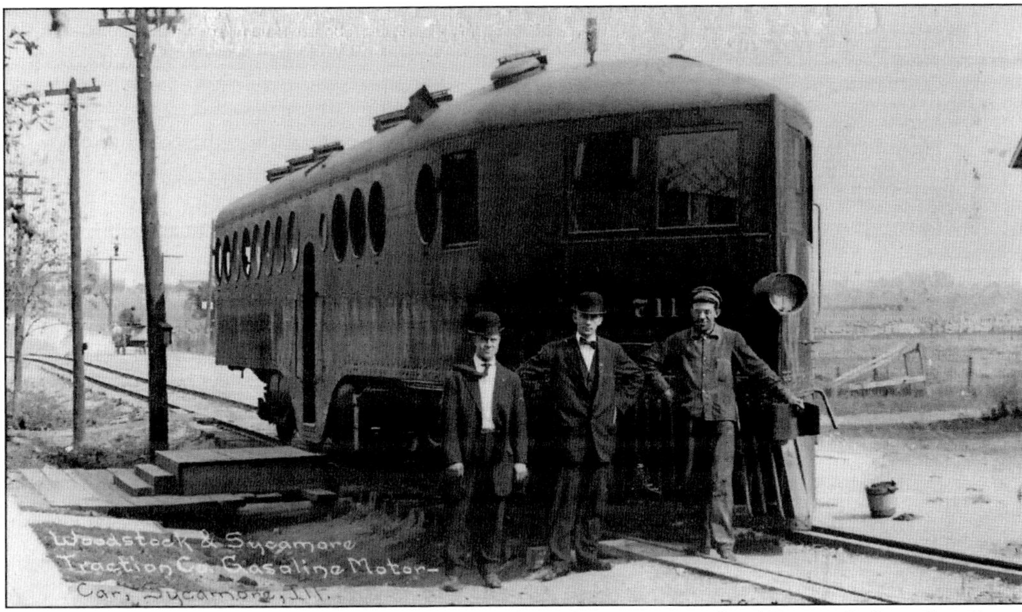

Lloyd Hoover (left), Henry "Hick" Nulle (center), and motorman Lloyd Ritsenthaler take a break near the No. 711 McKeen car across from the Sycamore Feed Mill in 1910. The car would later continue its route through Genoa. The McKeen car was also nicknamed "Gunboat," "Battleship," and "Peanut Roaster."

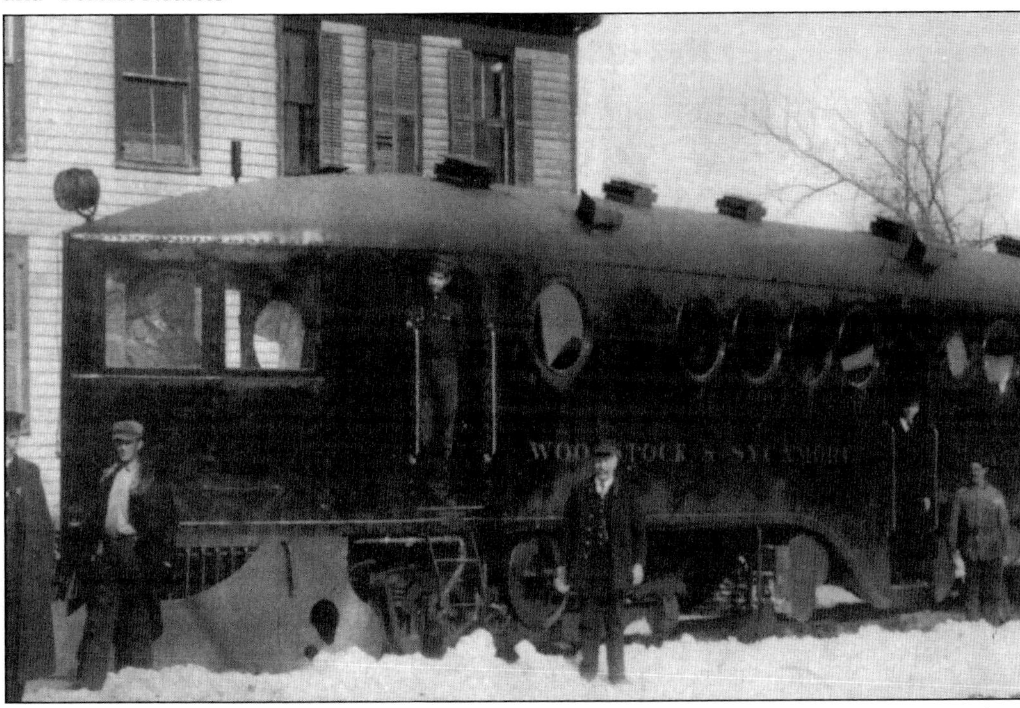

The No. 711 McKeen car faces south beside the Pacific Hotel in Genoa. The city was the northern terminal until 1913, when the Marengo section was connected. The interurban tracks in Genoa terminated south of the Chicago, Milwaukee, and St. Paul tracks. The Pacific Hotel had a ticket office and waiting room for passengers.

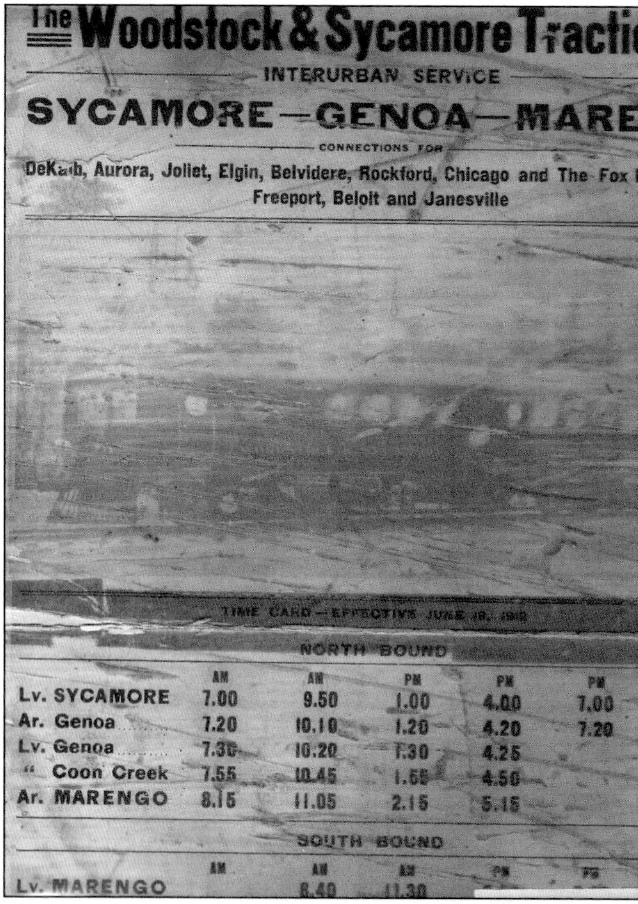

The Woodstock & Sycamore Tractio

INTERURBAN SERVICE

SYCAMORE—GENOA—MARE

CONNECTIONS FOR

DeKalb, Aurora, Joliet, Elgin, Belvidere, Rockford, Chicago and The Fox R
Freeport, Beloit and Janesville

TIME CARD—EFFECTIVE JUNE 18, [illegible]

NORTH BOUND

	AM	AM	PM	PM	PM
Lv. SYCAMORE	7.00	9.50	1.00	4.00	7.00
Ar. Genoa	7.20	10.10	1.20	4.20	7.20
Lv. Genoa	7.30	10.20	1.30	4.25	
" Coon Creek	7.55	10.45	1.55	4.50	
Ar. MARENGO	8.15	11.05	2.15	5.15	

SOUTH BOUND

	AM	AM	AM	PM	PM
Lv. MARENGO		8.40	11.30		

A schedule for the Woodstock and Sycamore Traction Company interurban railroad showed that passengers could make connections going to DeKalb, Aurora, Joliet, Elgin, Belvidere, Rockford, Chicago, Freeport, Beloit, and Janesville. A passenger leaving Sycamore at 7:00 a.m. could arrive in Marengo at 8:15 a.m. People wishing to reach Hampshire would disembark at the Coon Creek stop.

Passengers huddle inside one of the roadside shelters built by the Woodstock and Sycamore Traction Company from 1911 to 1918. The buds on the trees and lack of coats suggest that the people are enjoying a warm spring day. The shelter with only a roof and no walls would not provide any warmth on cold weather days.

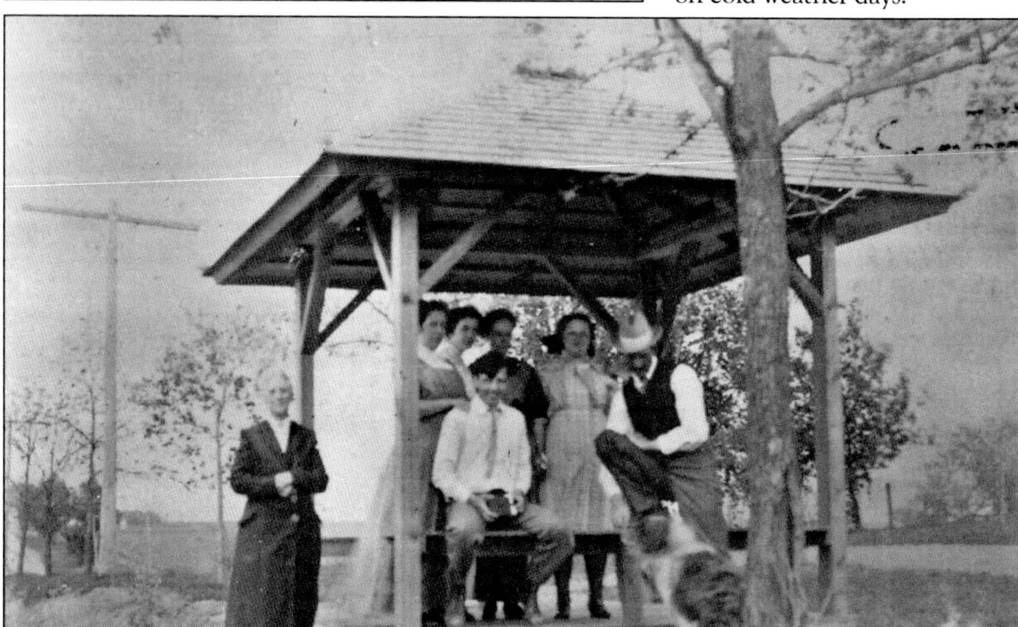

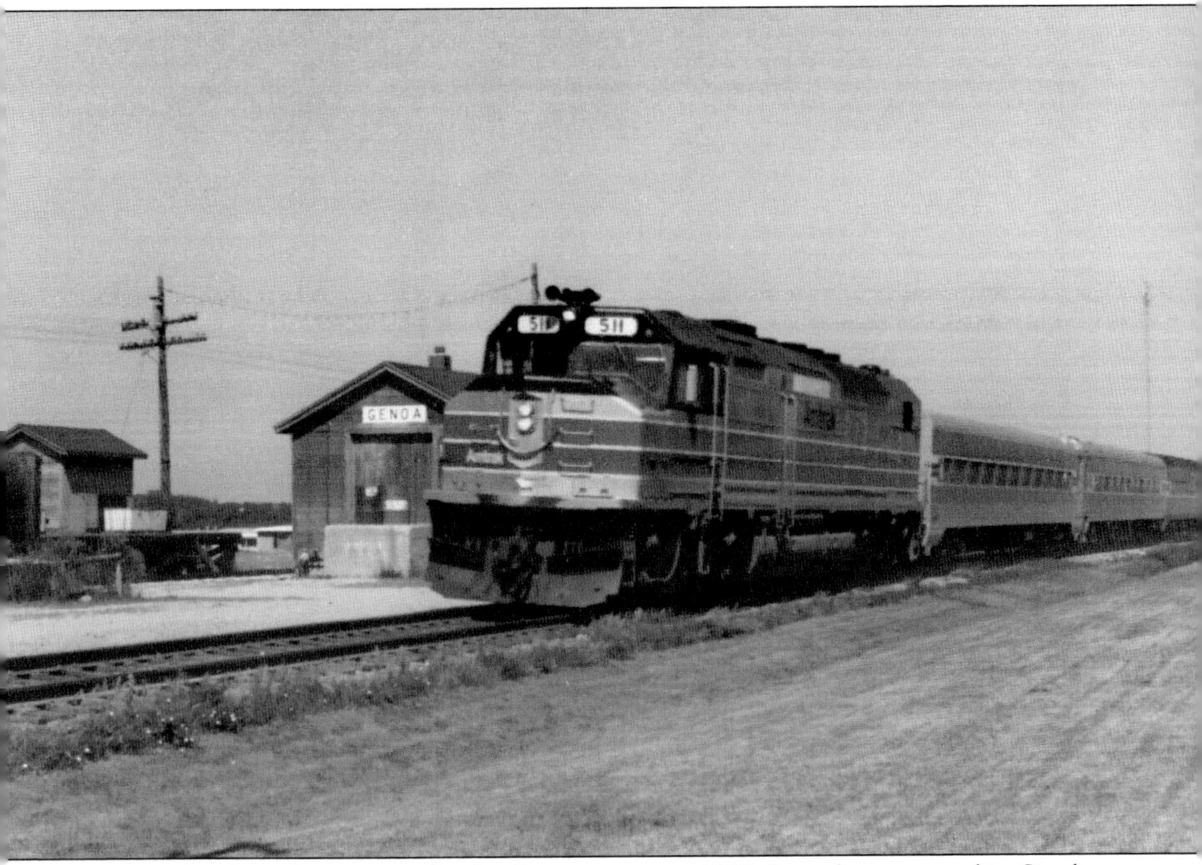

The No. 511 Amtrak train runs by the Genoa station in 1977. Amtrak was created in October 1970, when Congress passed the Rail Passenger Service Act. On May 1, 1971, while Richard Nixon served as U.S. president, Amtrak began its nationwide rail system dedicated to passenger service. The Amtrak station in Genoa was located along Sycamore Street. When the train stopped at the station in the morning, the engineer and his crew would sometimes walk a few blocks in order to have breakfast at the Huddle Inn at 225 West Main Street in Genoa. The Huddle Inn was once owned by Donald Weaver. Another former owner of the Huddle Inn was Irene Faye Harmon. She was born in Genoa in 1918 and died at age 86 in 2005. Amtrak service in Genoa ended in 1981. The building that was once home to the Huddle Inn now houses Cutters and Co. Family Hair Care.

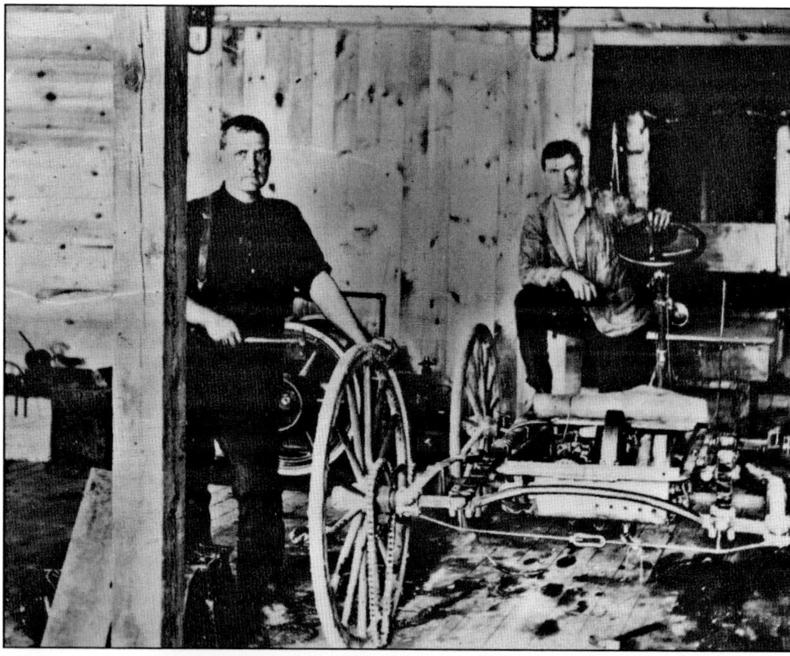

T. J. Hoover and Arch Hoover work on the "Practical Automobile" in 1906. The car had rubber tires, a chain drive on both sides, and a leather-covered wheel. The brothers added the automobile line to their machine shop on West Main Street in Genoa. They stopped making the car in 1909.

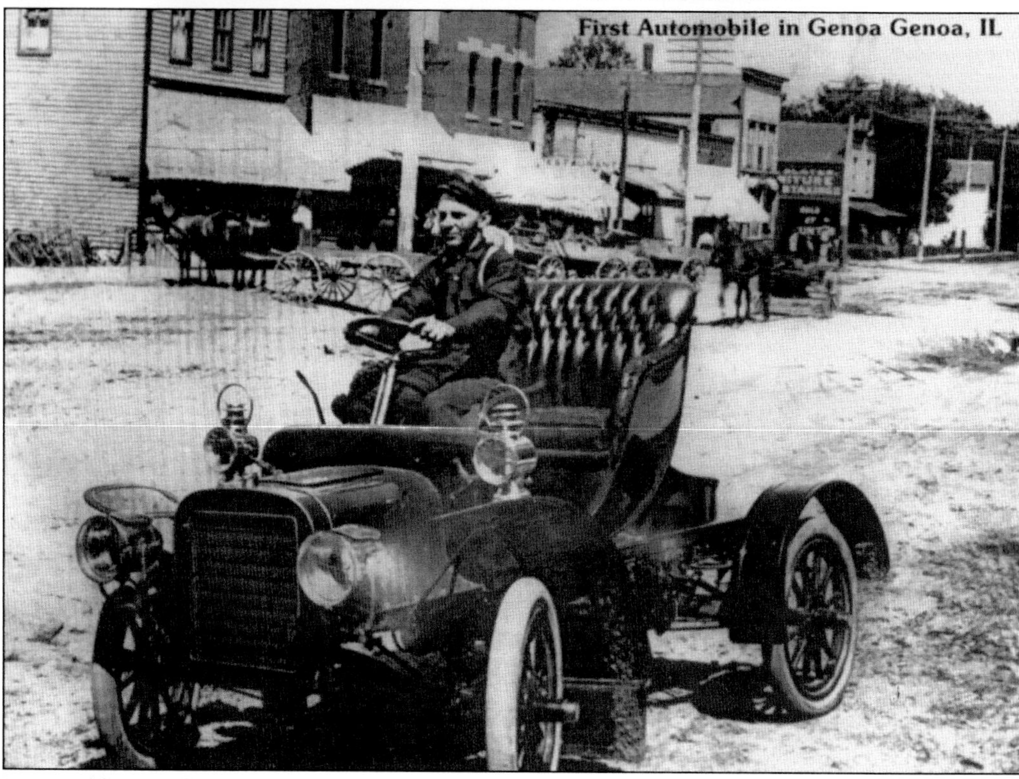

Lee Wylde was the owner of the first automobile in Genoa. He is shown driving his Cadillac down Main Street. Wylde and Bill Cooper often traveled to different states to race horses. They also participated in horse races held in Genoa. The racetrack was located north of where Custom Aluminum Products, Inc. is now located.

Three

Enterprising Entrepreneurs

Certain types of businesses in Genoa and Kingston have continued to stay in the same general location, while other buildings have hosted a variety of entrepreneurs. A fire in 1908 burned down many Main Street businesses in Kingston. One of the destroyed buildings was a bar located at Main Street and Illinois Route 72. The two buildings that were constructed on the site in 1918 house The Varsity Pub. The Genoa Public Library building was used through the years as a furniture store, undertaking business, hospital, cardboard box factory, and grocery store. Victoria's Crossing in Genoa is located in the former State Bank building that was constructed in 1903. The former Duval's Variety Store is now home to MCR Framing/Cattywampus in Genoa. A Genoa gasoline station, later a restaurant, is now home to Wild Thyme Herb Garden. The Genoa Café was once the Slater and Douglass store. The Eureka Electric Company facilities, founded in 1903, had many names in later years: Cracraft-Leich Electric, Leich Electric, General Telephone and Electronics Corporation, and then AG Communication Systems (AGCS). The facilities now house Sycamore Precision, Custom Aluminum/Casco, and the City Municipal Center building on First Street.

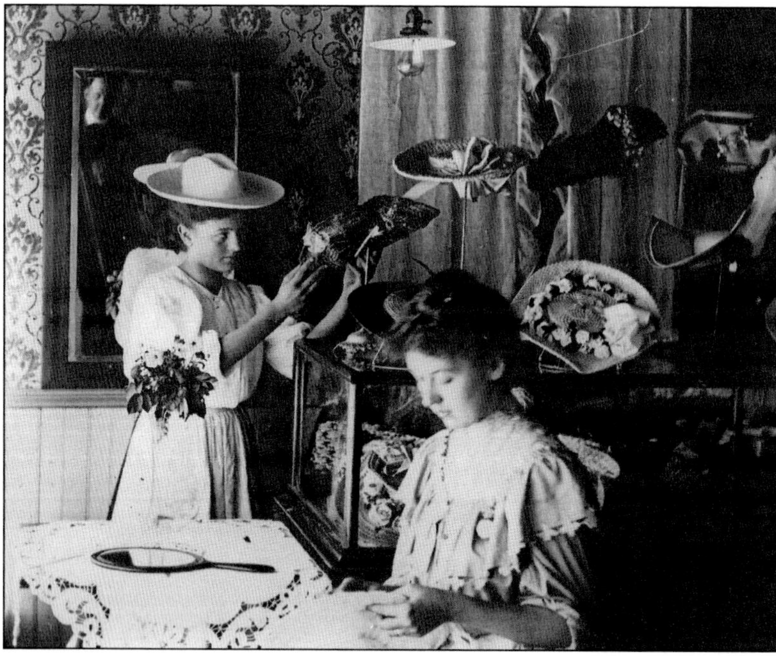

Seen here around 1900, Annette Duval (standing), owner of The Hat Shop on West Main Street in Genoa, waits on a customer, Hazel Robinson Farmiloe, who was the wife of a Methodist preacher. Annette was the wife of Lou Duval, a butcher who worked with his brother Fred at Duval Brothers Meat Market. Fred's wife, "Leafy," played the piano for silent films.

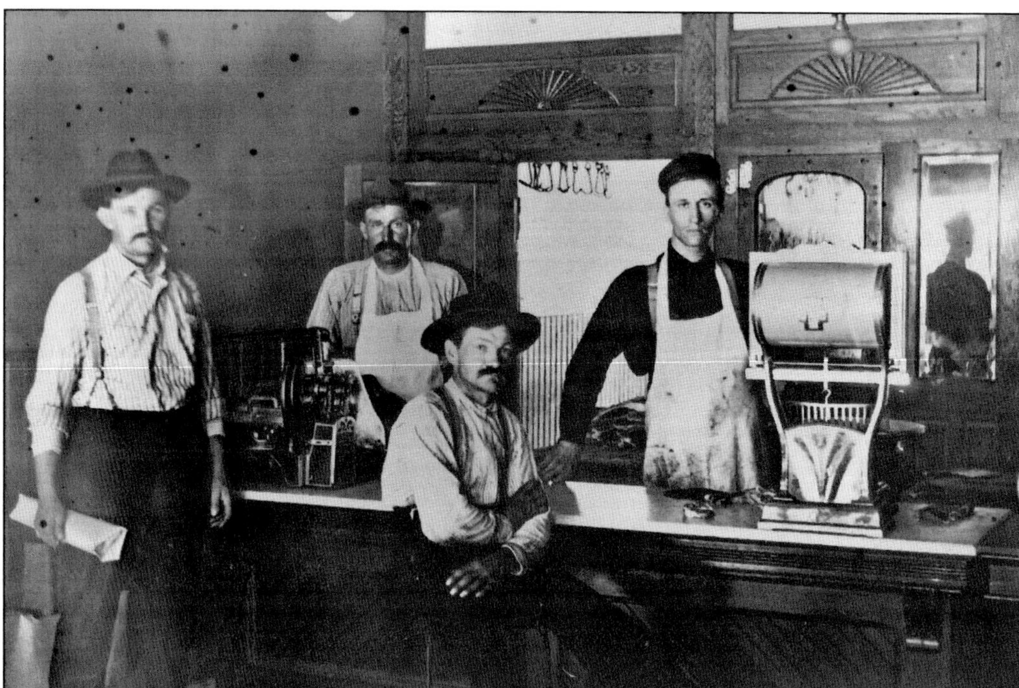

Fred Duval (left) stands behind the counter of Duval Brothers Meat Market at 405 West Main Street in Genoa. His brother Lou stands near the scales, while two customers stop by to order meat. The building that housed the meat market was constructed in 1900. It was later used for Fred E. Wells Dry Goods and now by All Natural Chiropractic.

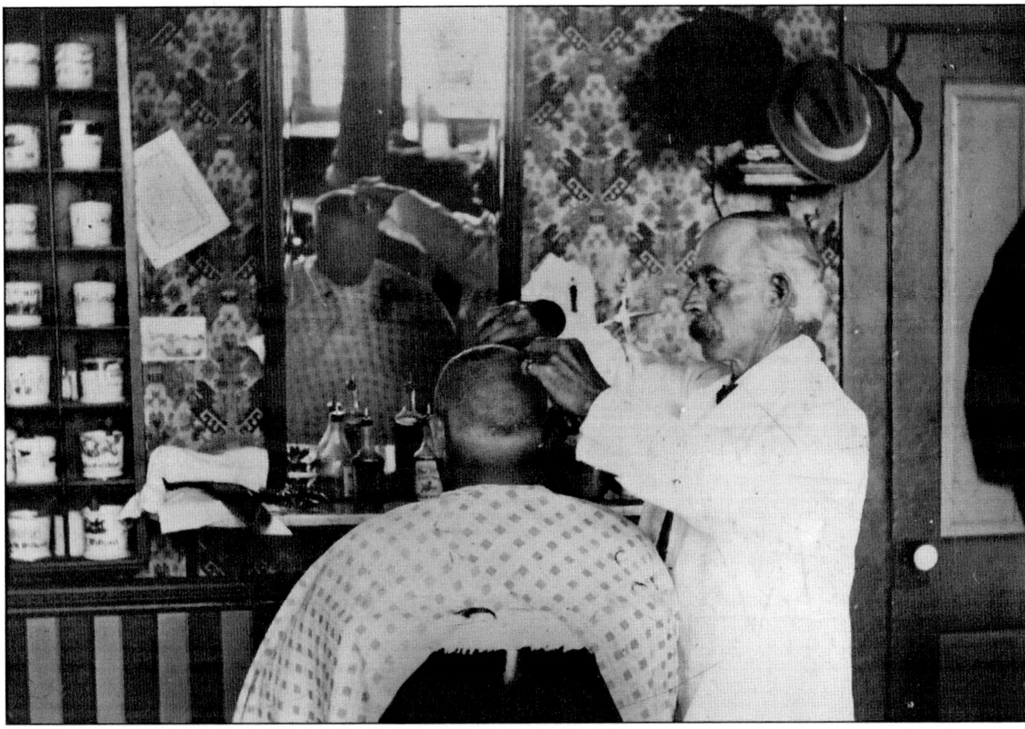

George Johnson cuts a customer's hair at Johnson and Marquart Barbershop at 408 West Main Street in Genoa in 1901. Johnson's partner in running the three-chair barbershop was Fred W. Marquart. Frank Grajek, assisted by Charles Maderer, ran another barbershop in Genoa around that time.

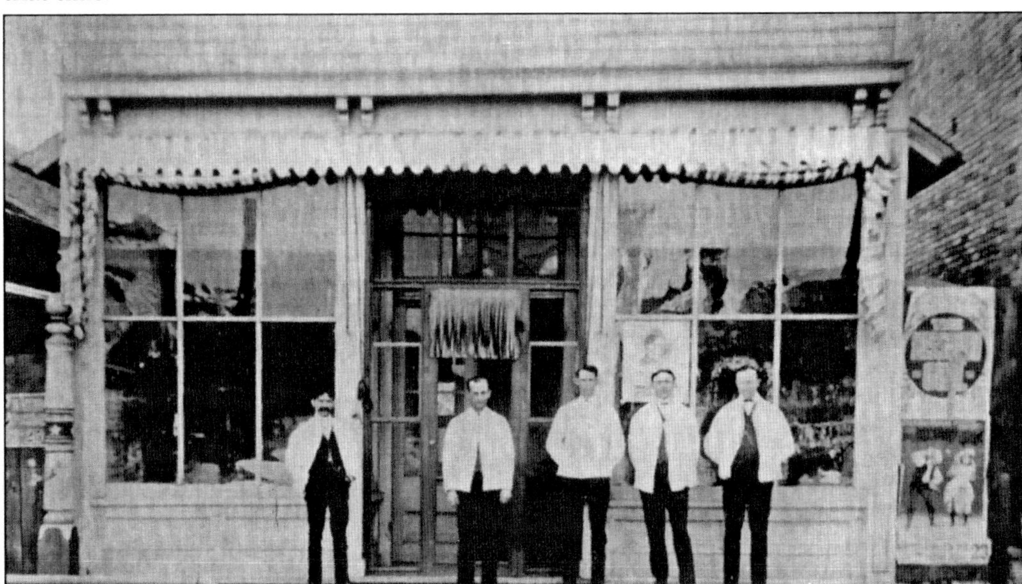

Barbers John "Jack" O'Brien (far left) and Archie Fuller (far right) wait for customers at Kingston Barbershop on Main Street in 1900. Small-town barbers, with their steady hands, were sometimes asked to act in place of the local surgeon in the event of an emergency.

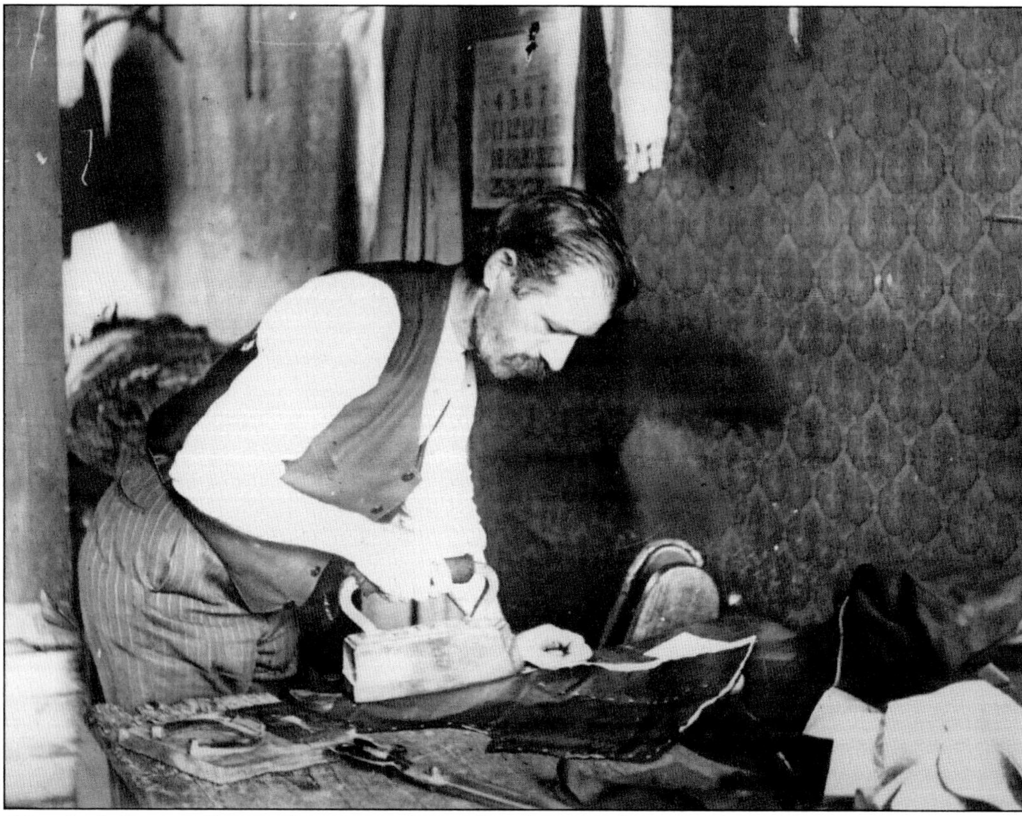

Olin Soderberg pulls out the iron at his tailor shop on the 300 block of West Main Street in Genoa. Soderberg was known for always wearing a black overcoat. He was walking home from work one night when he was killed by some Sycamore joyriders with poor headlights.

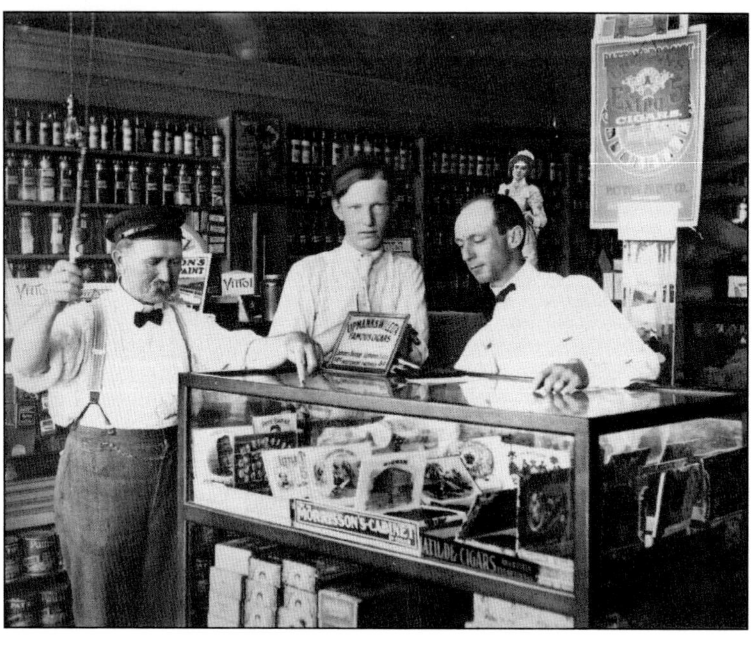

Charles Deerdruff (left), Sandy Crawford (center), and Lewis Carmichael check out the cigars in the glass case at Carmichael's Drugstore at 318 West Main Street in Genoa. Deerdruff was a barber and photographer. The store was sold to L. F. Scott and Edgar Baldwin during the 1920s. The building was later used for Larson's Department Store. The building today houses Jeffrey Caron Optometry.

Blanche Patterson, her husband, George (center), and Earl Brown relax inside the Genoa Post Office at the northeast corner of Main and Monroe Streets on June 30, 1906. George once served as a postmaster in Genoa. A mail route was first established from St. Charles through Genoa in 1837. Postage in 1906 was 2¢ per ounce.

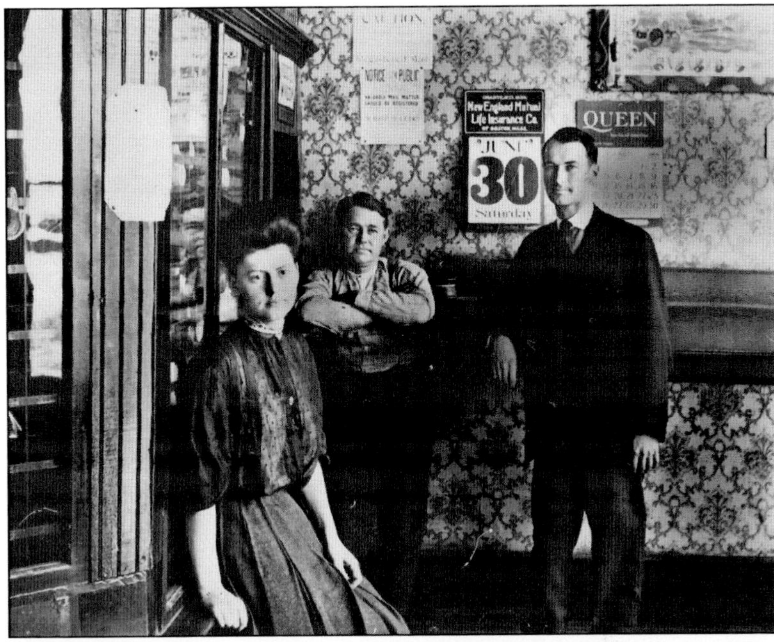

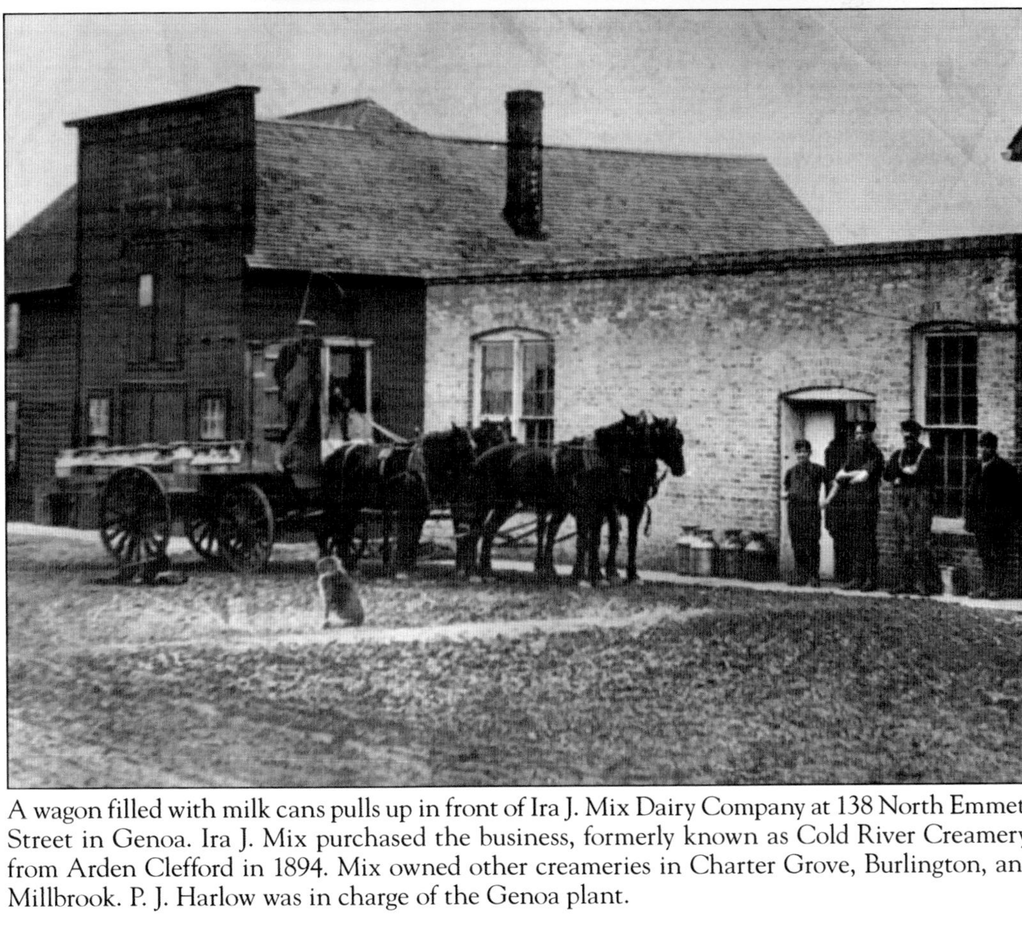

A wagon filled with milk cans pulls up in front of Ira J. Mix Dairy Company at 138 North Emmett Street in Genoa. Ira J. Mix purchased the business, formerly known as Cold River Creamery, from Arden Clefford in 1894. Mix owned other creameries in Charter Grove, Burlington, and Millbrook. P. J. Harlow was in charge of the Genoa plant.

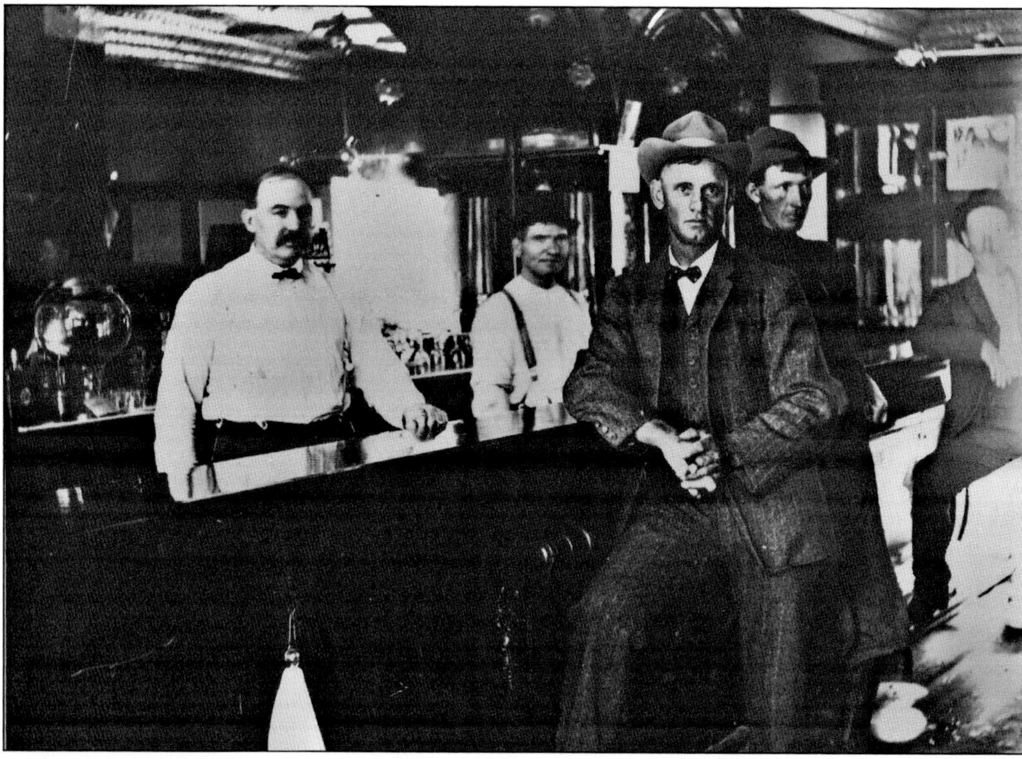

Edgar "Catfish" Richard (above, left) tends bar with Frank Adams at Catfish Richard's Saloon in the early 1900s at 217 West Main Street in Genoa. The customers, from left to right, are John R. Corson, an unknown man, and Bill Snow. The building was later used by Dr. James Hirsch around 1985. Today the building houses Prairie State Winery, which is owned by Rick and Maria Mamoser. Shown behind the counter at the winery (below) is tasting room manager J. T. Anesi. Since 1998, Prairie State Winery has won many awards in Illinois and the Midwest for its different wines. From the first vintage of 500 gallons to more recent vintages of nearly 10,000 gallons, Rick and Maria produce wines made exclusively from Illinois-grown grapes, including those raised in their own vineyard.

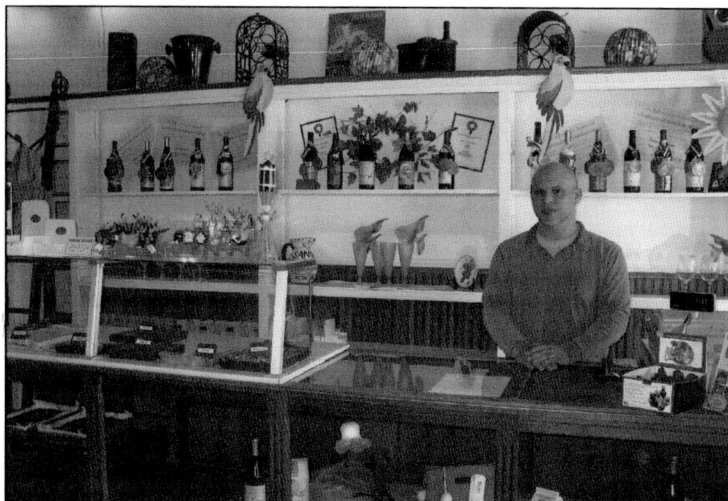

GENOA
NORTH SIDE OF MAIN STREET

EMMETT STREET | GENOA STREET

1913

233		225	221					
General Store	Barber	Tavern	Tavern	Restaurant & Saloon	Cigar Store	Meat Market	Tavern	Clothing
H. H. Slater & Ira Douglas	Cully Foster	Harvey Ide	Billy Lloyd	Richardson (Catfish)	Wylde	Holroyd	Godding	Bixby Hughes

1985

233		225	221	217	213	209	207	201
TV Sales	Vacant Lot	Cafe	Clothing	Dental Office	Attorney Office	Accounting	Real Estate	Package Liquor
Ed Link			Ken Whitesell	Dr. Hirsch	O'Grady & Cromley	Larson	L. Russin	

1999

233		225	221	217	213	209	207	201
Downtown Cafe	Vacant Lot	Cutters Hair Design	Crumpets Tea Room & Ice Cream	Prairie State Mercantile	Becker Law Office	Genoa Dental Office	Midwest Real Estate	Genoa Package Liquors
Ed & Donna Konecny		Betty Bolger Jennifer Kohler	John & Ann Seisser	Maria & Rick Mannoser	Atty/Mrs. Robert Becker	Sherrie Purdue	Lillian Russin	

A diagram shows businesses along the north side of Main Street bordered by Emmett and Genoa Streets during the years 1913, 1985, and 1999. Businesses in Genoa today receive support from the city, Genoa Main Street, Inc. and the Genoa Area Chamber of Commerce. Genoa became an Illinois Main Street–designated community in 1996. Genoa Main Street is a preservation-based economic development program founded by community volunteers. The chamber was established in 1956 to advance the general welfare and prosperity of Genoa. Its motto is "Moving forward with a purpose." Events such as open-air markets, the Harvest Moon Festival and Back Roads Tractor Run, Dinner and a Movie on Main Street, Genoa Days in June, and Celebrate the Season in December all help to promote Genoa businesses and bring visitors to the city.

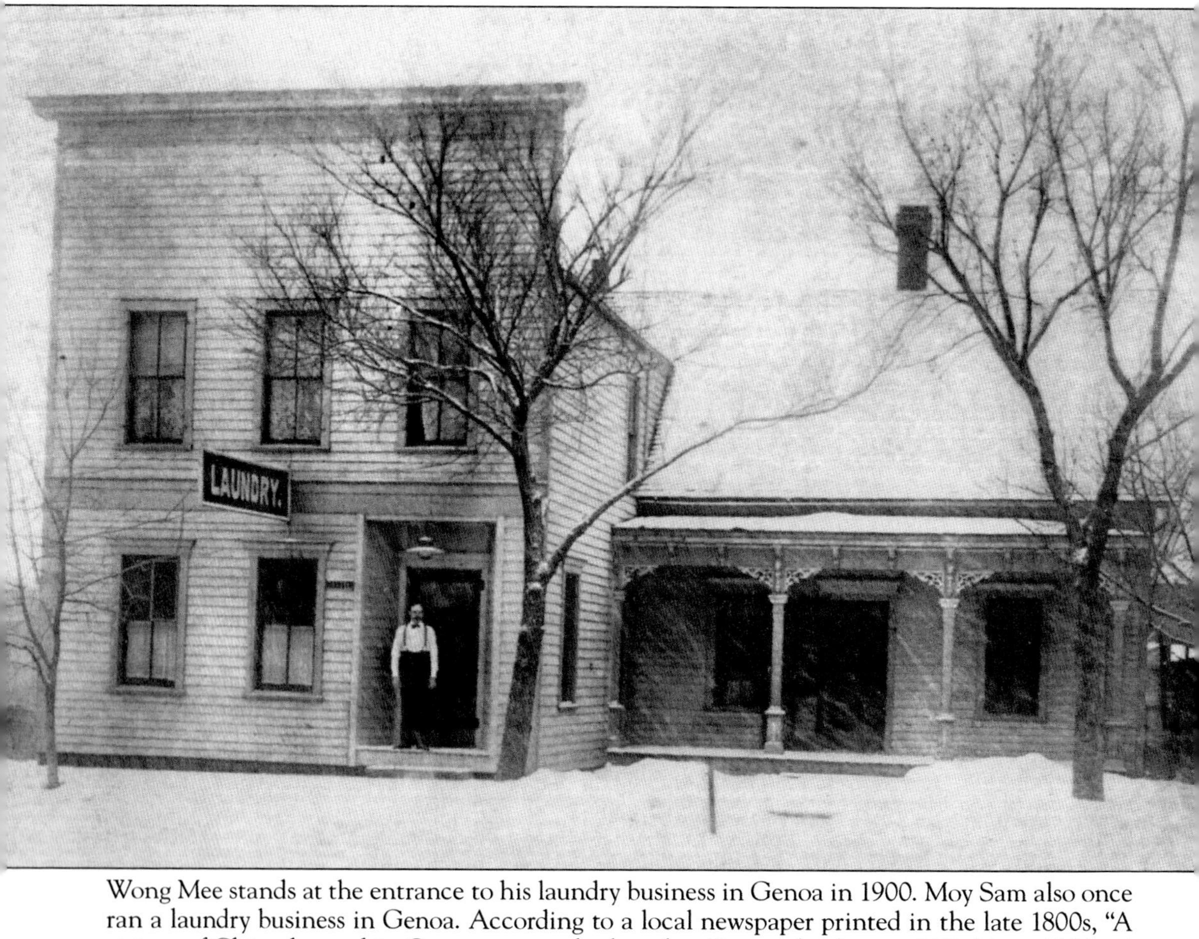

Wong Mee stands at the entrance to his laundry business in Genoa in 1900. Moy Sam also once ran a laundry business in Genoa. According to a local newspaper printed in the late 1800s, "A citizen of China located in Genoa operated a laundry. One night, he was killed in cold blood for a very few dollars. The criminals escaped and were never apprehended." It is uncertain if the victim was either Wong Mee or Moy Sam. In 1882, Chinese immigrants in the United States were affected by the Chinese Exclusion Act, a federal law signed by Pres. Chester A. Arthur that provided a 10-year moratorium on Chinese labor immigration. When this act expired, it was extended for another 10 years in the form of the Geary Act. The Magnuson Act in 1943 allowed Chinese immigration for first time since 1882 and permitted Chinese nationals to become naturalized citizens.

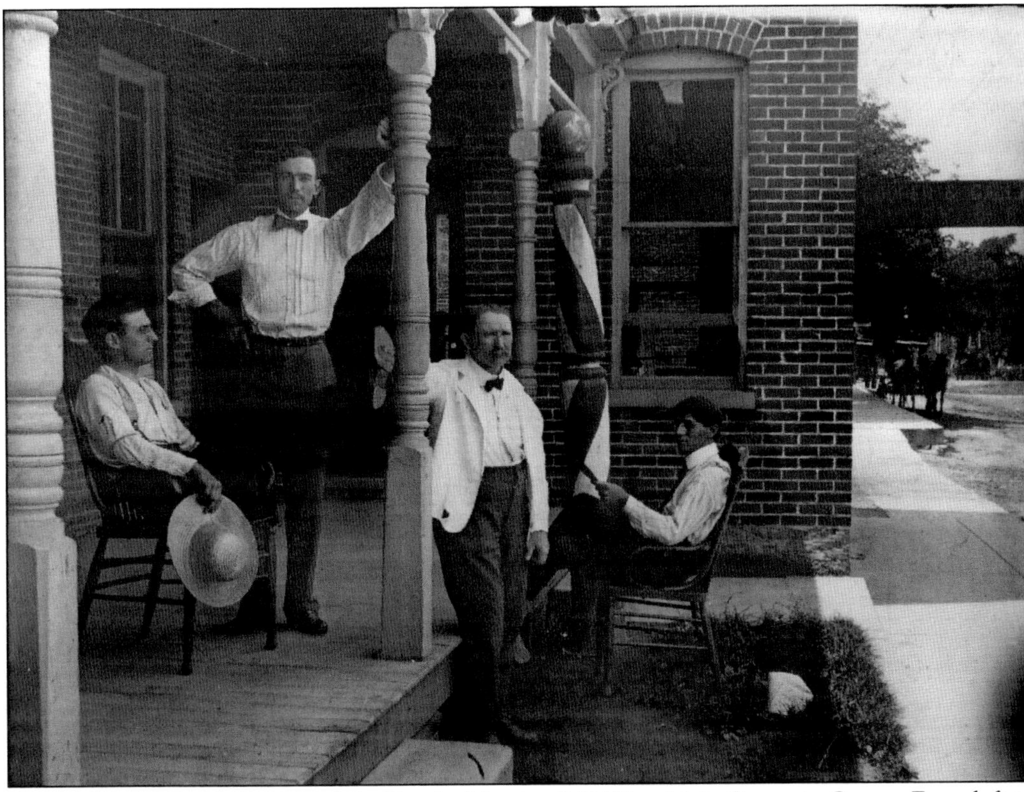

Four men relax on the porch of the Eureka Hotel at 240 West Main Street in Genoa. From left to right are Charles Saul Sr., Charles Maderer, photographer Charles Deerdruff, and an unknown man. Deerdruff and E. J. Buss (not pictured) were both well-known photographers in Genoa. In the early 1900s, Buss photographed many of Genoa's homes.

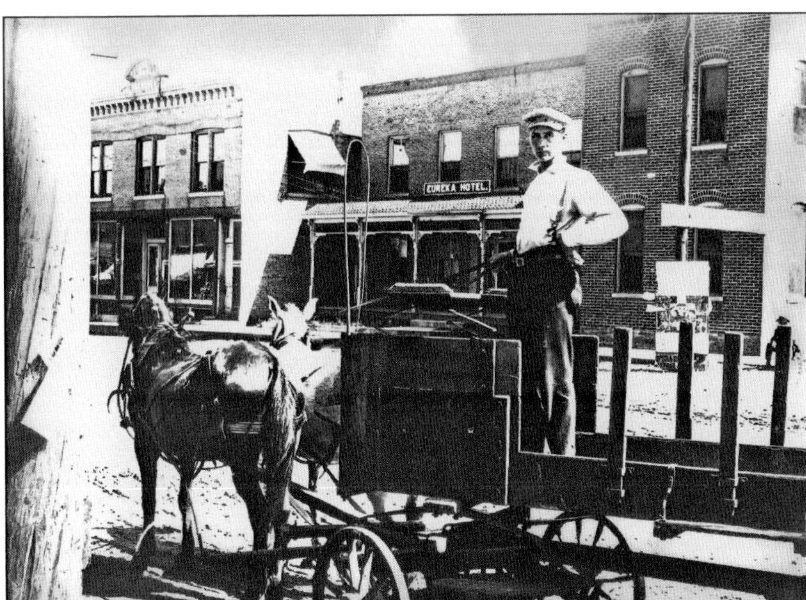

Bill Prain brings a dray loaded with baggage that he collected at the railroad station. The luggage belongs to guests staying at the Eureka Hotel at 240 West Main Street in Genoa, which was owned by James Merriman. The hotel no longer exists.

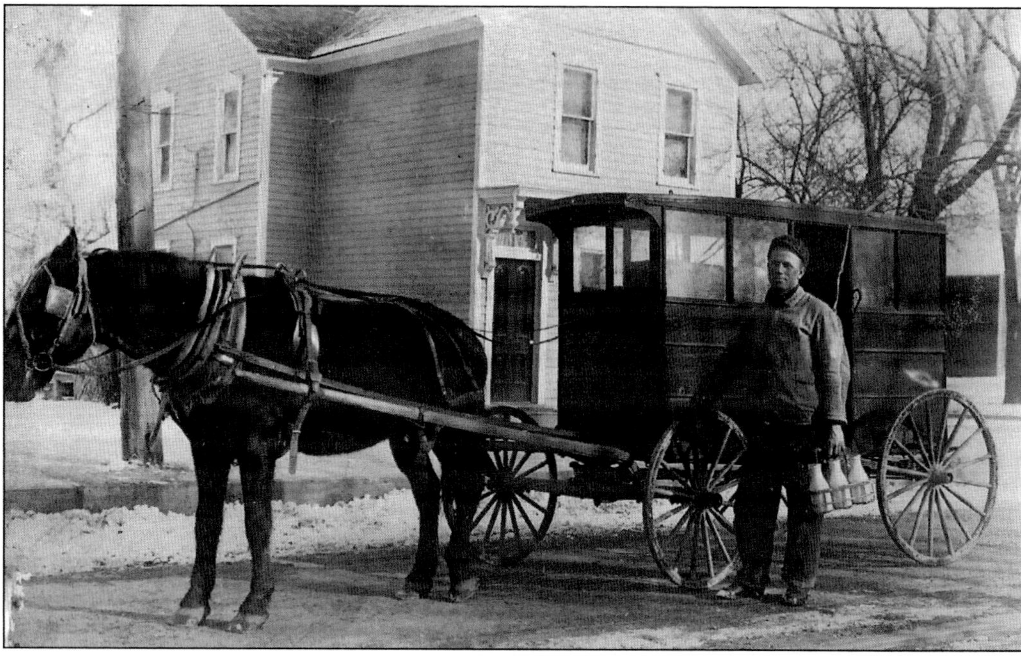

The Stott milk wagon halts along Main Street in Genoa in 1915. The building behind the milk wagon currently houses AT Cyber Systems at 101 West Main Street. J. E. Stott served as Genoa village president from 1905 to 1907 and again in 1911 before Genoa became a city. T. J. Hoover took over the reins as city mayor from 1911 to 1915.

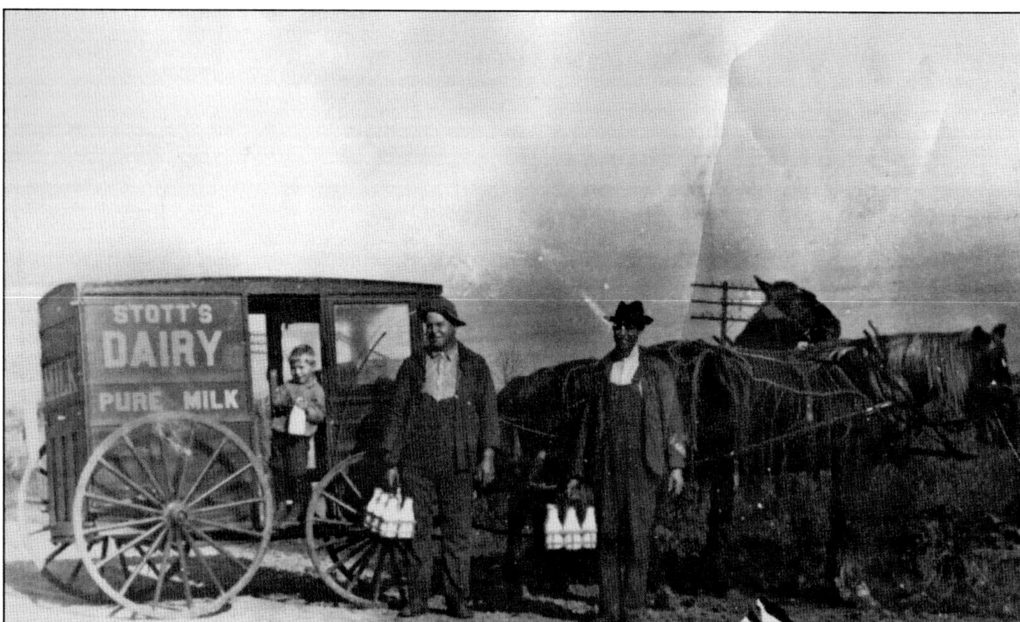

Stott's Dairy was located west of town and east of the Illinois Central railroad underpass on Belvidere Road. Pictured are Howard Stott (in wagon), Vic Stott (center), and an unknown hired man. Vic Stott once hired an Italian man to work at his dairy business. When World War I started, the man returned to Italy and joined the Italian army.

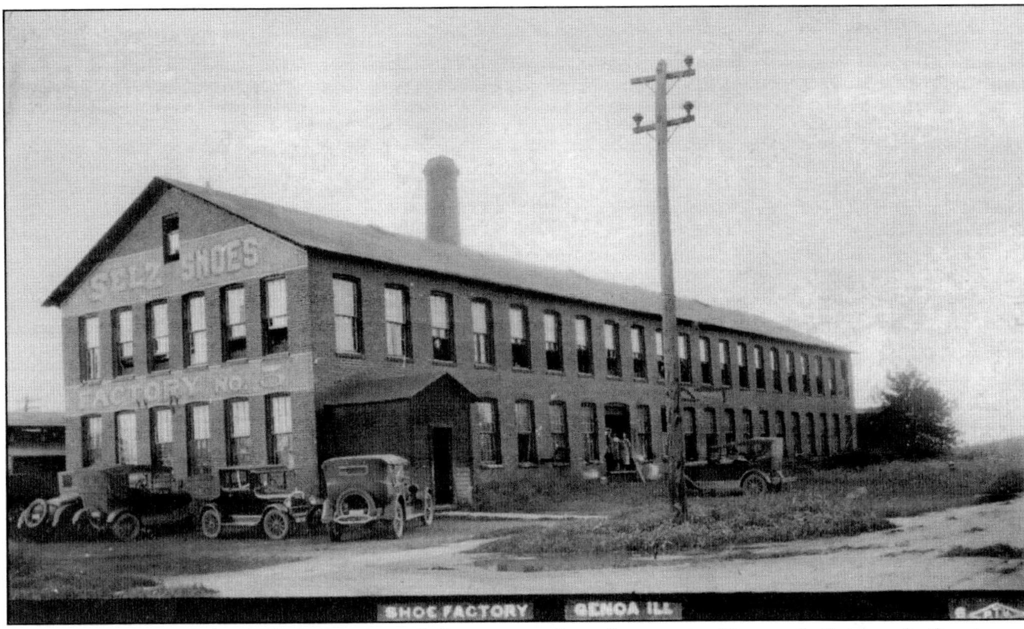

Here are views of the Selz Schwab and Company shoe factory in Genoa before and after it was destroyed by fire. The building originally housed the Garden City Shoe Company. Selz Schwab took it over in 1891. By 1901, the company had one factory in Genoa, one in Chicago, one in Elgin, and two in Joliet. According to an article in the *Hampshire Register*, in December 1920 three robbers stole 180 pairs of shoes worth $600. The factory closed in 1929 and remained empty until the fire in 1931. Nine-year-old Jeannette (Jean) Wager Hughes; her mother, Edith Wager (center); and her grandmother Mary Wager are shown among the factory's charred remains. Edith once worked at the factory. Her husband, Charles, was a fireman who helped to extinguish the fire. The Wager family lived a half block away from the factory.

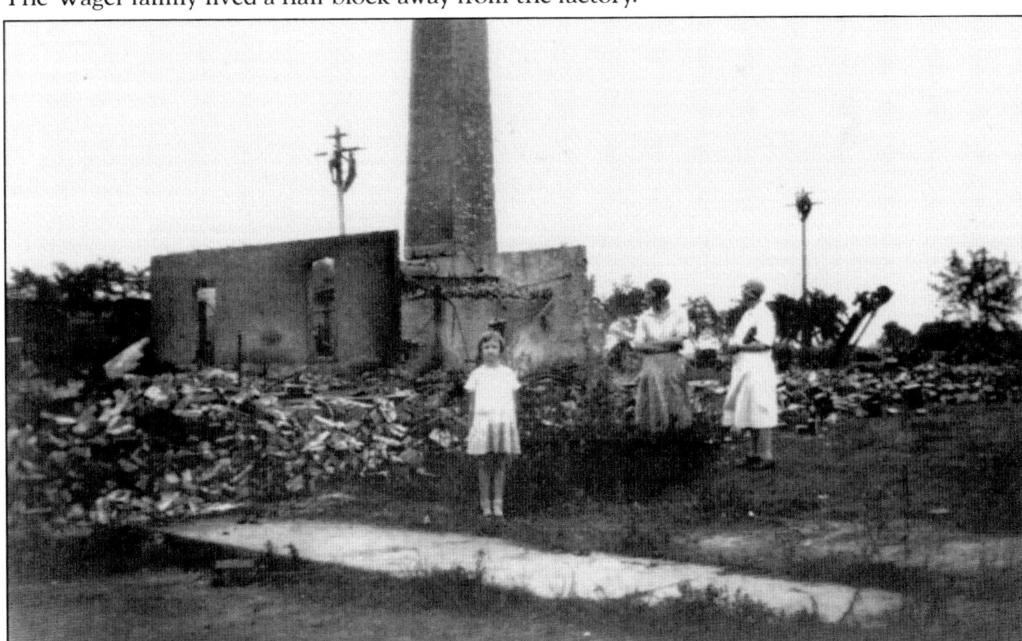

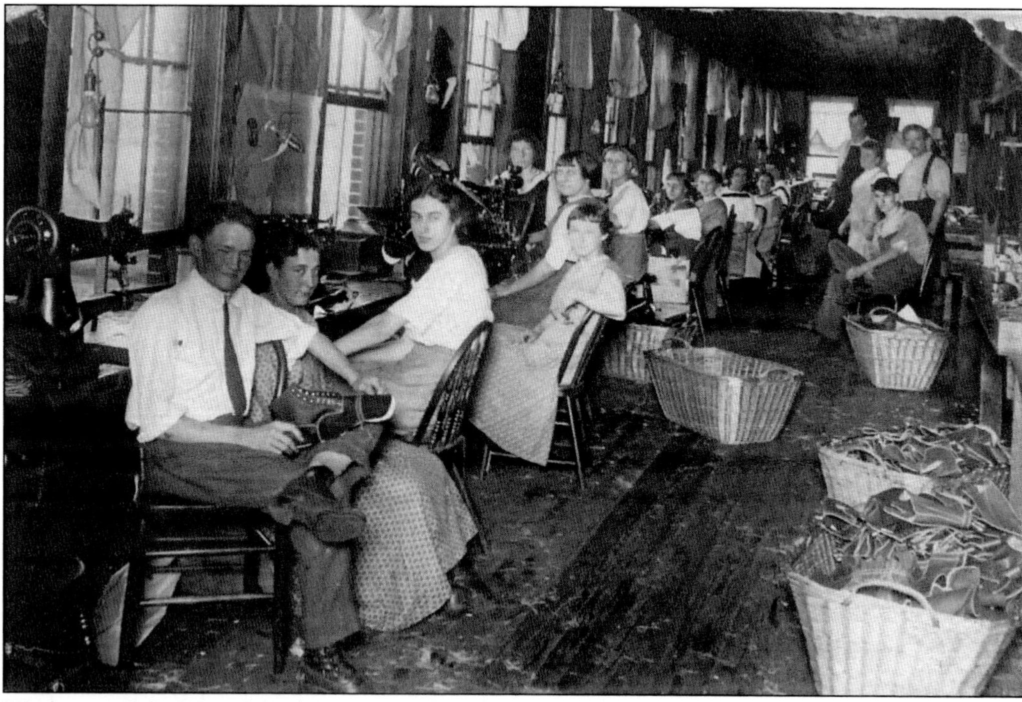

Workers at Selz Schwab and Company shoe factory take a break in 1912. Pictured from front to back are Earl Shattuck, Myrtle Sherf, Ida Crawford, Bertha Johnson, Mable Bennett, Ida Houtz, and Nellie Durham. The company at one time employed from 100 to 150 people. Emmanuel Adler was the superintendent of the Genoa plant.

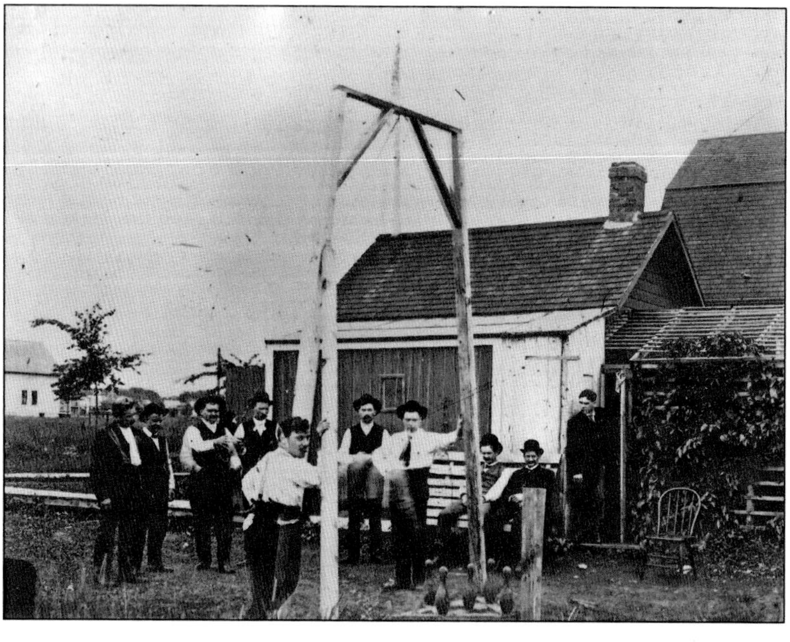

Members of the Selz Schwab and Company men's club bowl a game of 10 pins without an alley. The bowling ball hangs on a rope from a wooden archway. For this outdoor exercise, some men simply unbuttoned their coats while others played in shirtsleeves. A few men decided they would just like to watch the game.

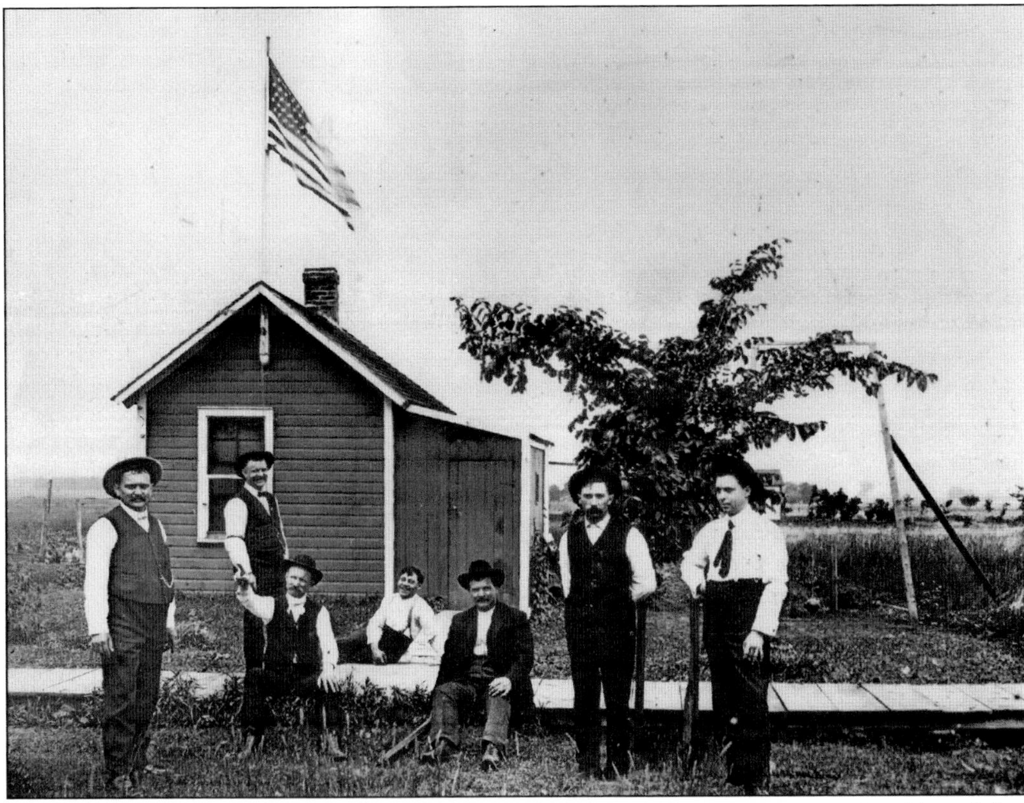

Members of the Selz Schwab and Company men's club enjoy leisure time together. From left to right are Paul Lapham, John Dodgsworth, Billy Kitler, Charles Saul, Bill Snow, "Pee Wee," and Otto Lockner. The men's club was closed by the company when it was discovered that some members were allowing women to attend the meetings.

Earl Brown (left), his father, Dillon S. Brown (seated), and Charles A. Brown (Dillon's brother and Warren Brown's grandfather) get together at Exchange State Bank in Genoa. The bank was established in 1882 and owned by Charles and Dillon. Exchange State Bank handled general banking and insurance and also sold steamship tickets to foreign countries.

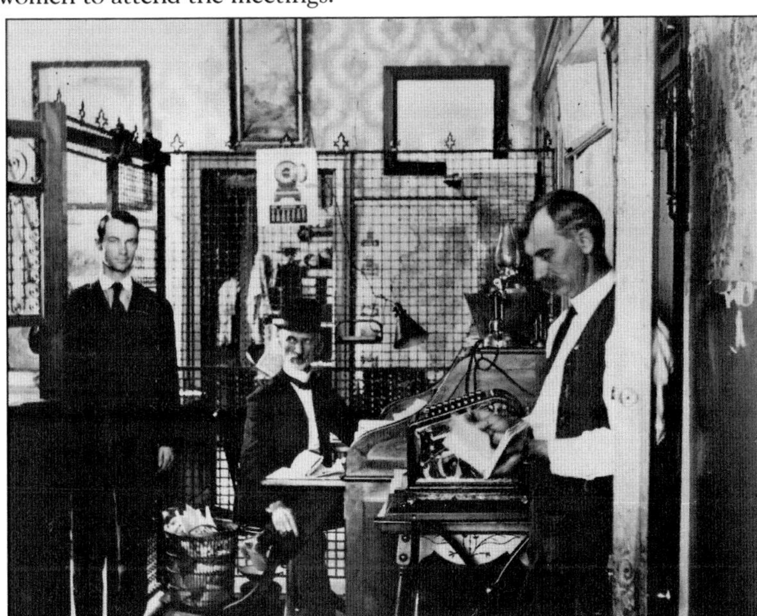

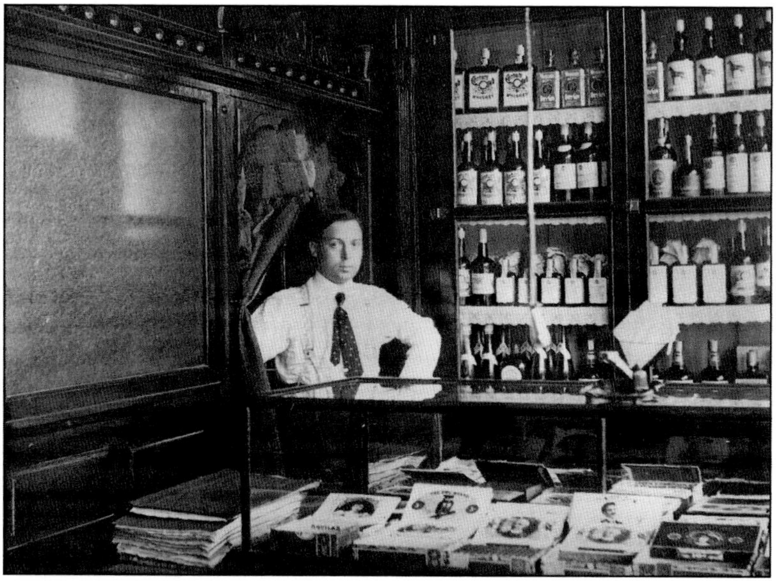

Harvey Ide's Liquor Store at 225 West Main Street in Genoa, pictured here around 1900, was considered the cleanest and most respectable saloon in town. Ide was a member of the Genoa Gun Club, which fostered both shotgun and rifle experts. The liquor store building now houses Cutters and Company Family Hair Care.

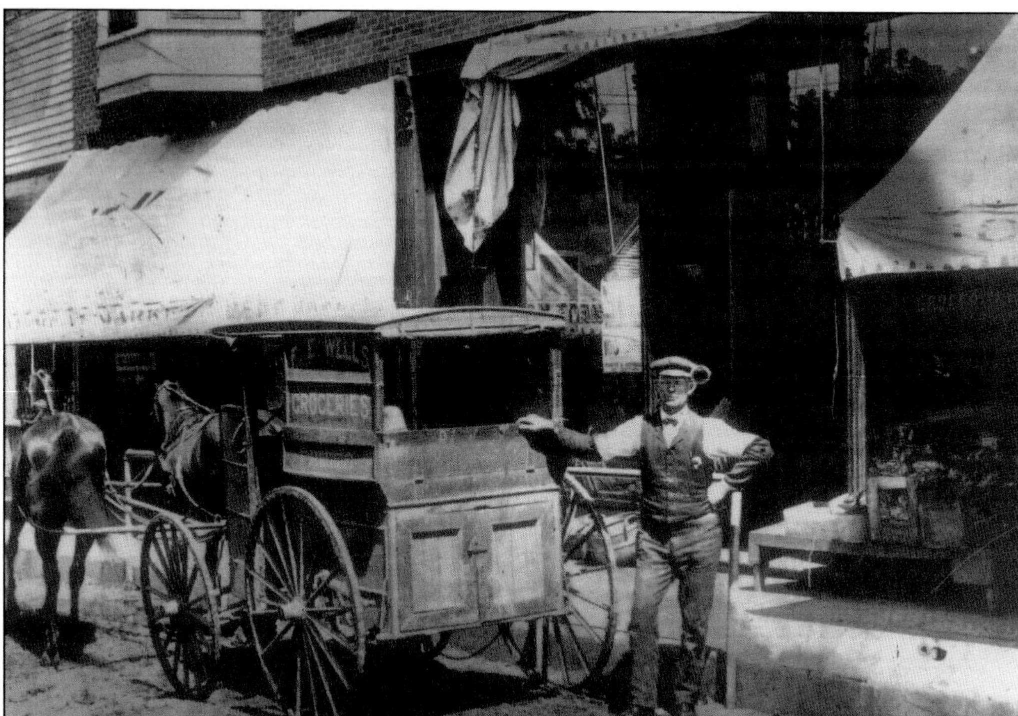

Fred E. Wells stands next to a horse-drawn delivery wagon for his grocery store along Main Street in Genoa. The grocery store building was constructed around 1900. Schoolchildren left grocery orders at the store on their way to school. Deliveries were made between 10:00 a.m. and 2:30 p.m. Fred E. Wells also sold shoes on the side.

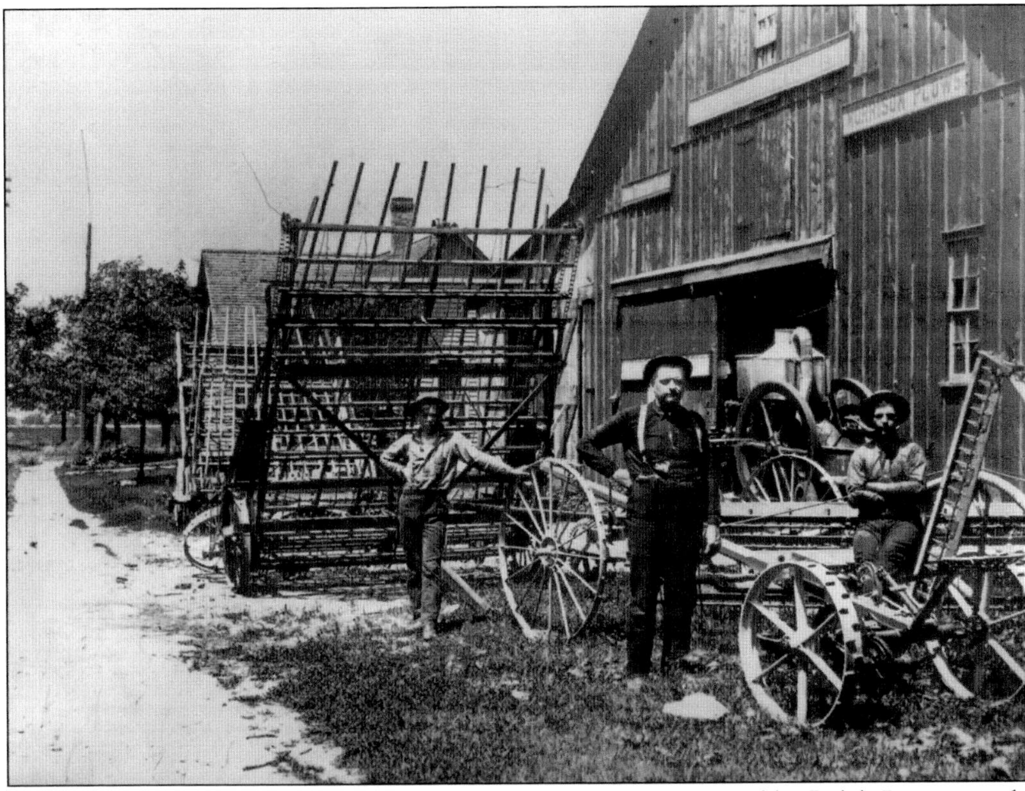

Larry Kiernan (left), his father, James (center), and machinery assembler Ralph Patterson take a break at Kiernan's Farm Machinery at 527 West Main Street in Genoa around 1900. The agricultural implement business was an agent for Deering machines and Advance threshers and engines. The company also did steam-fitting business.

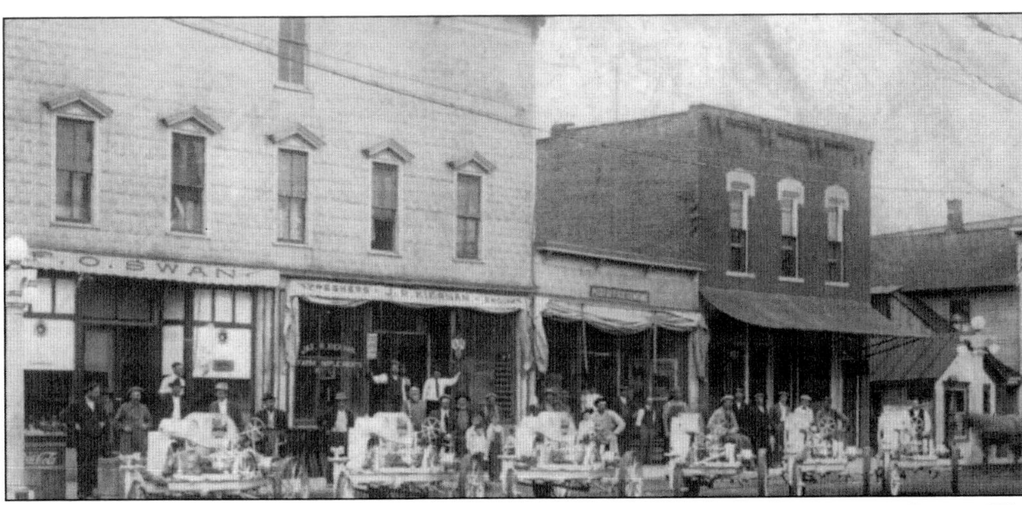

Big Bull tractors arrive at J. R. Kiernan's farm implements store on Main Street in Genoa. The Big Bull tractor was built from 1915 to 1920. The large, protruding spine on the front wheel of the three-wheel tractor was designed to keep it running in the furrow. The vehicle was once hailed as the ultimate in tractors.

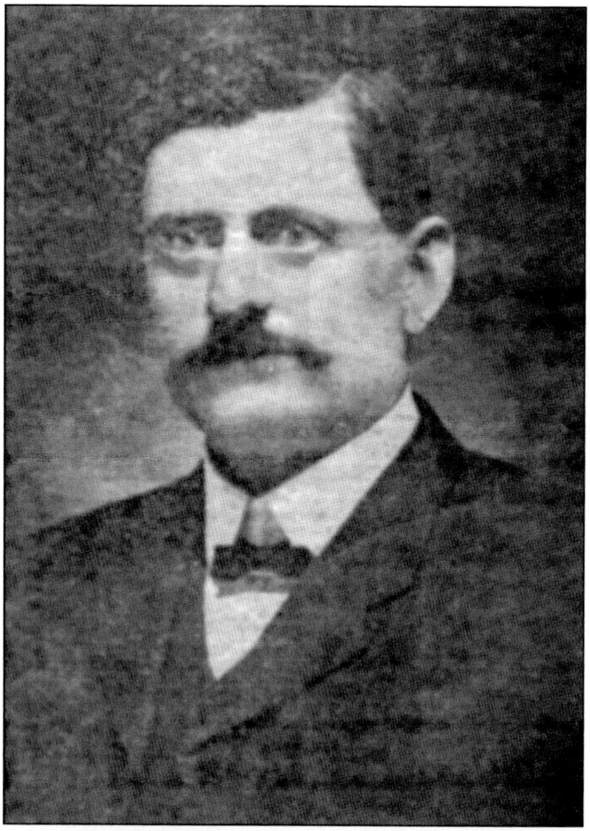

James R. Kiernan was born in Kingston Township in 1864. He lived on his father's farm until 1891, when he started a business in Genoa as a dealer of agricultural implements. He also handled buggies, wagons, and International Harvester merchandise. Kiernan and his first wife, Emma Hosker, had four children: Nellie, Dela, Lawrence, and Anna.

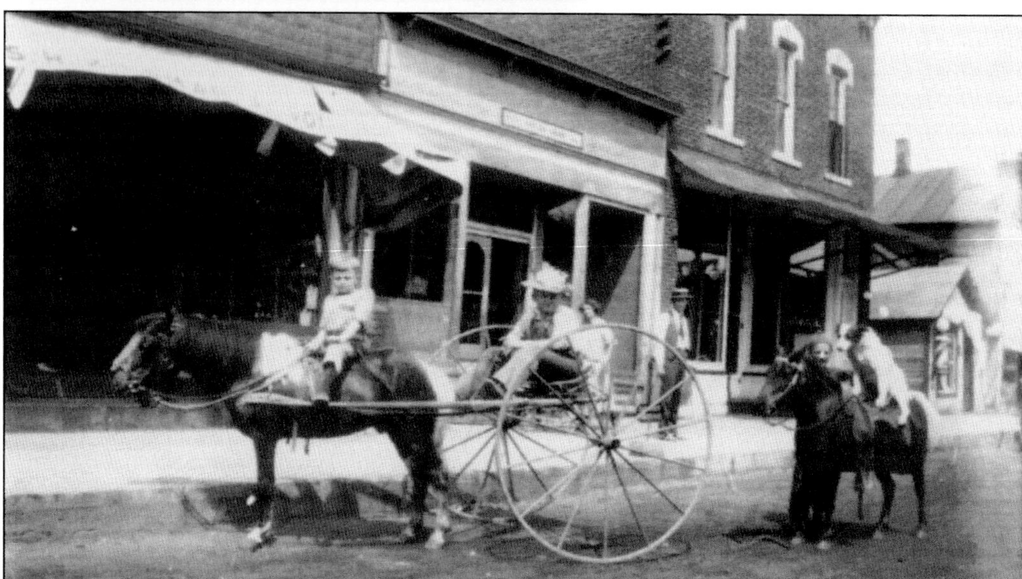

Grandchildren of James R. Kiernan pose with their ponies and dog in front of their grandfather's farm implements store along Main Street in Genoa. Kiernan built his business up gradually to the point where he earned $25,000–$30,000 a year. After Kiernan's first wife died at age 43, he married Mary Casey of Burlington, Illinois.

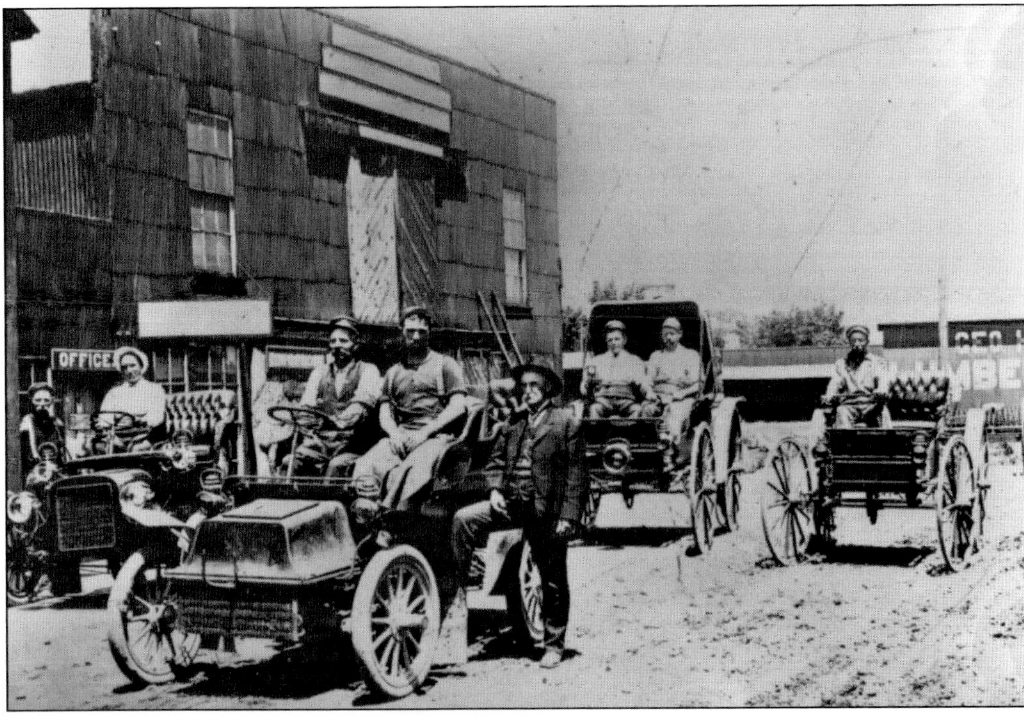

Four automobiles converge on Bob Gallagher's Livery Stable on North Genoa Street, which later became Barker's Lumber Yard. Jack Godding is on the far left driving a Cadillac, Frank Tischler Jr. is the passenger in the front car, and Frank Tischler Sr. is a passenger in the car directly behind; the other men in the photograph are unknown.

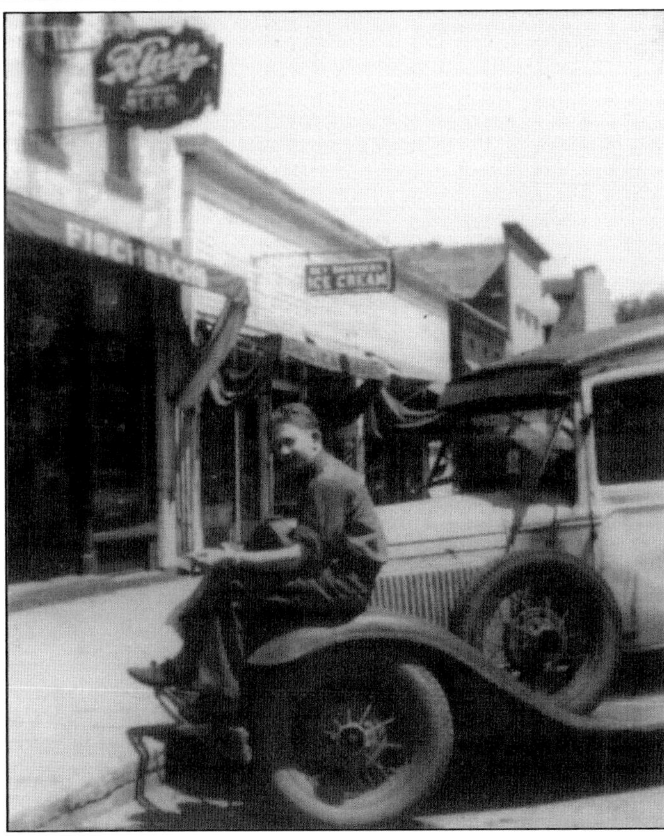

Clyde "Shrimp" Bradford, a meat cutter at Tischler's Certified Mart at 221 West Main Street in Genoa, perches on Tischler's grocery delivery truck in 1938. Edward J. Tischler bought Swan's Grocery Store, while Frank Swan bought Frazier's Grocery Store at 401 West Main Street. The two stores were across the street from each other. Bradford later became a driver's license examiner in DeKalb.

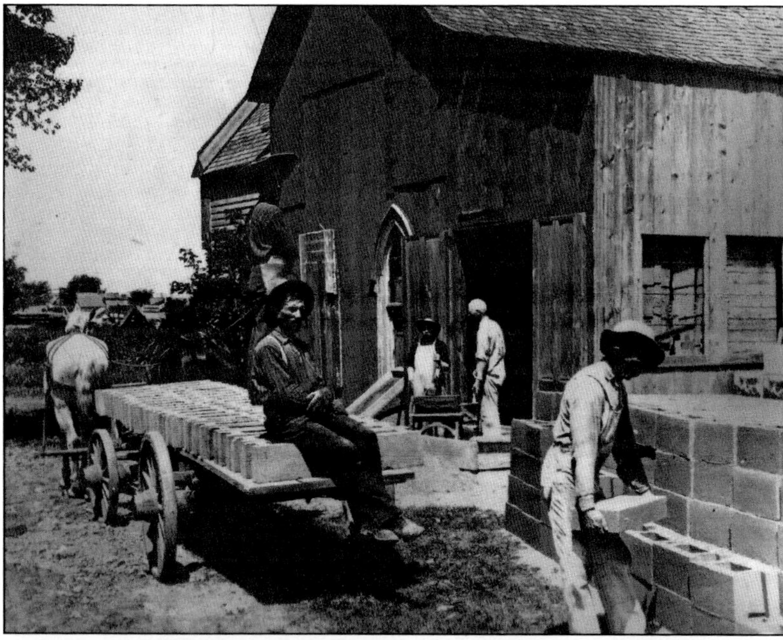

Cement blocks are loaded onto a dray. The blocks were hauled to the construction site for the Slater and Douglass store at 233 West Main Street, which was built in 1876. Lew Doty sits on the completed blocks, while Ace Snyder is shown carrying another block.

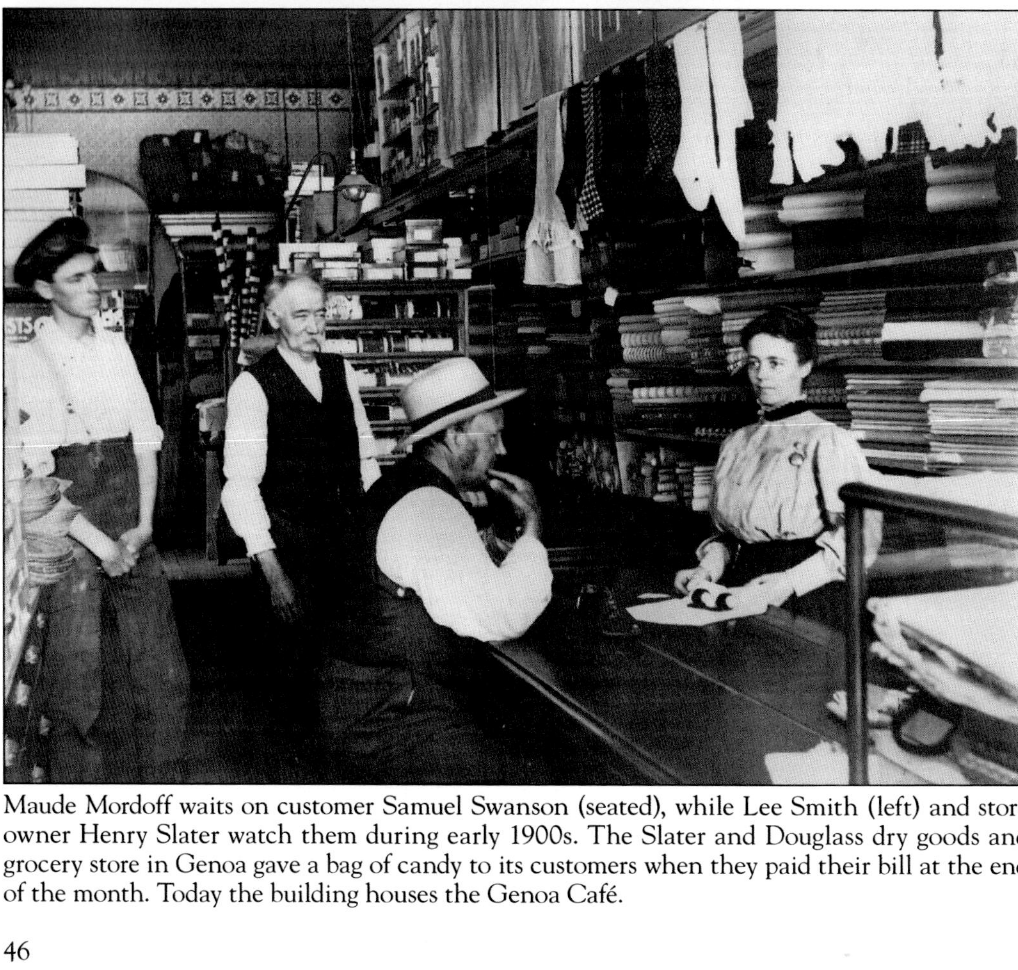

Maude Mordoff waits on customer Samuel Swanson (seated), while Lee Smith (left) and store owner Henry Slater watch them during early 1900s. The Slater and Douglass dry goods and grocery store in Genoa gave a bag of candy to its customers when they paid their bill at the end of the month. Today the building houses the Genoa Café.

Henry H. Slater was a partner with Ira Douglass at the Slater and Douglass dry goods and grocery store at 233 West Main Street in Genoa. Pictured are Henry Slater and his wife, the former Amarette Stiles. She was the great-grandmother of Robert Slater and Betty Slater Romke. The Slater and Douglass store was known as the "Old Reliable" because customers could usually find whatever they needed. The store carried a complete line of drugs, medicines, paints, oils, dry goods, groceries, and shoes. Douglass had a second store in Kingston.

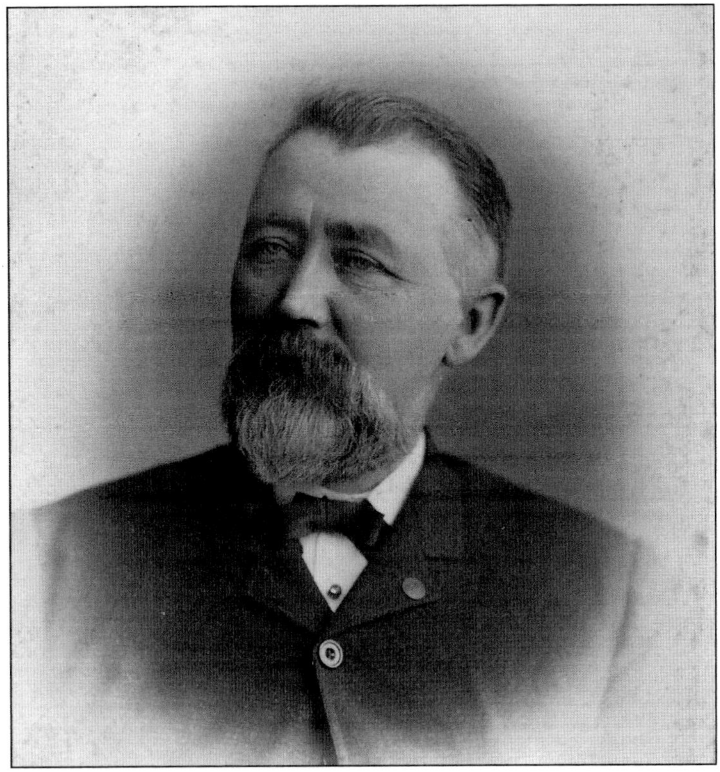

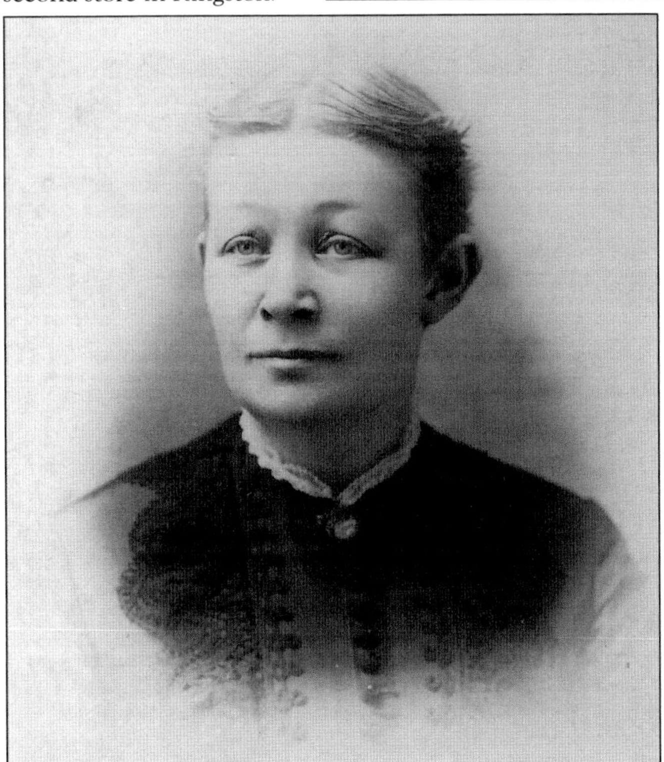

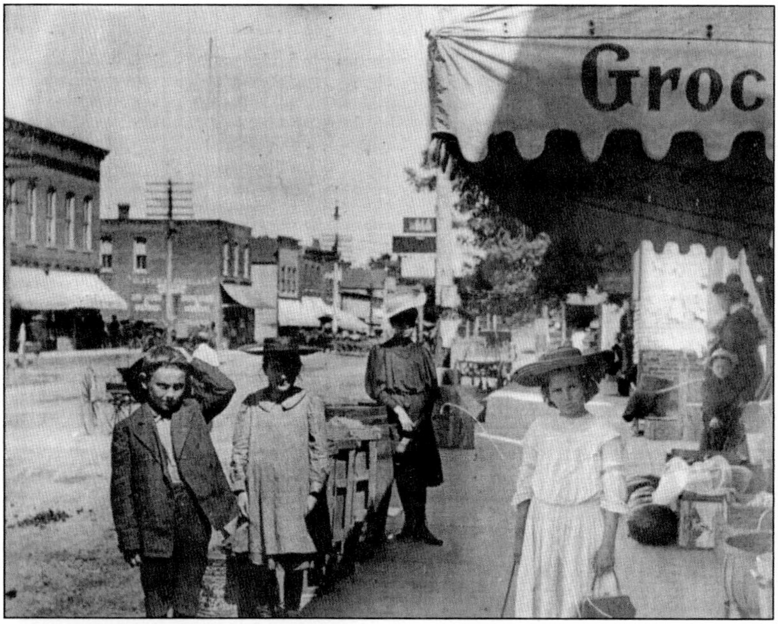

Genoa shop owners during the early 1900s were bothered by flocks of sparrows that whitewashed their buildings with bird droppings. Frank Swan, owner of Swan's Grocery Store along Main Street, paid children a penny for every dead sparrow they brought in. The well-dressed children standing in front of Swan's store were probably not interested in the task.

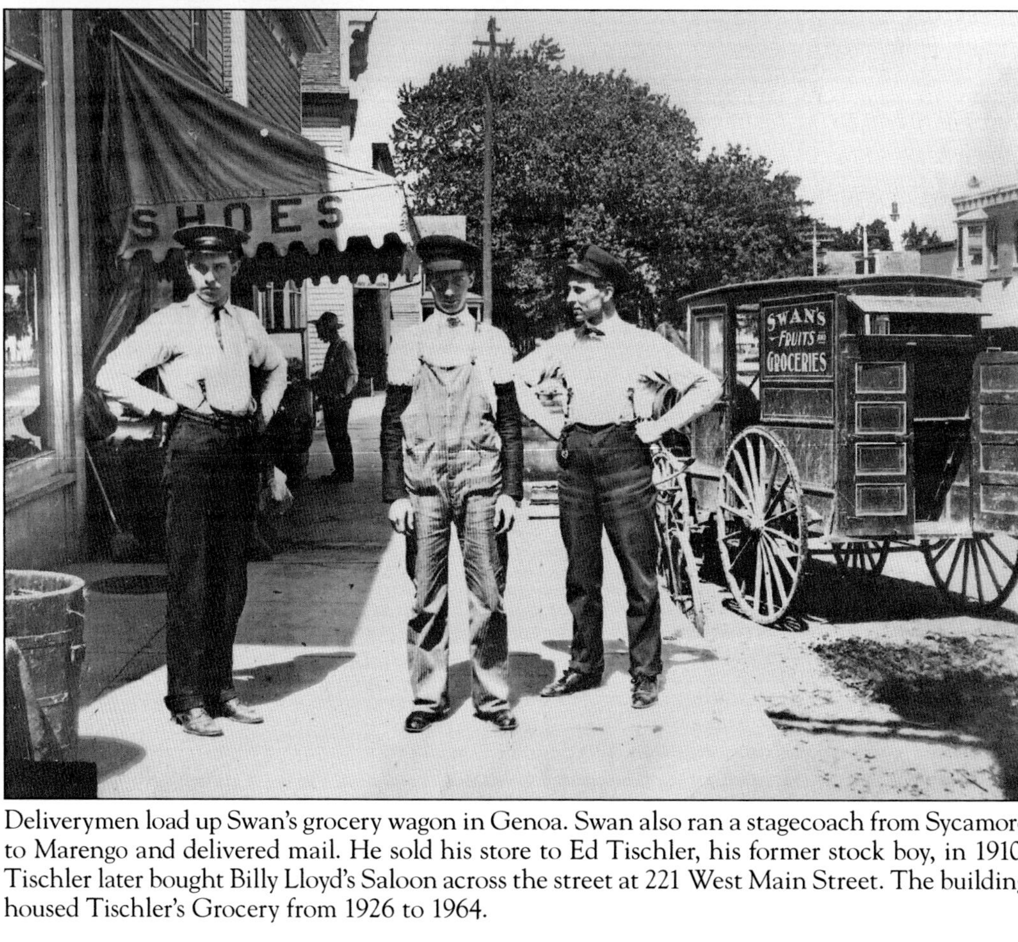

Deliverymen load up Swan's grocery wagon in Genoa. Swan also ran a stagecoach from Sycamore to Marengo and delivered mail. He sold his store to Ed Tischler, his former stock boy, in 1910. Tischler later bought Billy Lloyd's Saloon across the street at 221 West Main Street. The building housed Tischler's Grocery from 1926 to 1964.

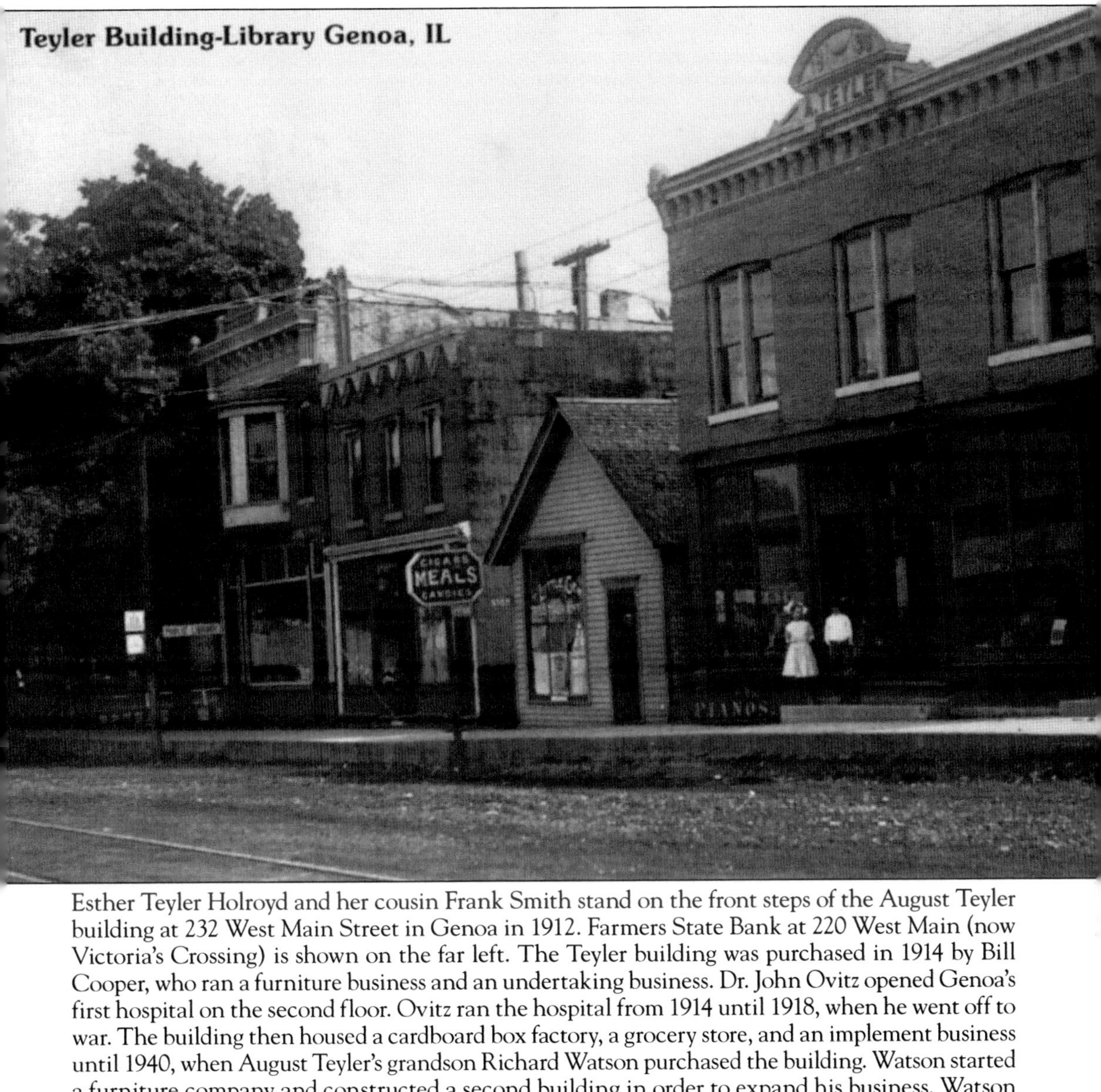

Esther Teyler Holroyd and her cousin Frank Smith stand on the front steps of the August Teyler building at 232 West Main Street in Genoa in 1912. Farmers State Bank at 220 West Main (now Victoria's Crossing) is shown on the far left. The Teyler building was purchased in 1914 by Bill Cooper, who ran a furniture business and an undertaking business. Dr. John Ovitz opened Genoa's first hospital on the second floor. Ovitz ran the hospital from 1914 until 1918, when he went off to war. The building then housed a cardboard box factory, a grocery store, and an implement business until 1940, when August Teyler's grandson Richard Watson purchased the building. Watson started a furniture company and constructed a second building in order to expand his business. Watson rented the facility to John and Bill Rauschenberger in 1955 for Rauschenberger Furniture. Frank DiMario purchased the building in 1970 and sold it to the Genoa Public Library in 1977.

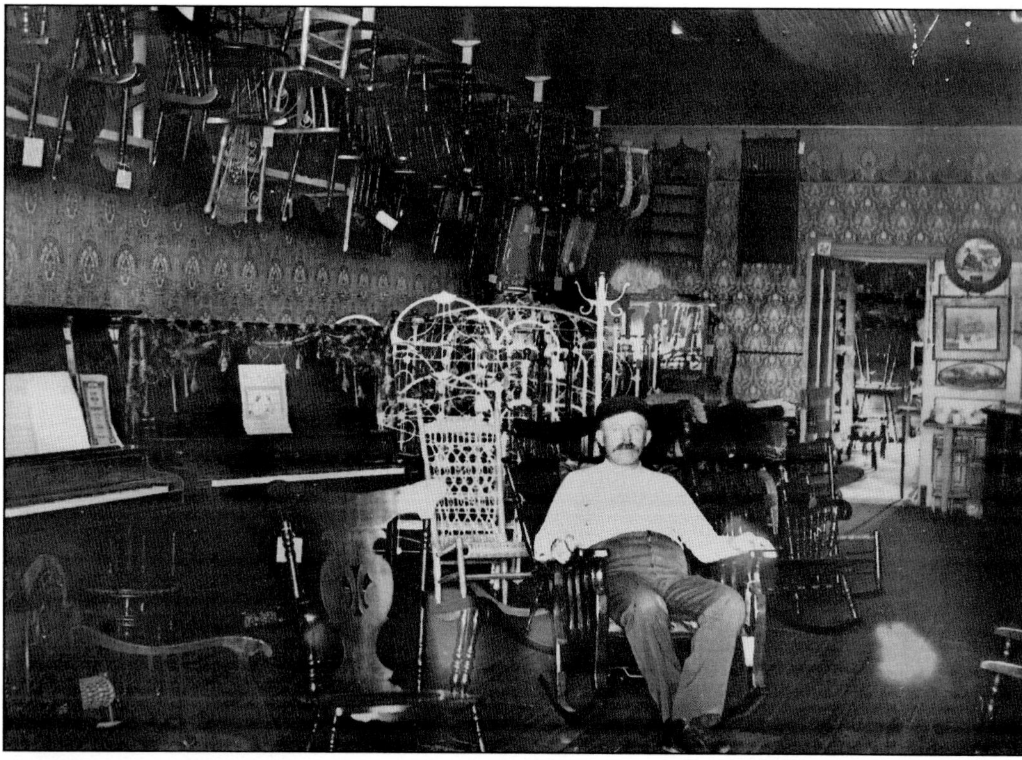

In 1895, August Teyler built a two-story brick building at 232 West Main Street in Genoa. The foundation was made from stone hauled from Joliet. Teyler sold Thompson Pianos made in Genoa along with furniture, German and French china, glassware, semi-porcelain, crockery, and lamps. He also worked as an undertaker. In 1914, Teyler lost his life in a train accident.

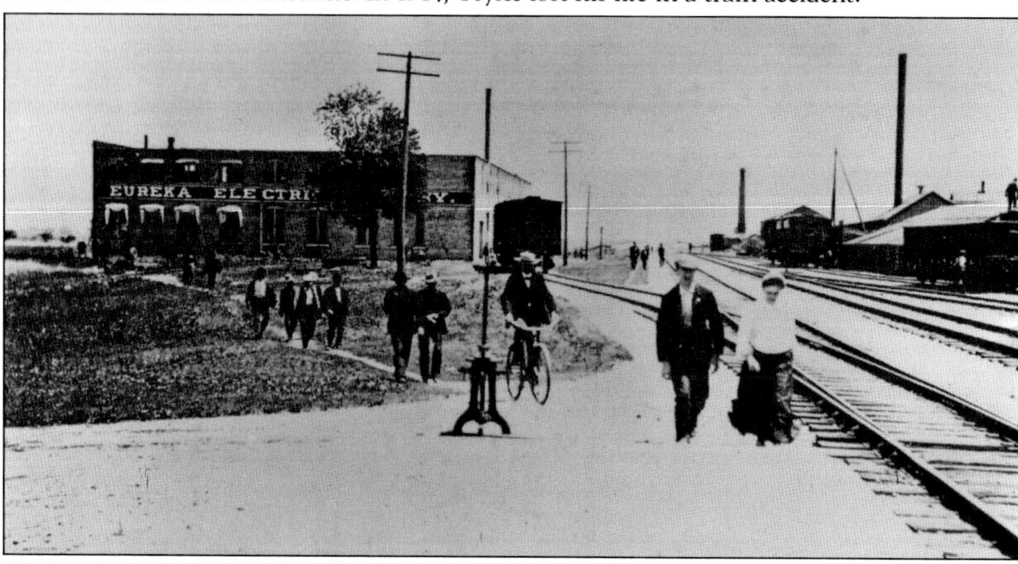

Workers leave for home after a hard day's work at Eureka Electric Company. Fred Ruelman rides his bicycle, while C. H. Van Wie and Birdie Evans choose to walk. In 1904, Eureka Electric produced switchboard drops, ringing and listening keys, and switch hooks and transmitters for local and central energy work.

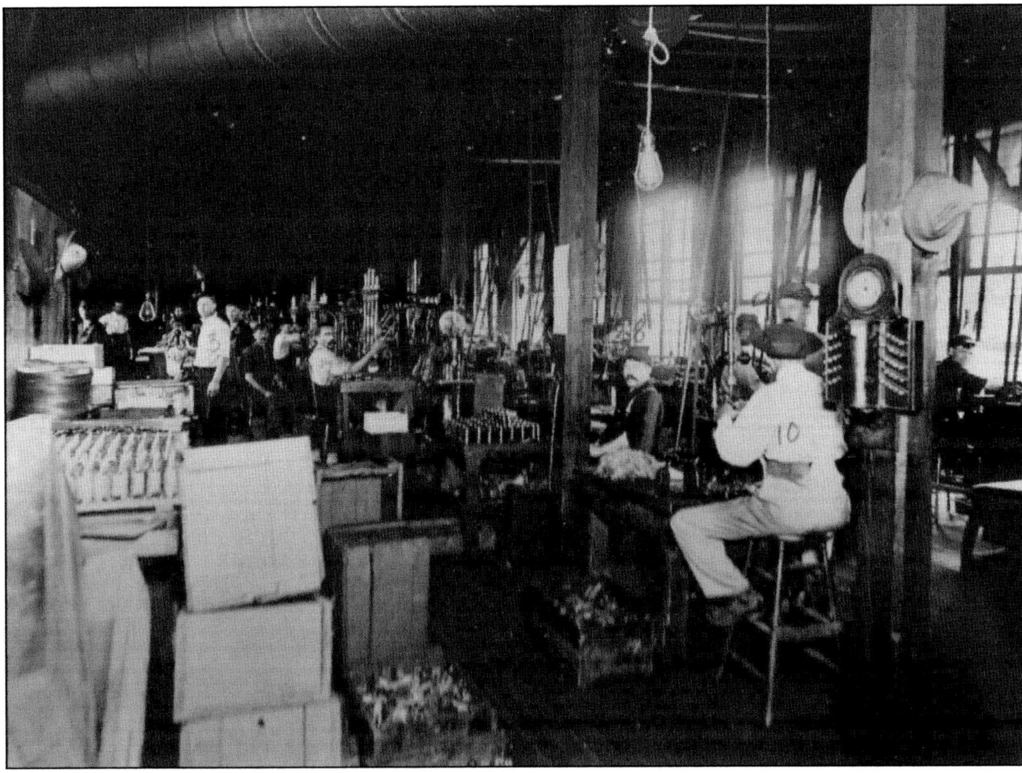

Leich Electric Company was an outgrowth of Eureka Electric Company. Ace Snyder, shown in a white outfit and seated on a stool, is putting in a hard day's work at Leich Electric in Genoa around 1920. Shown peering above Snyder's hat is company foreman Fred C. Duval. All of the machines ran from power shafts on the left side.

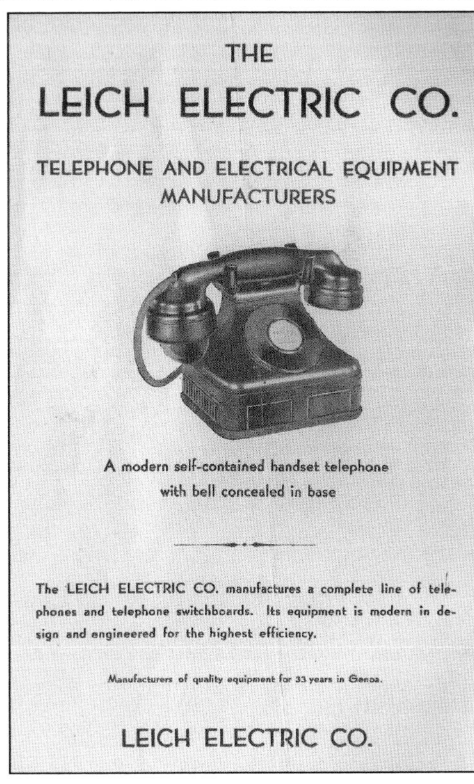

During the early 1900s, Leich Electric Company made the first vibrating ringing converter to operate from a 60-cycle alternating current. It was also known for its harmonic ringing equipment that was used for both manual and automatic switchboards. A pulsating harmonic system was introduced into the magneto field. Leich also made signaling relays for railroads and built several railroad dispatching boards.

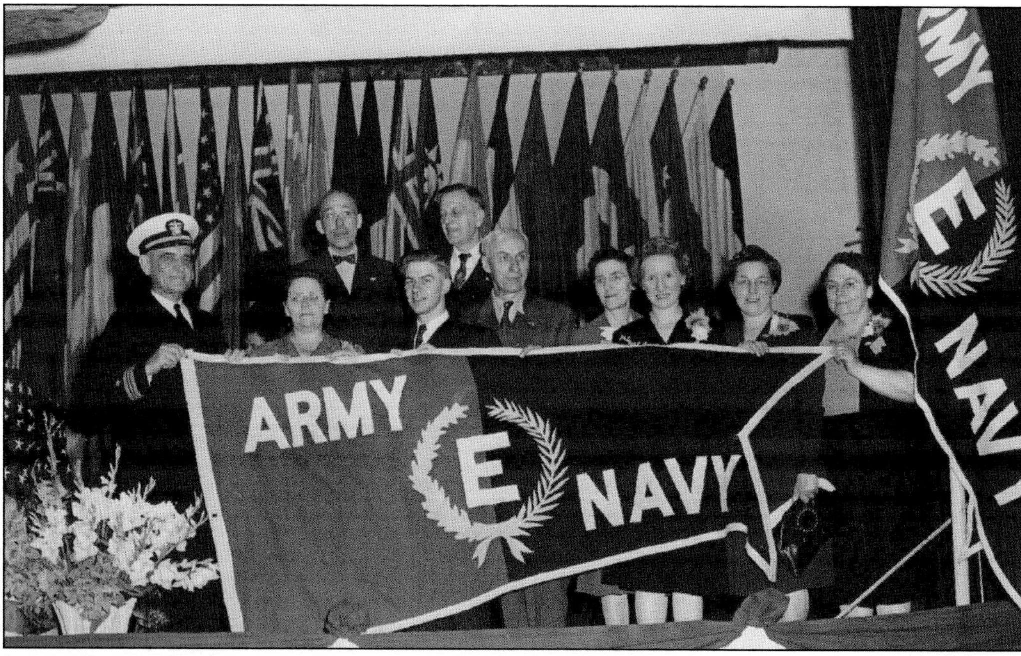

Leich Electric Company in Genoa won the Army-Navy "E" Award twice during World War I and World War II for excellence in production of military switchboards. At the 1944 award presentation, standing from left to right next to an unknown U.S. Army officer, are (first row) Mrs. Petman, Milt Durham, Pete Rosenke, Margaret Hutchison, Emma Hoehn, Anna Hoehn, and Dolly Nelson; (second row) William Schnur and James Forsythe.

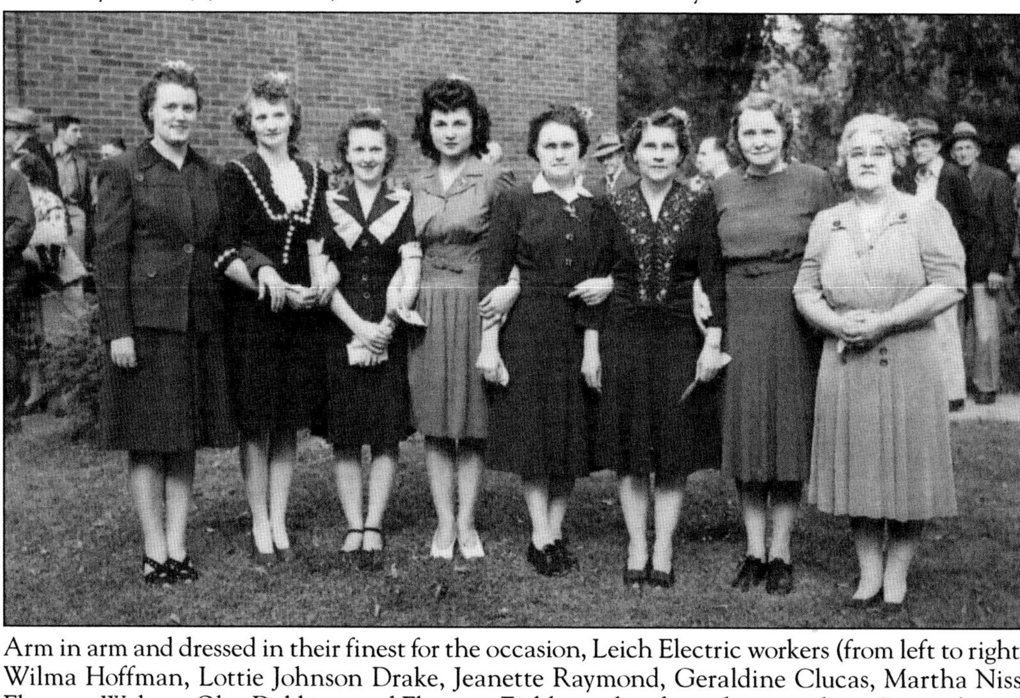

Arm in arm and dressed in their finest for the occasion, Leich Electric workers (from left to right) Wilma Hoffman, Lottie Johnson Drake, Jeanette Raymond, Geraldine Clucas, Martha Niss, Florence Wolters, Olga Dobbins, and Florence Eickler gather for a photograph on September 15, 1944, for the presentation of the Army-Navy "E" Award in Genoa.

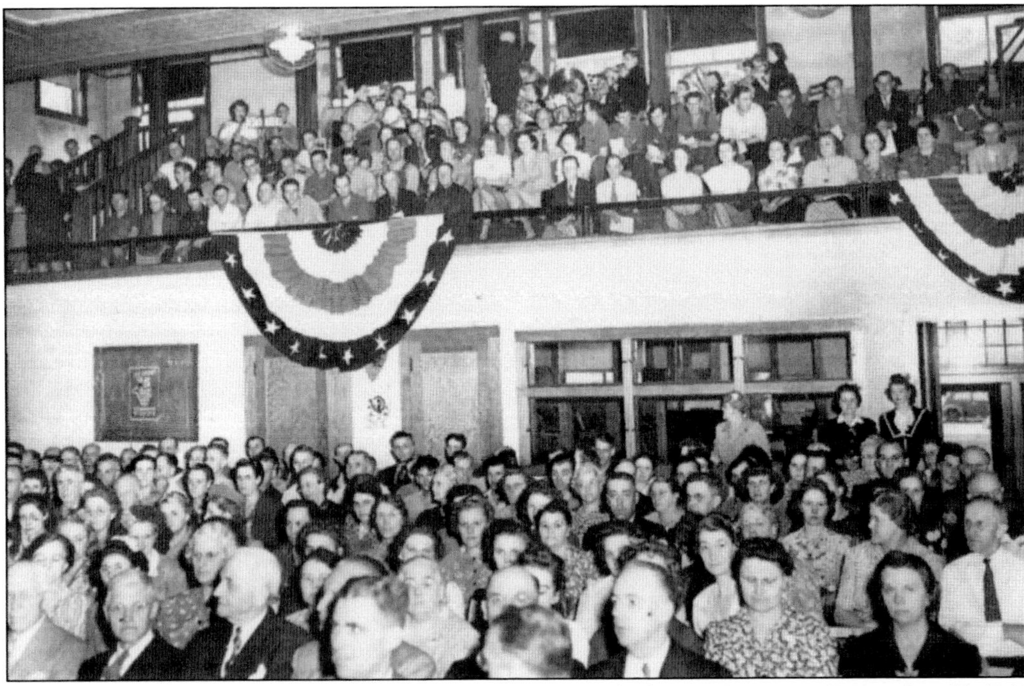

A crowd filled both floors of the Leich Electric Company facility in Genoa on September 15, 1944, for the presentation of the Army-Navy "E" Award. When Cracraft-Leich became Leich Electric Company in 1917, its first job was to produce telephones for the government during World War I. Leich Electric employees once worked 26 consecutive hours for an emergency shipment overseas.

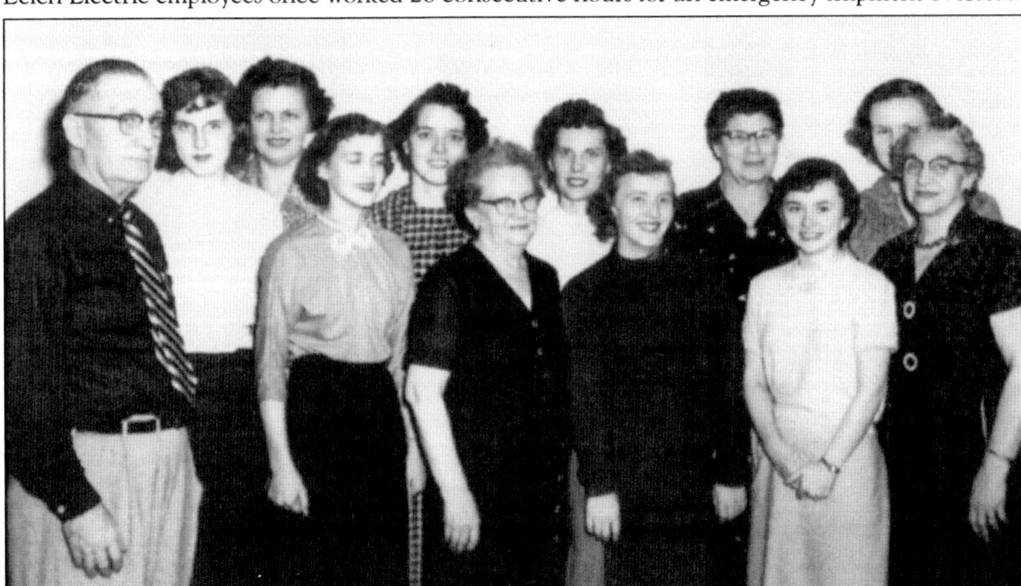

In 1950, Leich Electric Company in Genoa became a wholly owned subsidiary of General Telephone and Electronics Corporation (GTE). GTE workers, shown from left to right in 1956, are (first row) Martha Loy, Ella Hohn, Dorothy Lorenson, Shirley Kimey, and Lena Holmes; (second row) Elmer Prain, Judy Hackman, Marie Loreson, Ann Swanson, Elaine Carroll, Susie Winterton, and Barbara Ramsey.

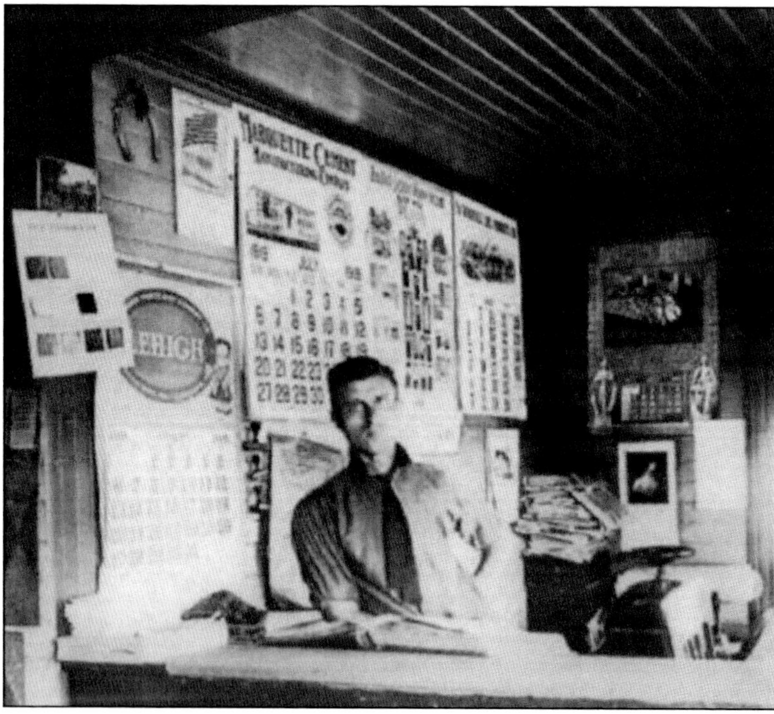

Orrin Merritt Sr. was a manager at Tibbets and Cameron Lumberyard in Genoa in 1919. His son Orrin Merritt Jr. had a Borden distributorship for 14 years and was a payroll manager for Automatic Electric and DeKalb Ag. Orrin Jr.'s son Orrin Merritt III taught biology at Genoa-Kingston High School. He is now vice president of Kishwaukee Valley Heritage Society Museum.

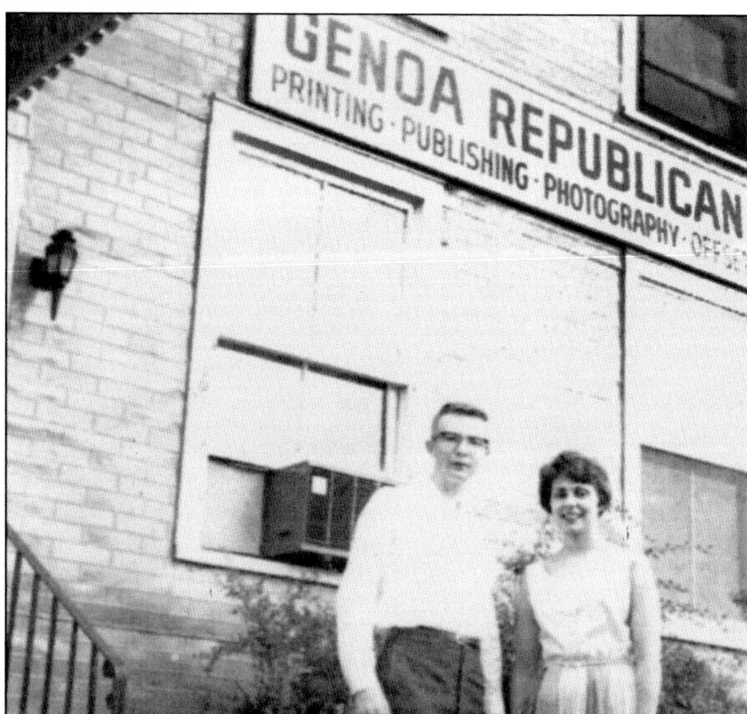

Barry Schrader and Kay (Wirsing) Schrader stand before the Genoa Republican Building during the 1960s. The *Genoa Republican* newspaper was started in 1902. Charles D. Schoonmaker bought the *Republican* and the *Genoa Journal* in 1904, combining them into the *Genoa Republican-Journal*. The Schraders bought the publication in 1966 and sold it in 1968. The newspaper no longer exists.

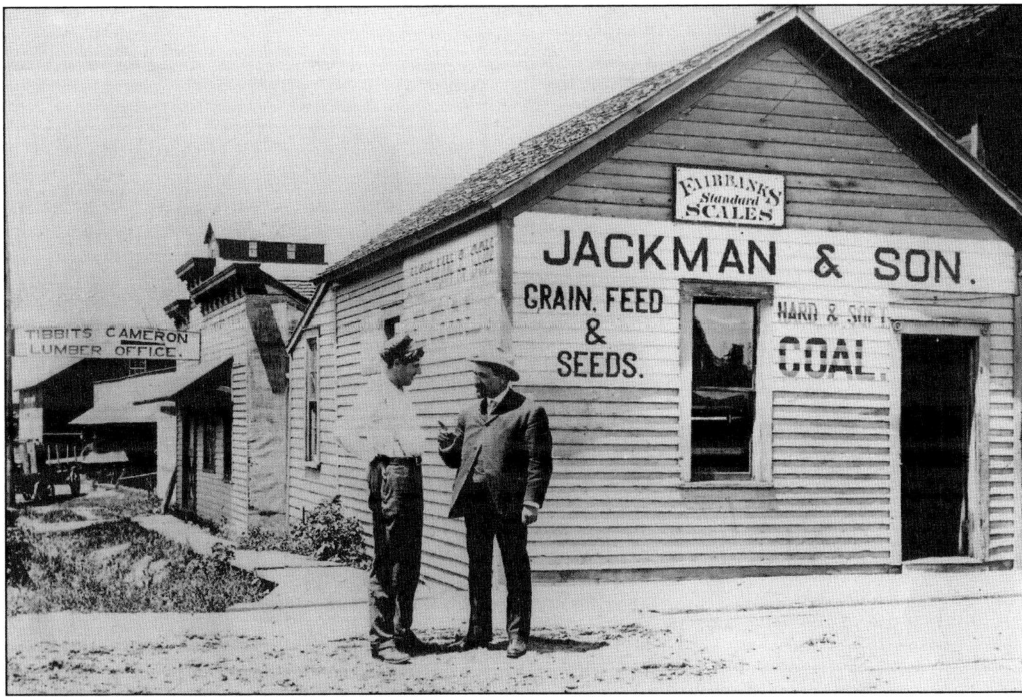

Doc Mordoff (right) chats with Will Jackman at Jackman and Son Grain, Feed, and Seeds. The company was located at 201 North Sycamore Street in Genoa. The Tibbets Cameron Lumber office is shown in the background. The grain elevator was built by Jackman in 1890. The business was sold to Zeller and Son in 1914 and then to Frank Merriman in 1937.

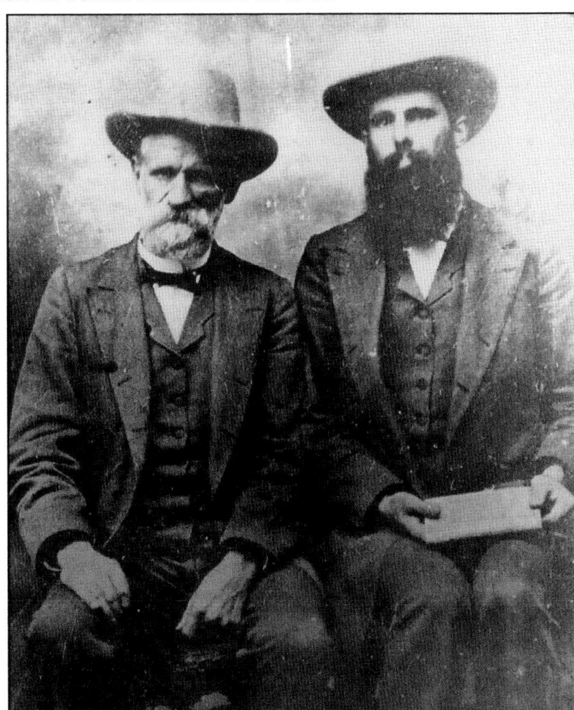

Posing here together, Almon Brown Strowger (left) and his nephew Walter S. Strowger invented the automatic telephone switch, which eliminated the need for a human telephone operator. Automatic Electric Company acquired the right to manufacture and sell Strowger automatic stepping switches. Automatic Electric merged with General Telephone and Electronic in 1955 and used the Leich Electric facility in Genoa, a GTE subsidiary, to manufacture the Strowger system.

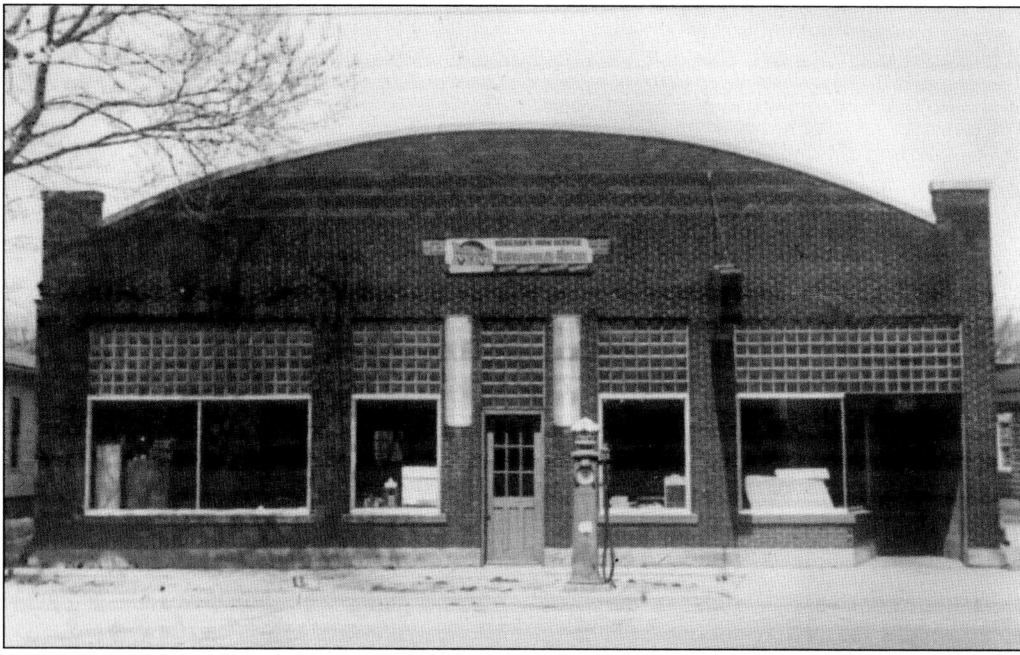

Farmers could find what they needed at Wyman Hodgson Farm Store at 527 West Main Street in Genoa in 1950. The facility was formerly known as Bill Whipple's store before it became a farm store. It later became Earl and Janet Tischler's Supermarket (1965–1969), Carol and Nick Tabone's Genoa IGA, and Roberta Brown's Market. It is now a Dollar General discount store.

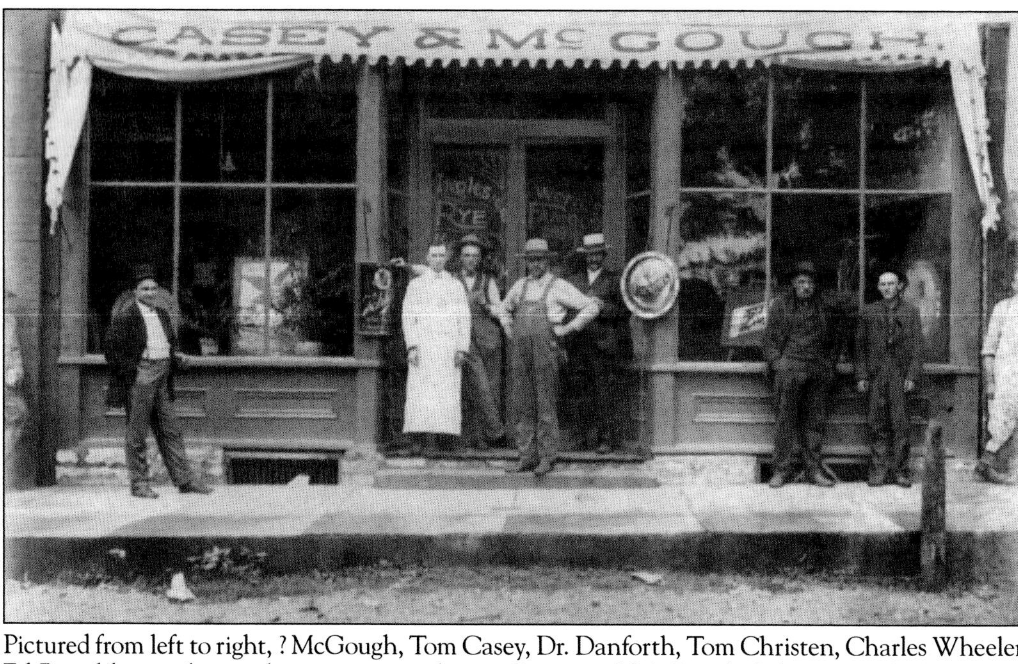

Pictured from left to right, ? McGough, Tom Casey, Dr. Danforth, Tom Christen, Charles Wheeler, Ed Beardsley, and an unknown man gather at Casey and McGough Saloon at 413 West Main Street in Genoa around 1900. The saloon burned down and was replaced with a cobbler shop. The building later housed Sh'Naningans for 17 years. Karlsbad Tavern has been at 413 West Main Street since 1994.

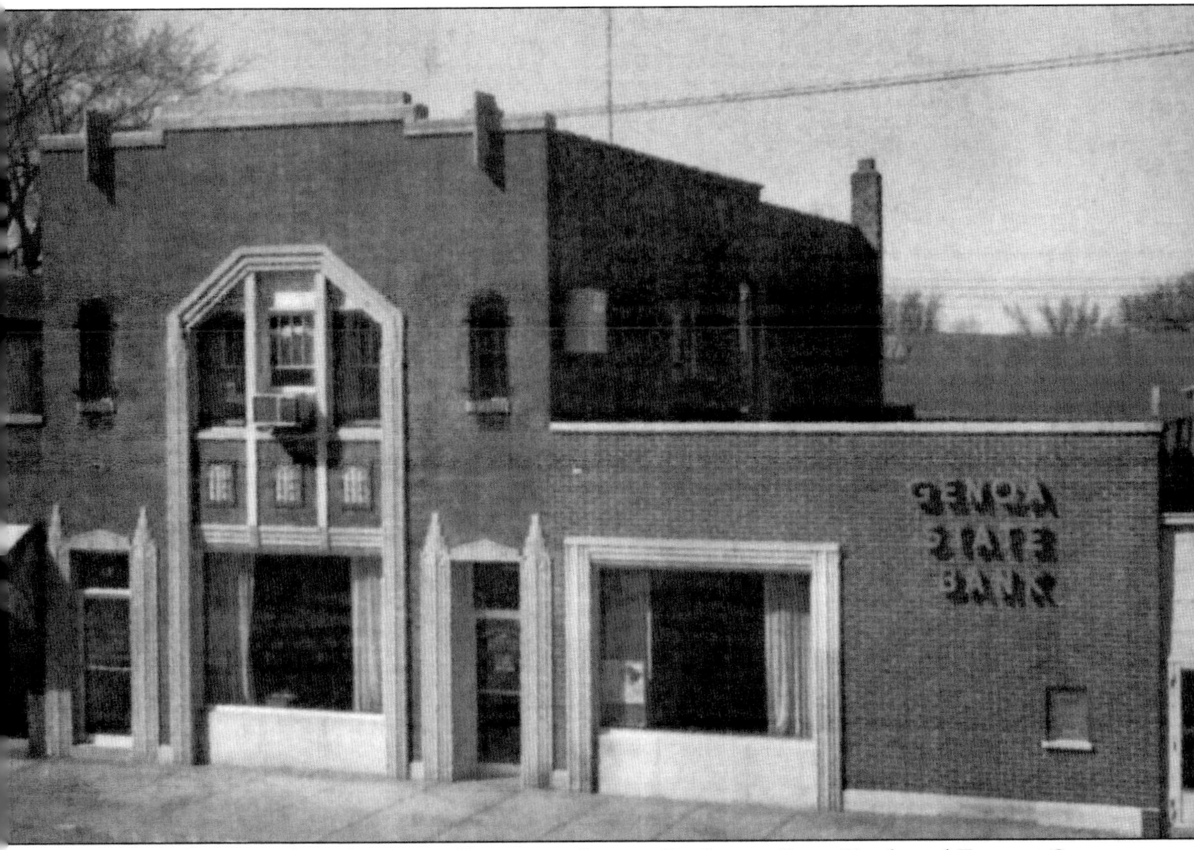

In 1929, the year when the Great Depression began, Exchange State Bank and Farmers State Bank in Genoa were closed by state officials. The banks had depleted cash reserves caused by frozen assets that were not immediately collectible. John Duval and E. J. Tischler of Genoa, along with Paul Nehring of DeKalb and other area residents, worked to start a new bank in Genoa. The Genoa State Bank opened on May 1, 1930, with Nehring as president. On June 25 of that same year, Genoa State Bank passed a resolution to take over the assets and liabilities of Kingston State Bank. In 1936, Kingston State Bank stockholders were discharged from any liability in connection with the bank takeover. Princeton National Bancorp, Inc., as holding company for Citizens First National Bank, purchased Genoa State Bank in 1986. Today the facility that once housed Genoa State Bank at 327 West Main Street now houses Citizens First National Bank.

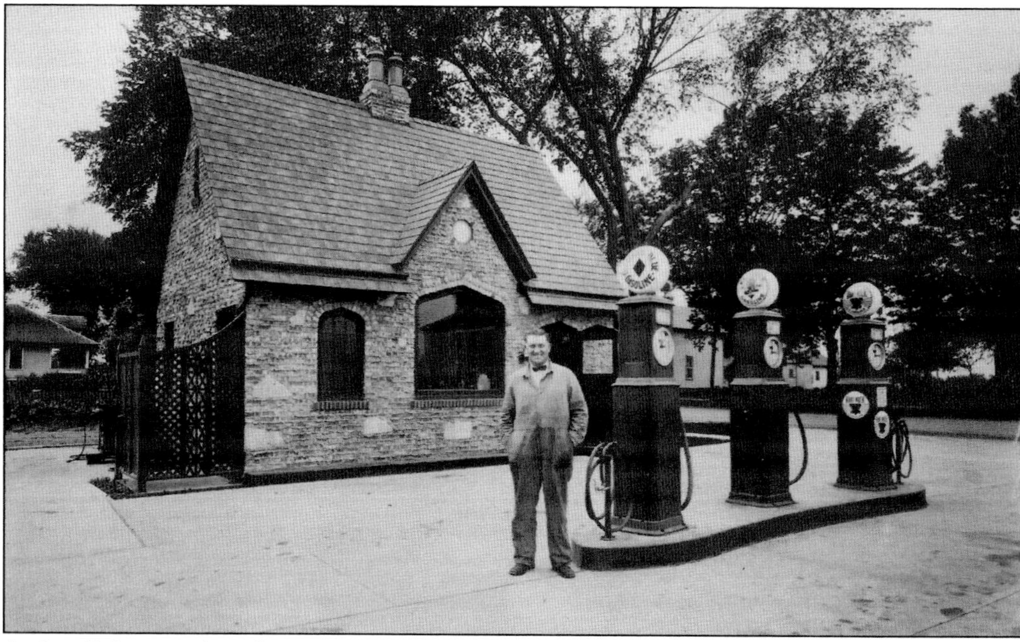

Arthur Baker stands at the gas station at 438 Main Street in Genoa in 1932. The site later became a used car lot, a car wash, and then an ice cream shop. When the Cooley family purchased the building, they ran it as a restaurant for 22 years. In 1998, the business changed to Wild Thyme Herb Garden, which is run by herbalist Evelyn Cooley. (Courtesy of Evelyn Cooley.)

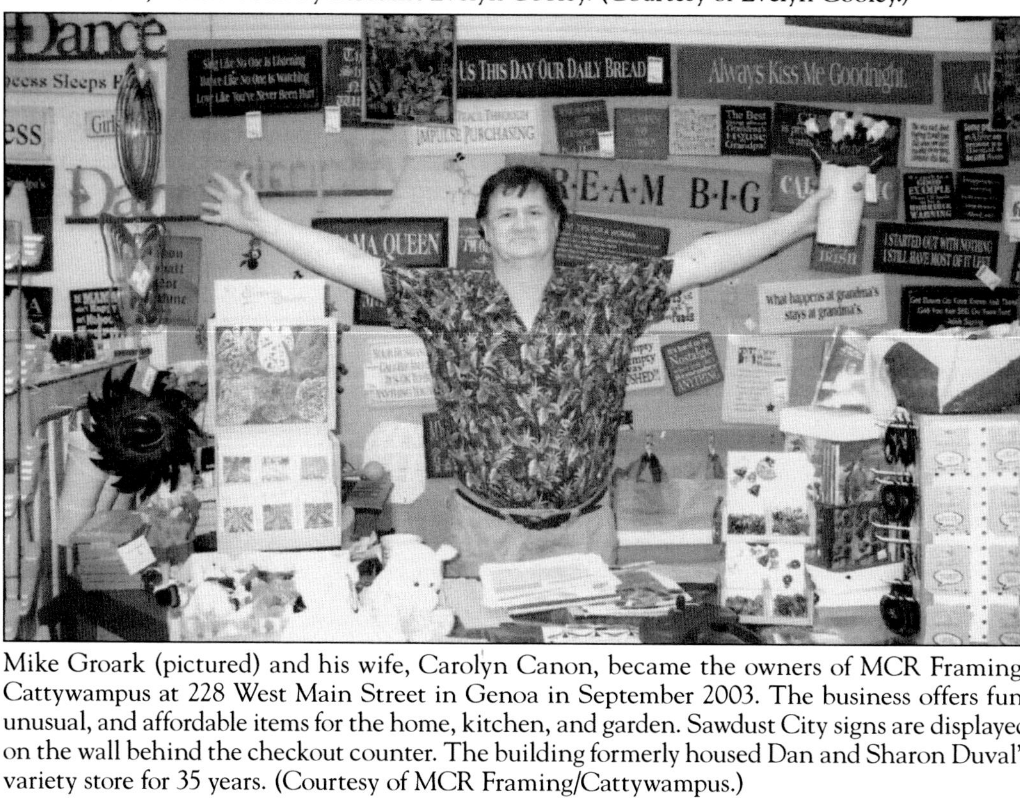

Mike Groark (pictured) and his wife, Carolyn Canon, became the owners of MCR Framing/ Cattywampus at 228 West Main Street in Genoa in September 2003. The business offers fun, unusual, and affordable items for the home, kitchen, and garden. Sawdust City signs are displayed on the wall behind the checkout counter. The building formerly housed Dan and Sharon Duval's variety store for 35 years. (Courtesy of MCR Framing/Cattywampus.)

Four

School Days

Students in Genoa and Kingston were originally taught in one-room schoolhouses. James Harrington Moore, a grandson of Thomas Matteson, recalled:

> The old log schoolhouse that sheltered the little kids, as well as the larger ones, was 28 by 24 feet. It faced east with a high fireplace in the west end built of stone that took in 4-foot wood. The desks were long, extending the entire length of the building, and were made of white wood lumber hauled from Chicago. Benches were split out of basswood logs hued until they were two or three inches in thickness, with holes bored in the ends and pins put in for legs, with no backs to rest against. They made our backs ache, but we managed very well, for we knew of nothing better. The cracks between the logs were filled with clay to keep out the cold. Many of the scholars came over three miles to school. Some stayed among the farmers and did chores for their board.

Many years later, Moore came back to Genoa and visited his former school. The building had been turned into a place to store farm machinery.

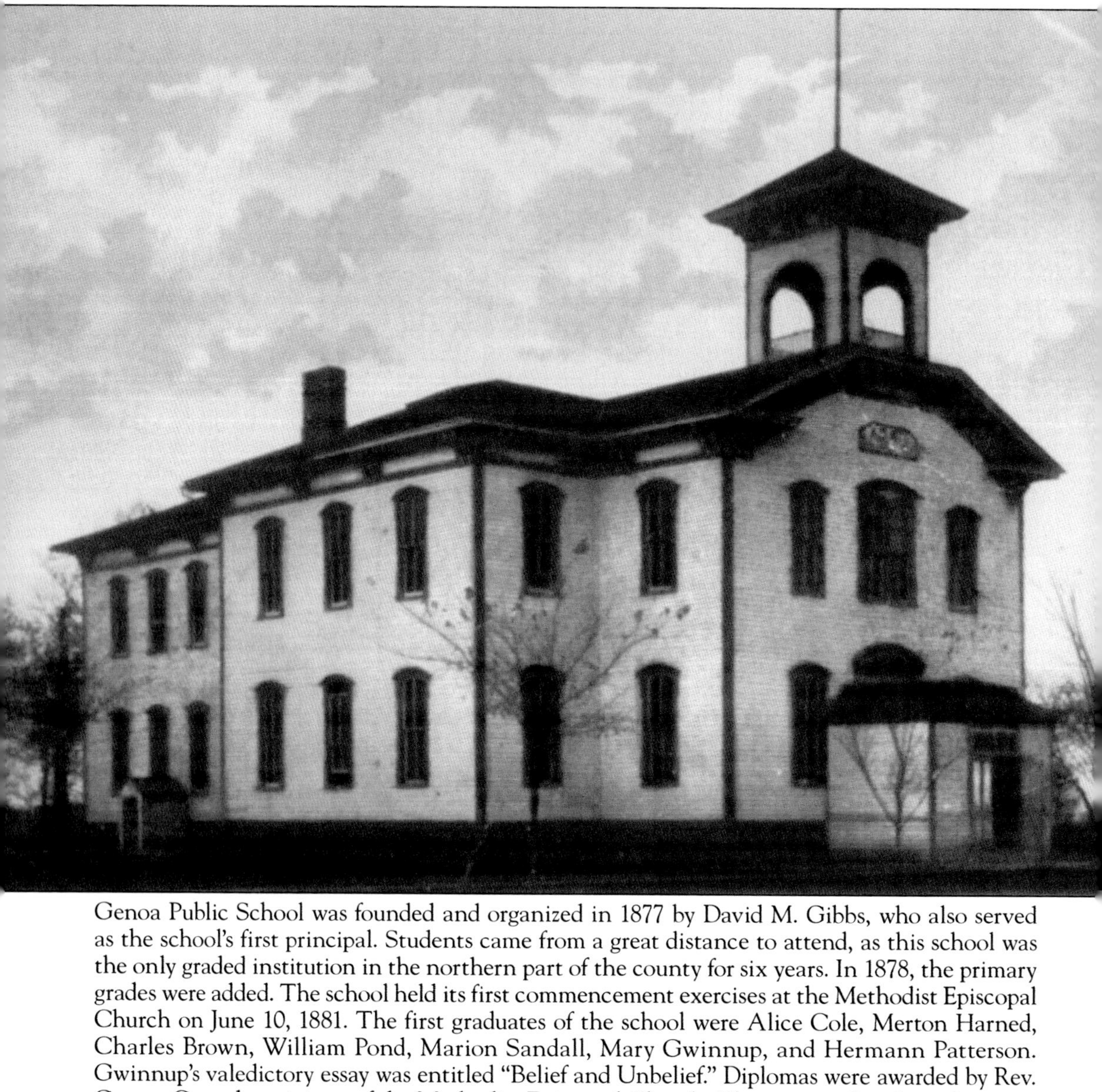

Genoa Public School was founded and organized in 1877 by David M. Gibbs, who also served as the school's first principal. Students came from a great distance to attend, as this school was the only graded institution in the northern part of the county for six years. In 1878, the primary grades were added. The school held its first commencement exercises at the Methodist Episcopal Church on June 10, 1881. The first graduates of the school were Alice Cole, Merton Harned, Charles Brown, William Pond, Marion Sandall, Mary Gwinnup, and Hermann Patterson. Gwinnup's valedictory essay was entitled "Belief and Unbelief." Diplomas were awarded by Rev. George Carr, the minister of the Methodist Episcopal Church. The course of study at that time was three years and was extended to four years in 1900.

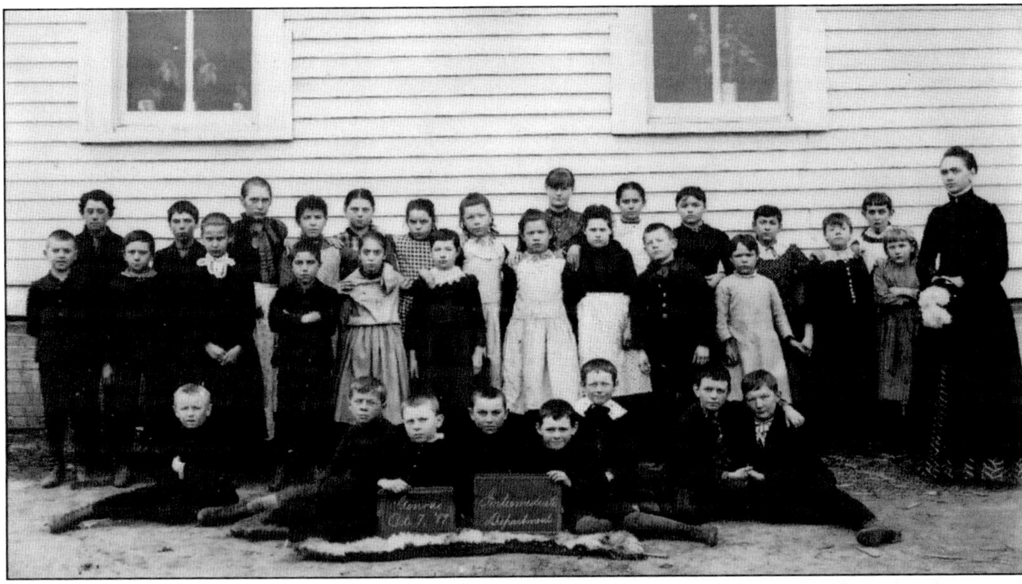

Genoa Public School intermediate students pose with their teacher in 1889. The school year was divided into three terms: winter term began in January and ended in April, spring term began in April and ended in June, and the fall term started in September and ended in December. The school taught primary, intermediate, and high school students.

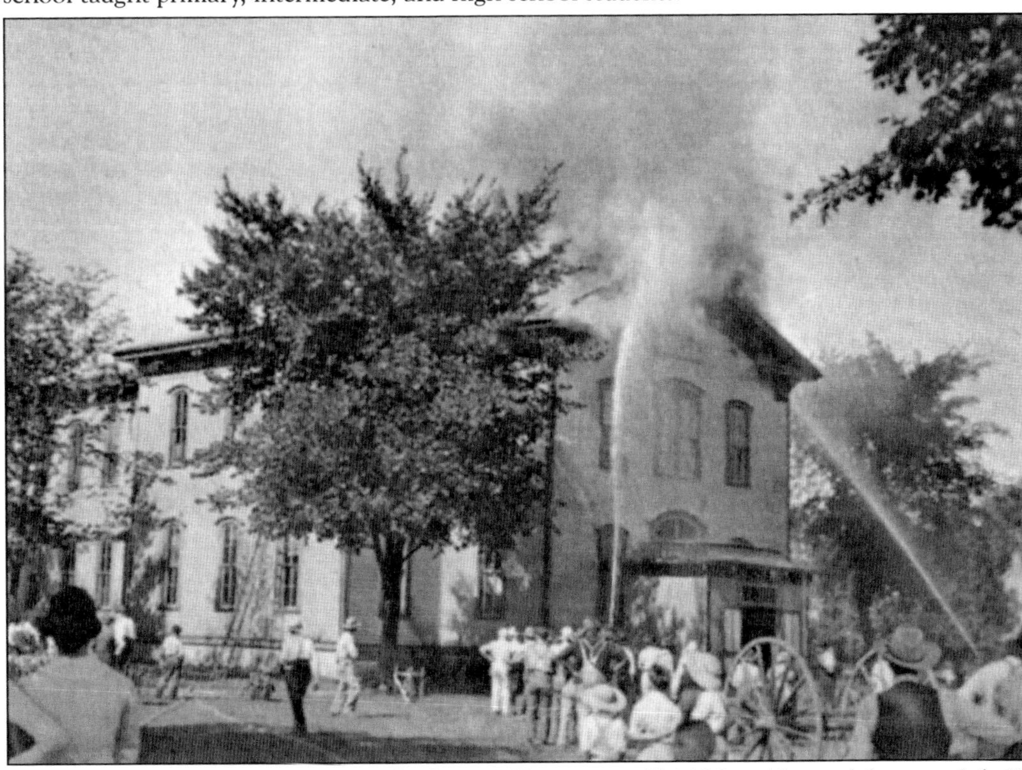

The Genoa Public High School was built in 1877 at a cost of $4,000 and burned down on July 29, 1918. The fire originated from a pile of brush that was being burned in the back of the building. The site is now occupied by Davenport Elementary School at 123 West First Street.

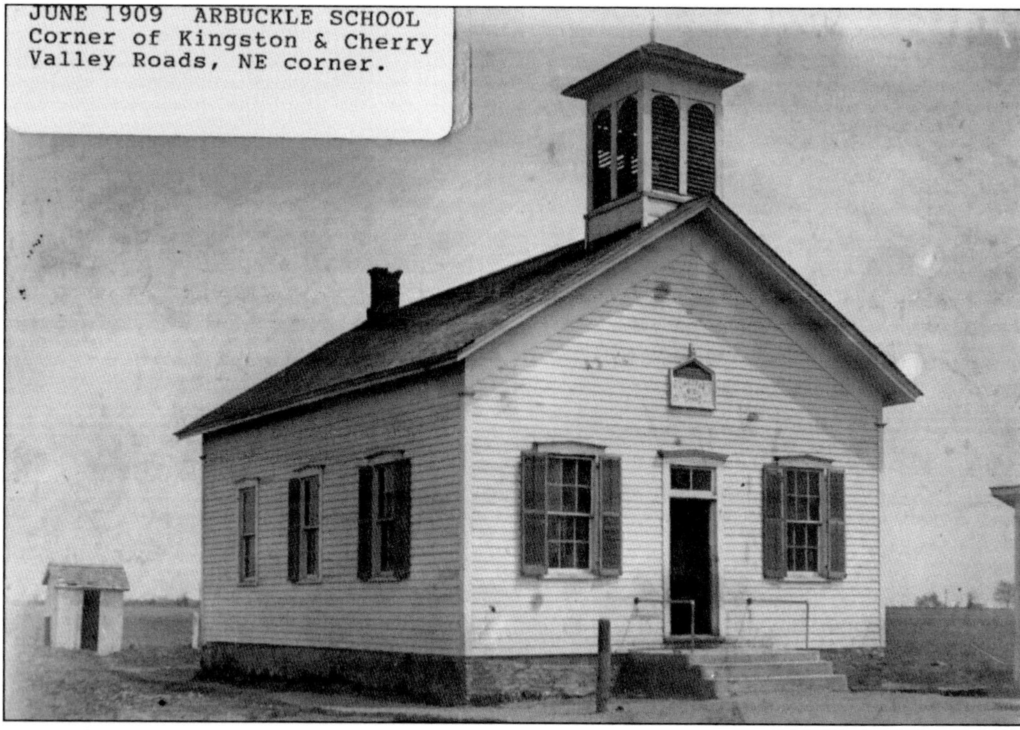

Pictured above is the Arbuckle School building as it looked in June 1909 at the northeast corner of Kingston and Cherry Valley Roads. Below, also around 1909, are the class and teacher of Arbuckle School. Teachers who taught at Arbuckle School included Gladys Vosburg (1906–1907), Minnie Koeller (1907–1908), Ruby Sergent (1908–1909), Marjorie Rowen (1909–1910), Dora Bell (1910–1914), Gertrude Hemenway (1914–1917), Hazel Nicolson (1917–1919), Dora Sheley (1919–1920), Zella A. Morehouse (1920–1925), Harriet Doty Wolf (1925–1926), Lois Sheley (1926–1928), Alice E. McConaghie Saunders (1928–1930), Floyd Montgomery (1930–1931), Esther Holroyd (1931–1934), Kelvin Saunders (1934–1936), Lois Kiefer (1936–1937), Gladys Chaplin (1937–1941), Mercedes Ranking (1941–1943), and Phyllis Kinkaid (1943–1947). The school consolidated with District 421 (Kingston Elementary) in 1948–1949 and then with Community Unit District 424 in 1949.

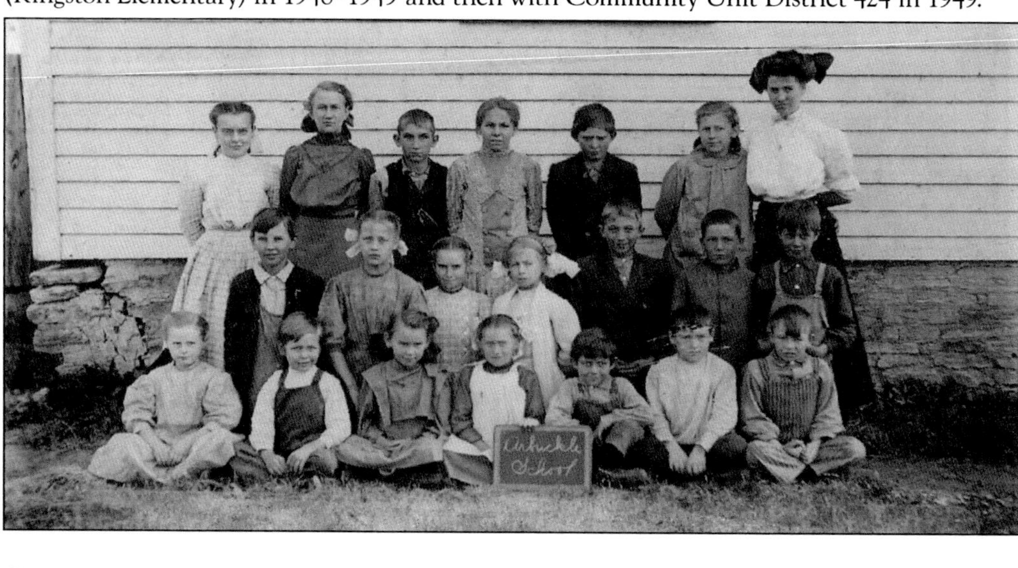

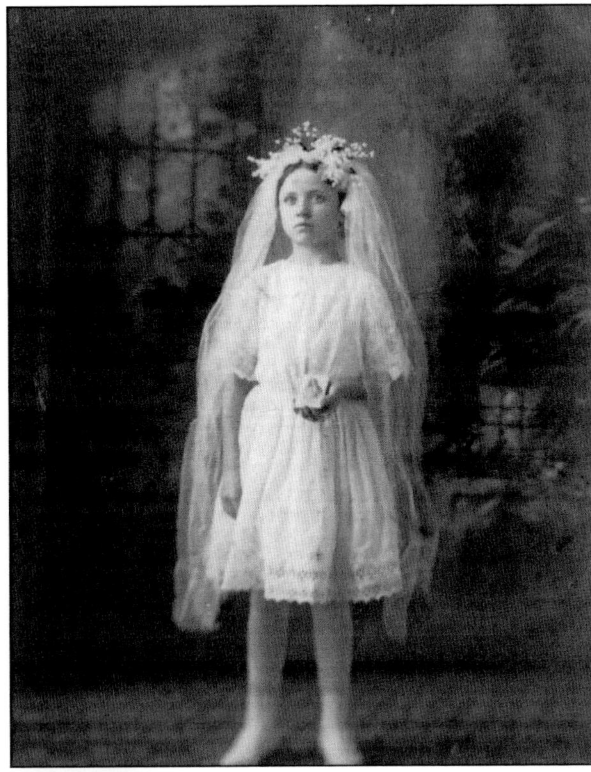

Kathleen Coffey is pictured at right as a child in her First Communion dress and below as a young woman. Kathleen became a teacher at Henrietta School in Kingston Township. Kathleen's sister Jane also became a teacher. Henrietta was once a village located between Genoa and Kingston. When the Milwaukee Road came into Kingston in 1875, two horse-drawn buses carried passengers to and from Henrietta and Kingston. The town of Henrietta no longer exists. Kathleen and Jane Coffey were devoted parishioners of St. Catherine of Genoa Church in Genoa. They left a bequest of $273,000 that retired the debt of the church complex, which was built in 1967.

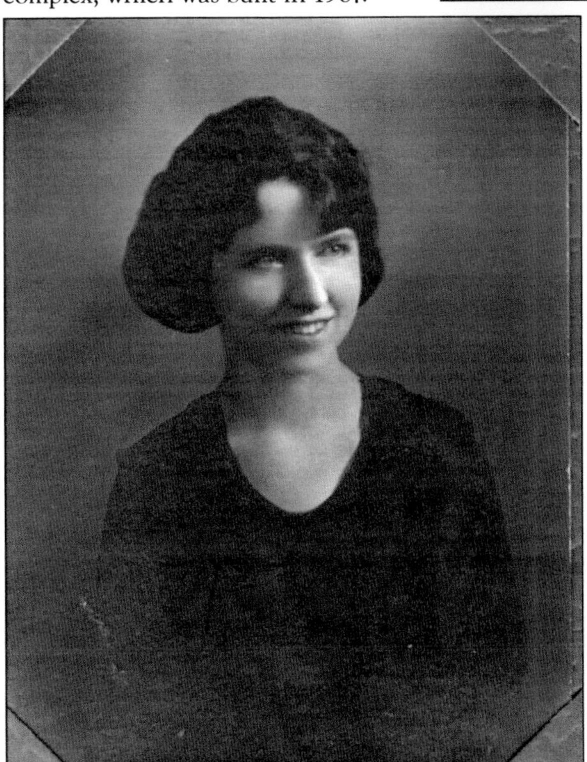

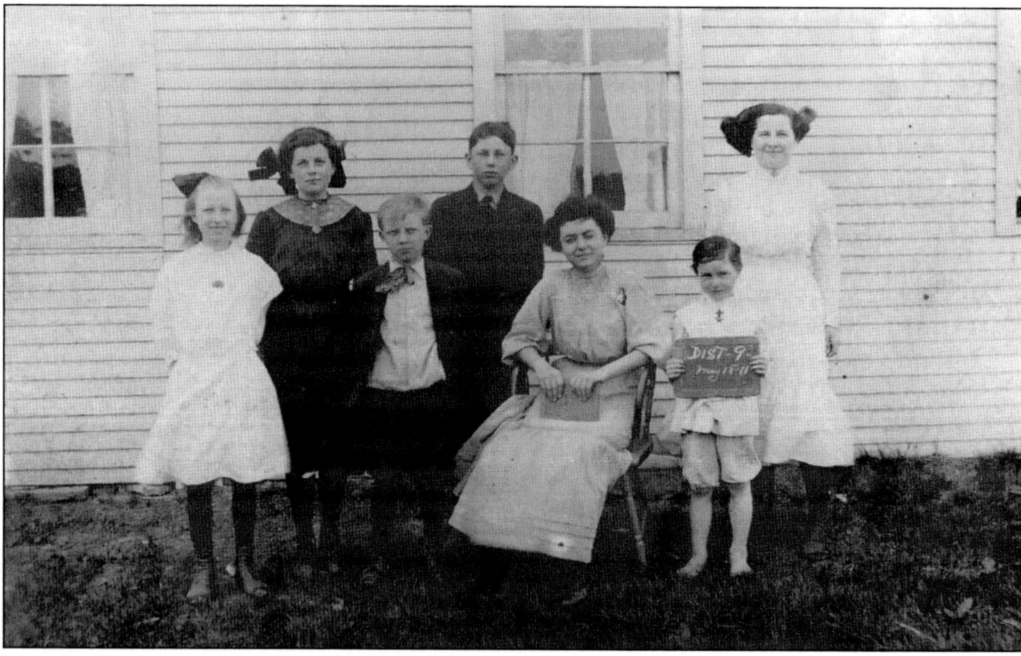

Jane Coffey, a teacher at the Olmstead School of District 9, poses with her students on May 18, 1911. Olmstead School was established after 1895 on the corner of Harrison and Ash Roads. The school closed from 1941 to 1948. It consolidated with Community Unit School District 424 in 1949.

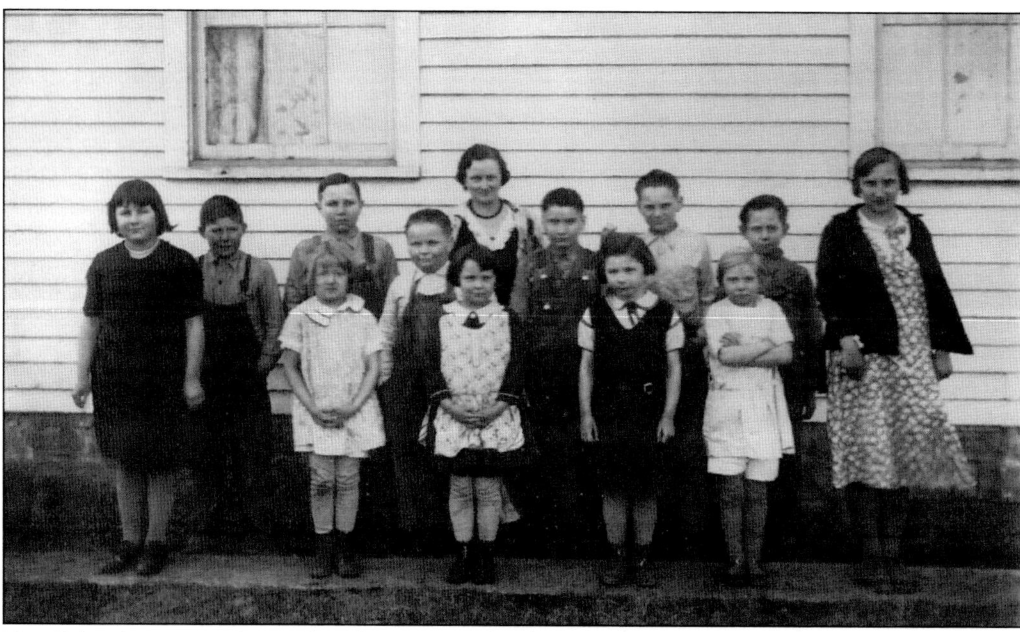

Ney School was once located at the corner of Polk and Melms Roads in Genoa. The 1932 class, pictured here with their teacher, included (first row) Helen Taglang, Virginia Benson, Jean Ellen Melms, Francis Reid, Victoria Workowski, and Shirley Williams; (second row) Albert Taglang, Verl Kiner, James Corson, Gladys Buck Welter (teacher), Harvey Engel, John Corson, and Emily Workowski.

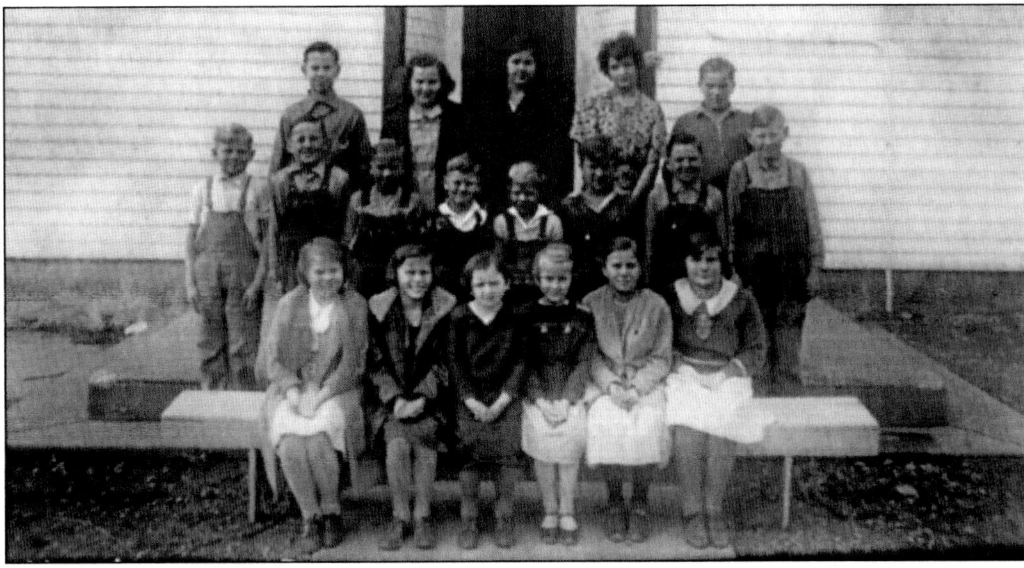

Helen McGaughey's New Lebanon School class gets together for a photograph in November 1935. The school was founded in 1895 and was led by Bay Fulkerson, who taught at the school from 1906 to 1907. The last teacher at the school, Martha Campbell, taught there from 1946 to 1949. The school consolidated with Community Unit School District 424 in 1949.

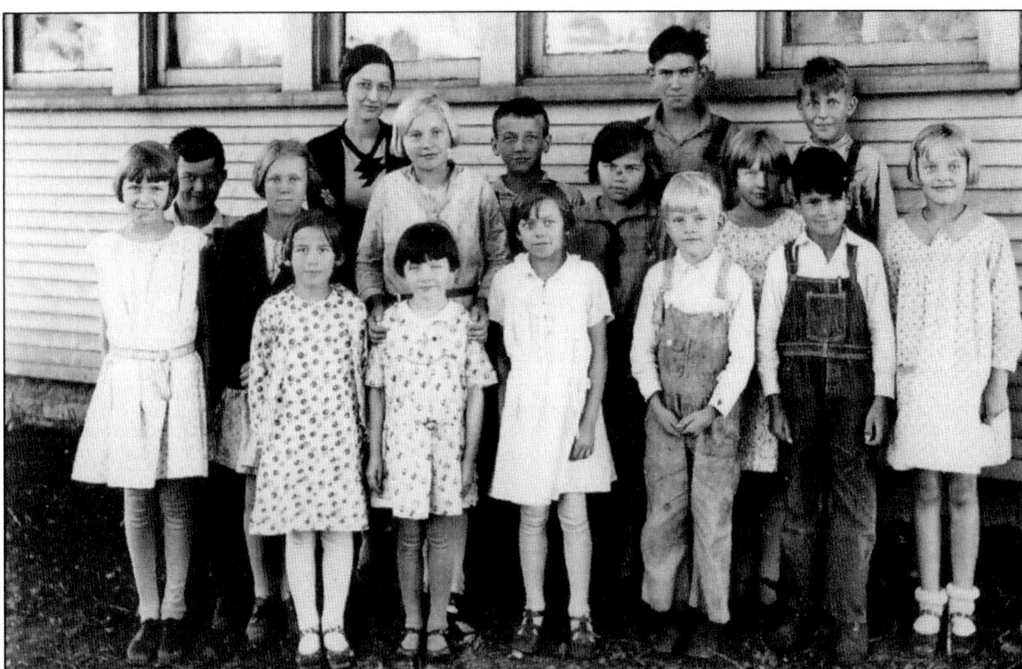

Students in Freida Kohne's 1932 class pose with their teacher in front of Derby Line School in Genoa. Pictured from left to right are (first row) Frances Worley, Guyla Brown, Phyllis Daniels, Harold Peterson, Harold Bernard, and Dorothy Peterson; (second row) Dorothy Florworth, Ruby Shearer, Betty Peterson, Helen Nelson, and Jennie Brown; (third row) James Lewis, Kohne, Clarence Worley, Roy Tewksbury, and Maylon Davis.

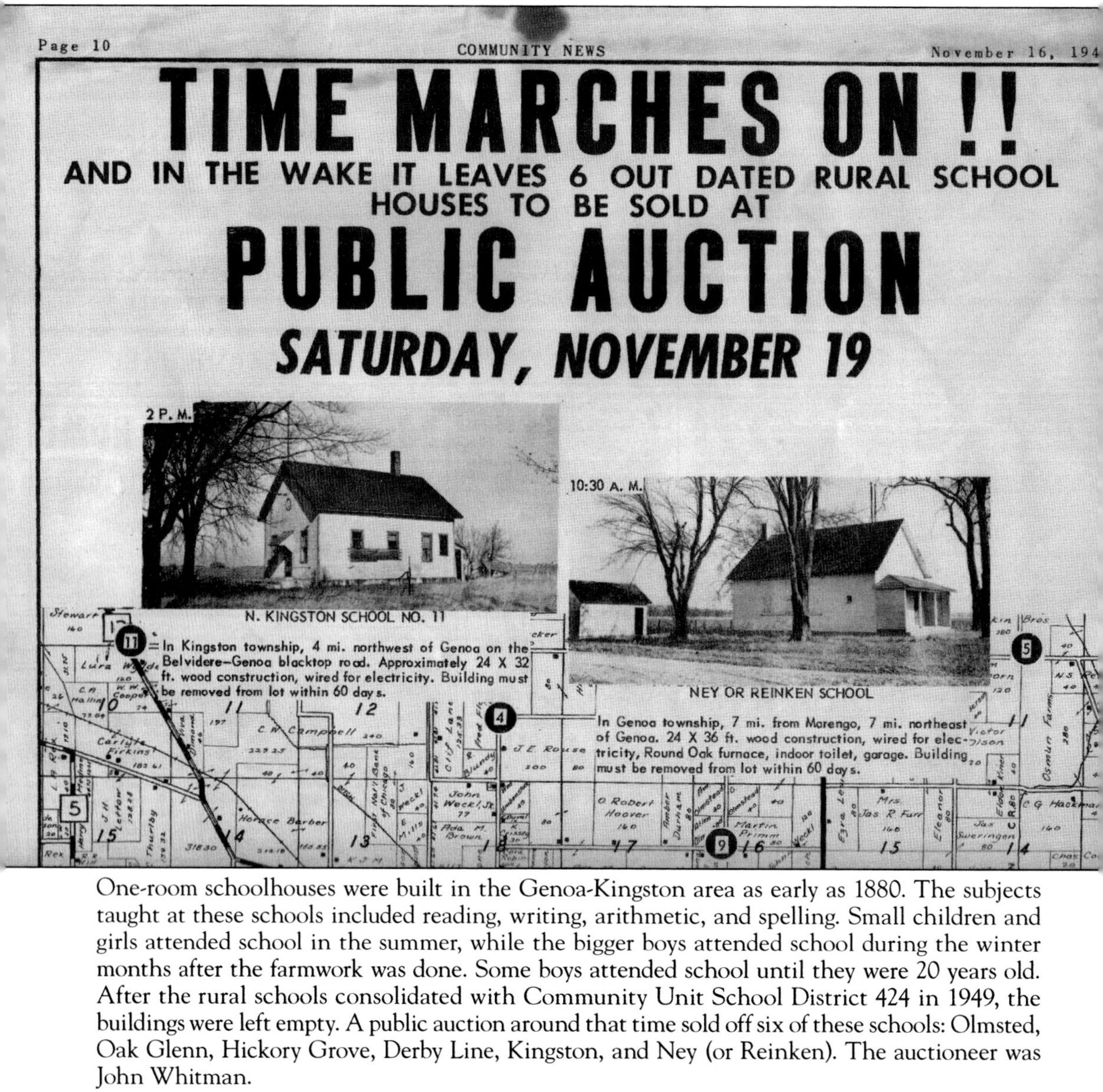

Page 10 COMMUNITY NEWS November 16, 194

TIME MARCHES ON !!

AND IN THE WAKE IT LEAVES 6 OUT DATED RURAL SCHOOL HOUSES TO BE SOLD AT

PUBLIC AUCTION

SATURDAY, NOVEMBER 19

2 P.M.

N. KINGSTON SCHOOL NO. 11

11 = In Kingston township, 4 mi. northwest of Genoa on the Belvidere—Genoa blacktop road. Approximately 24 X 32 ft. wood construction, wired for electricity. Building must be removed from lot within 60 days.

10:30 A. M.

NEY OR REINKEN SCHOOL

In Genoa township, 7 mi. from Marengo, 7 mi. northeast of Genoa. 24 X 36 ft. wood construction, wired for electricity, Round Oak furnace, indoor toilet, garage. Building must be removed from lot within 60 days.

One-room schoolhouses were built in the Genoa-Kingston area as early as 1880. The subjects taught at these schools included reading, writing, arithmetic, and spelling. Small children and girls attended school in the summer, while the bigger boys attended school during the winter months after the farmwork was done. Some boys attended school until they were 20 years old. After the rural schools consolidated with Community Unit School District 424 in 1949, the buildings were left empty. A public auction around that time sold off six of these schools: Olmsted, Oak Glenn, Hickory Grove, Derby Line, Kingston, and Ney (or Reinken). The auctioneer was John Whitman.

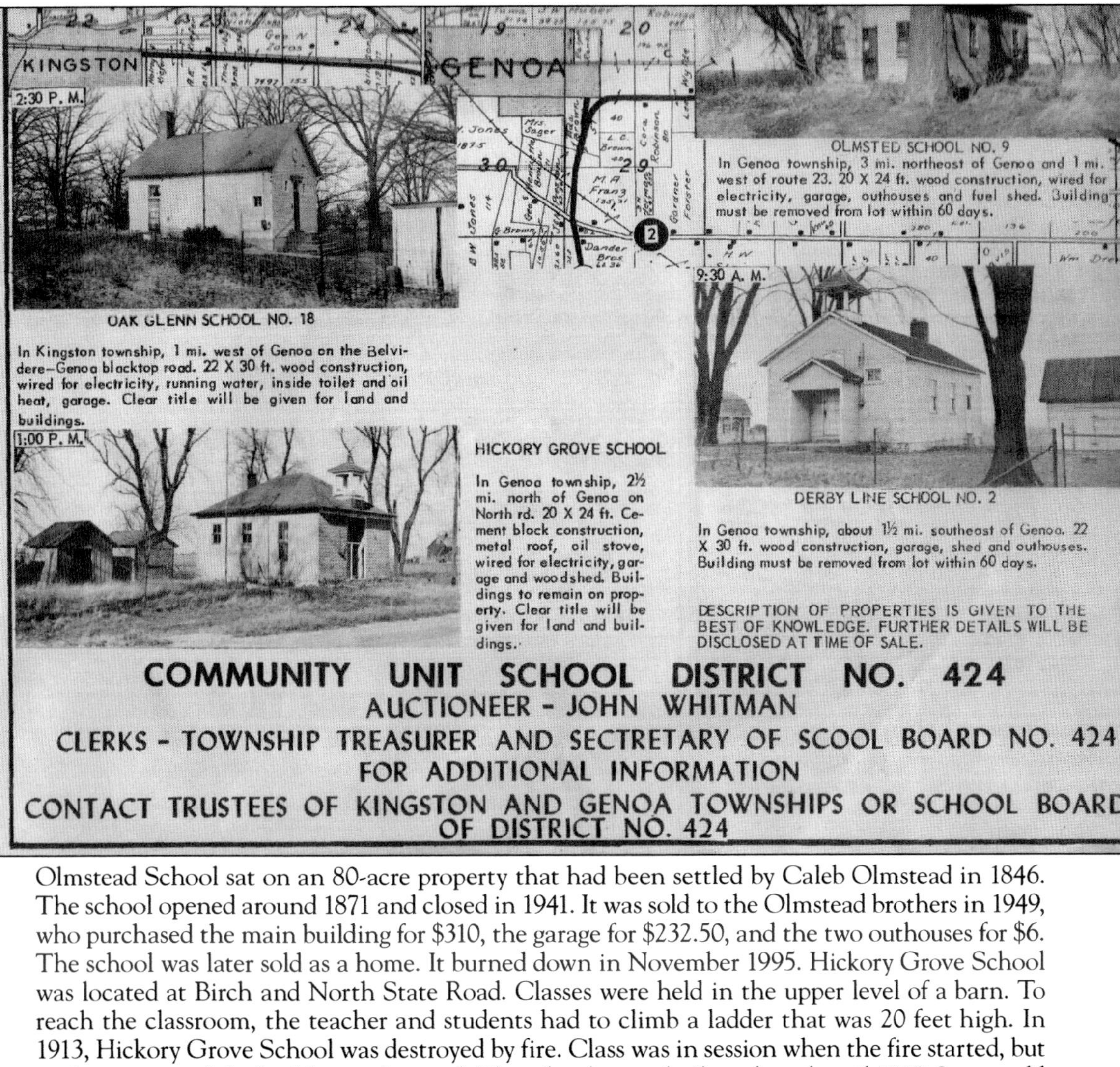

Olmstead School sat on an 80-acre property that had been settled by Caleb Olmstead in 1846. The school opened around 1871 and closed in 1941. It was sold to the Olmstead brothers in 1949, who purchased the main building for $310, the garage for $232.50, and the two outhouses for $6. The school was later sold as a home. It burned down in November 1995. Hickory Grove School was located at Birch and North State Road. Classes were held in the upper level of a barn. To reach the classroom, the teacher and students had to climb a ladder that was 20 feet high. In 1913, Hickory Grove School was destroyed by fire. Class was in session when the fire started, but students escaped the building unharmed. The school was rebuilt and used until 1948. It was sold to John Floto for $1,900. Derby Line School opened in 1880 with Celia Carnes as the first teacher. She was paid $25 per month. The school's pot-bellied stove was used for baking potatoes.

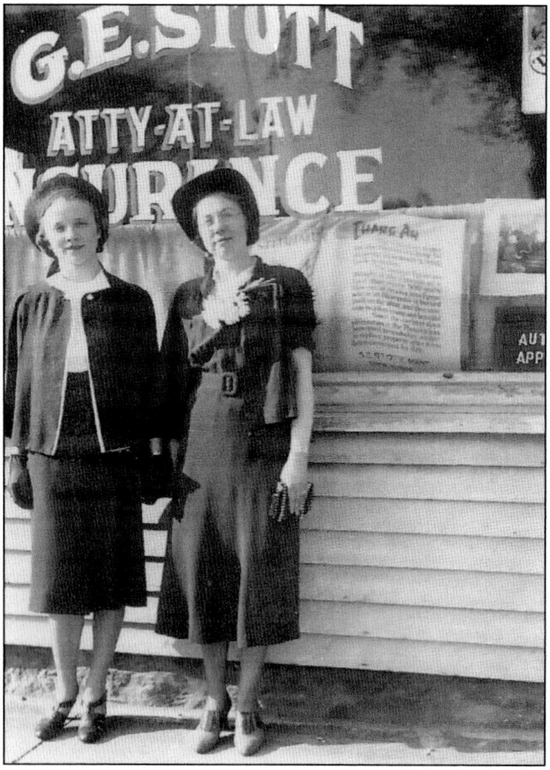

Schoolteacher Esther Tilley (right) and her friend Violet are shown standing outside the law office of G. E. "Ed" Stott along Main Street in Genoa in 1937. Stott held the office of city attorney and ran a large insurance and collecting business. The women's ensemble outfits reflect the style of 1930s fashion, which was a return to a genteel, ladylike appearance. Notice the women's hats, gloves, clutch purses, and fancy high heels.

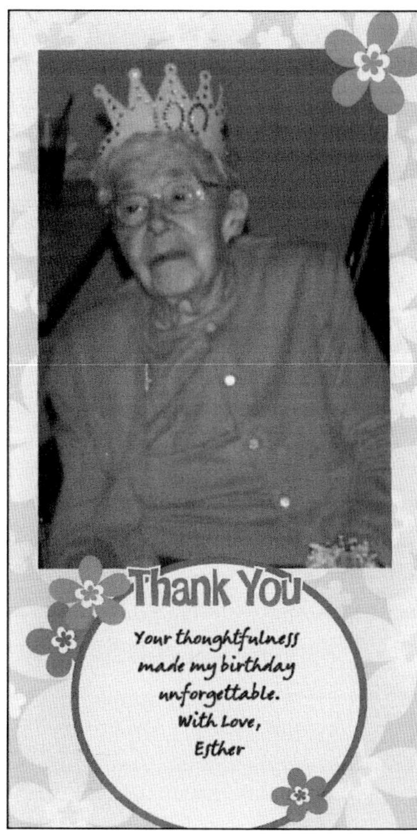

Esther Tilley was born in 1908 to Dr. T. N. and Effie Mae Austin. Her father operated his medical practice in Genoa. Tilley taught elementary school students in DeKalb County for 27 years. She spent some of those years teaching in a one-room schoolhouse. Pictured is the card Tilley sent on the occasion of her 100th birthday in 2008. (Courtesy of Susan Walker, Tilley's daughter and Genoa Public Library director.)

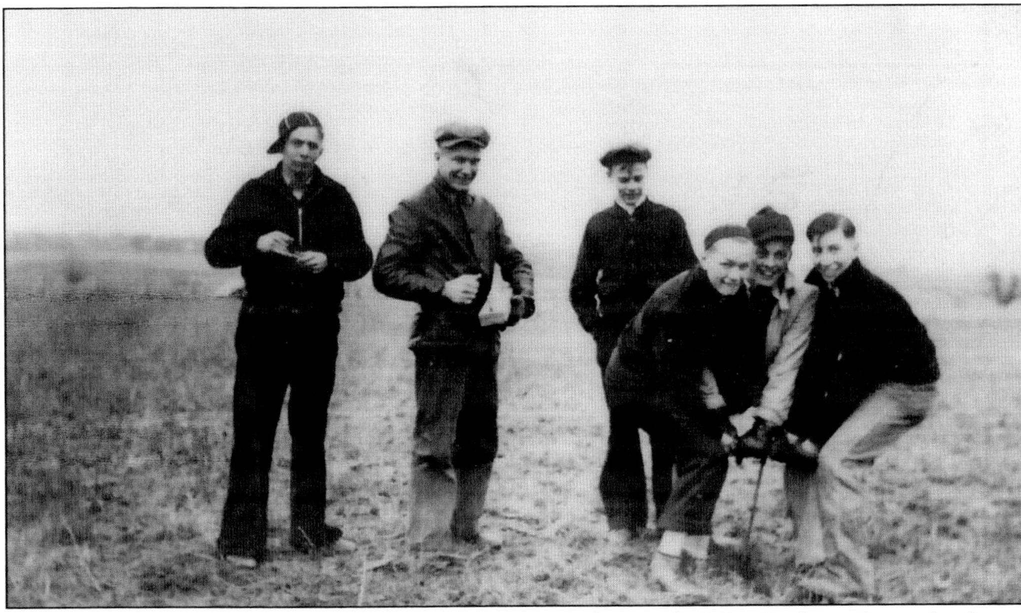

Students of the 1934 agriculture class at Genoa Township High School take soil samples from a farm. From left to right are Robert Coonley, Charles Coon, Robert Nelson, William Brendenmuhl, Charles Patterson, and Marion Hammer. Two years later, Congress passed the Soil Conservation and Domestic Allotment Act that encouraged soil conservation by paying benefits for planting soil-building crops instead of staple crops.

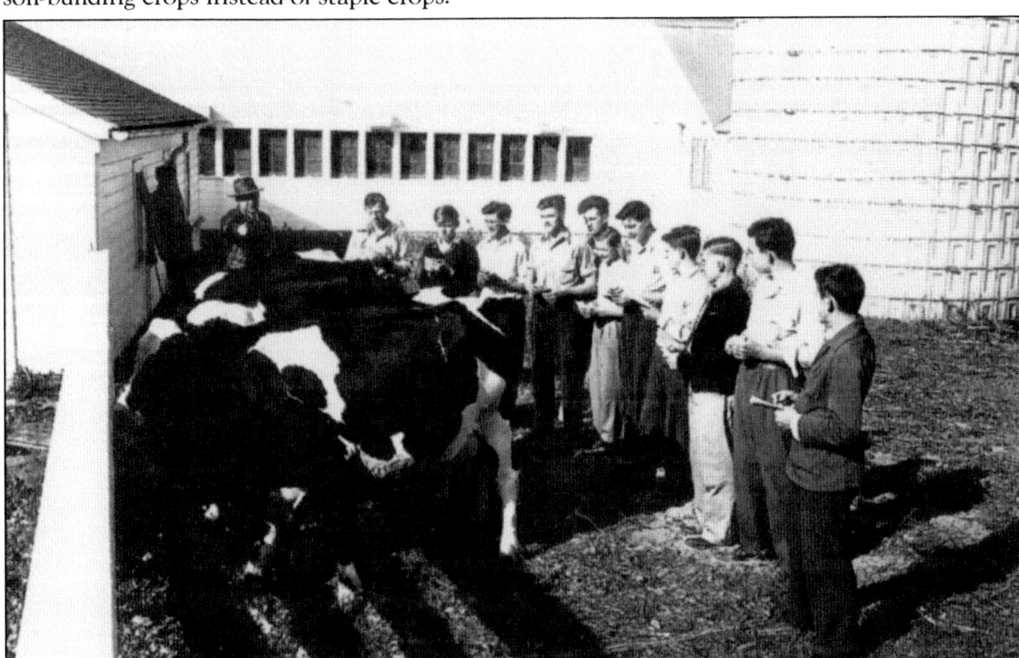

Genoa Township High School students visit Green Top Farm along Highway 23 south of Genoa in 1942 to learn more about farming. Their teacher is Merle Roberts. From left to right are Lawrence Ernesti, Howard Hermance, Glenn Pearson, Mark Stott, Dewy Lyle, Lavern Anderson, Myron Faber, Charles Ernesti, William Grollemond, Winston Evans, and Calvin Coon.

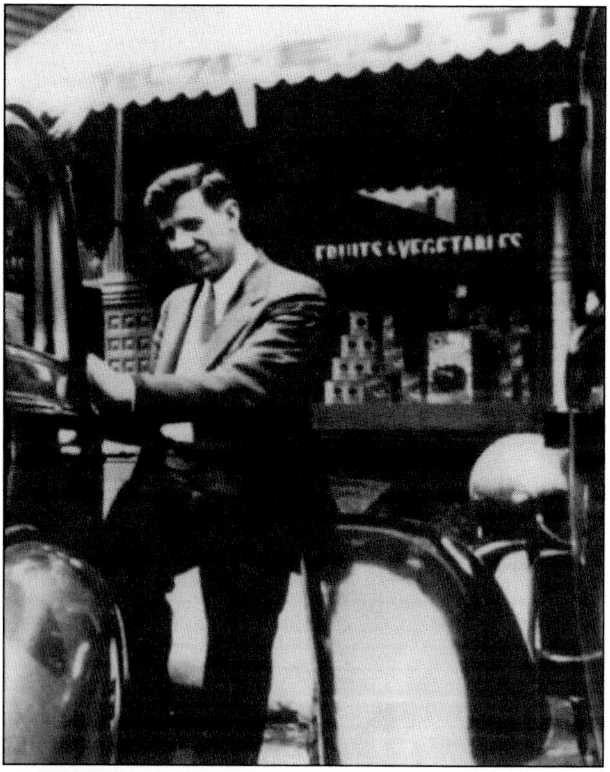

Genoa Township High School teacher Merle "Doc" Roberts prepares to get into his car in front of Tischlers Grocery Store in 1938. O. M. Barcus was the mayor of Genoa at that time. Roberts in later years worked with other Genoa area residents in establishing the annual Pioneer Day at the Kishwaukee Valley Heritage Society Museum.

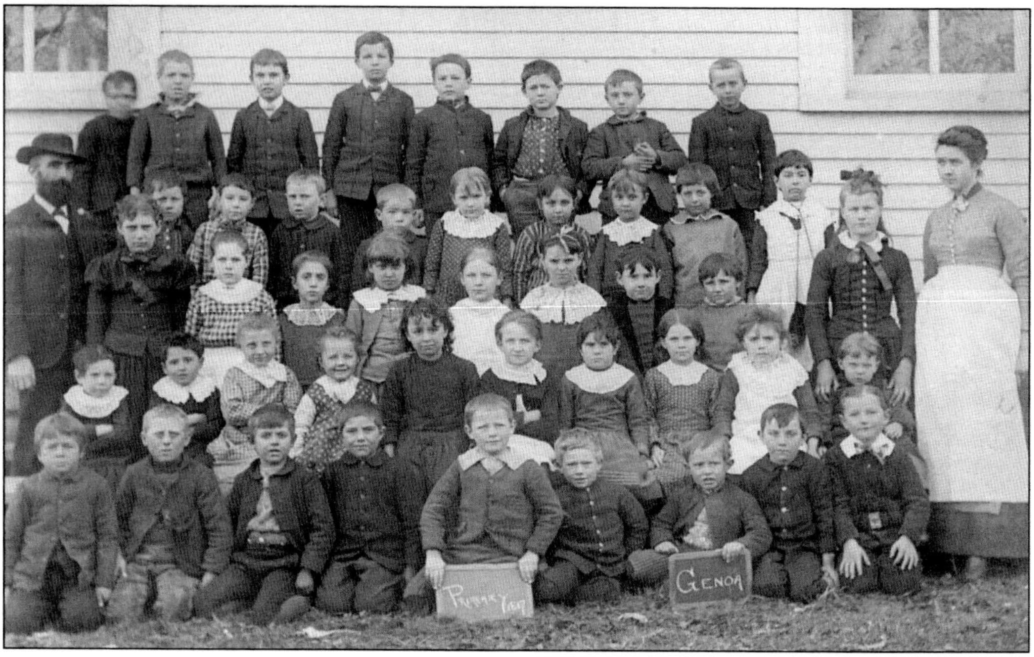

A primary class in Genoa gathers for a photograph in 1909. E. S. Clark was the superintendent of Genoa public schools at that time. The tuition for the 1908–1909 school year was $19 for the high school and $14.25 per school year for lower grades. The cost in 1905 to conduct the schools in Genoa for one year was $5,000. (Courtesy of Joiner Room.)

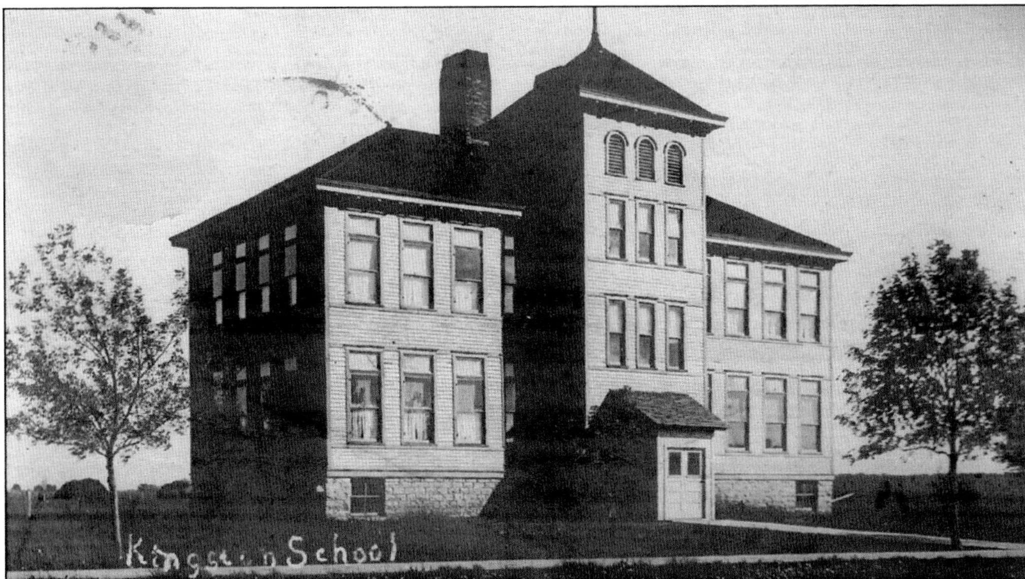

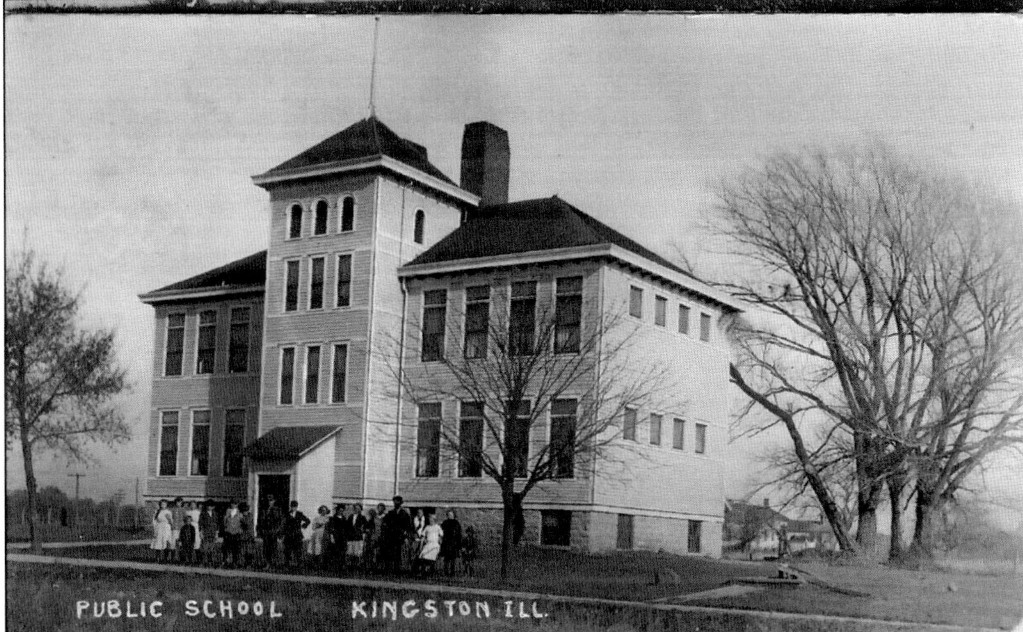

The first school in Kingston Township was held in a log house in 1840, with Harriett Russell as teacher. A schoolhouse was built in Kingston in 1881 for a cost of $3,304 and was located about a half mile east of the village. The average teacher's salary at that time was $29.48 per month. The school burned down in 1894, and a new school was completed on the same site in 1896 for a cost of $8,000. A brick addition, which had a gymnasium on the lower level and an auditorium on the upper level, was built in 1928. The school housed the grade school and a four-year high school until 1947. After that time, the building was used for kindergarten through eighth-grade classes. A fire destroyed the school on March 8, 1954. Elementary classes were temporarily held at White Oak Grange Hall, the Methodist church, and the Masonic Hall. A new school was built for a cost of $205,760 and is being used today for grades two and three. (Courtesy of Alice A. Paulson.)

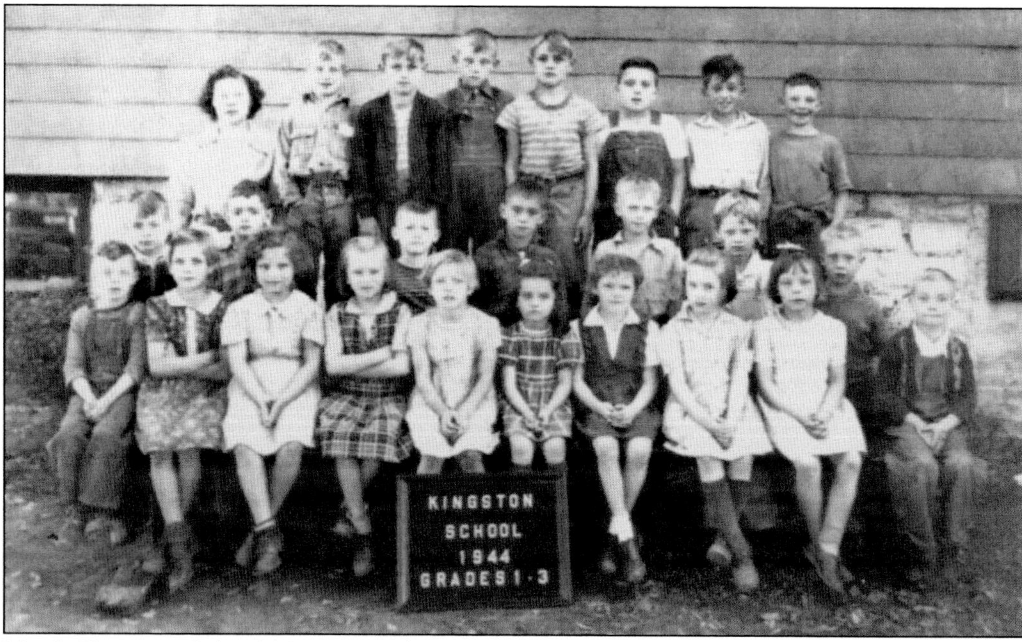

North Kingston School No. 11 was located at the northeast corner of Melms Road and the Belvidere-Genoa blacktop. Ruth Slater is shown here with her first-, second-, and third-grade students in 1944. The school's first teacher was Myrtle Holroyd, who taught in 1906 and 1907. Other teachers were Polly Branch (1907–1908) and Iram Basmett (1908–1909). The school consolidated with Community Unit School District 424 in 1949.

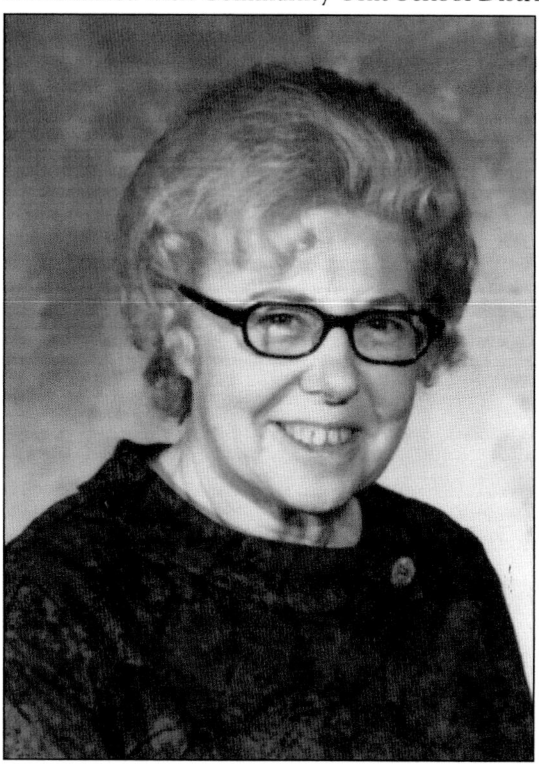

This is a photograph of schoolteacher Esther Tilley in 1966. She retired from teaching school in 1973 but continued to teach piano until she was 99 years old. She was featured with other teachers and students in a DVD in 2003 about local one-room schoolhouses entitled *One Room, One People*. A resolution was passed by the City of Genoa in October 2008 in recognition of Tilley's 100th birthday. (Courtesy of Susan Walker.)

Clarence Louderback was the first superintendent for Community Unit School District 424. He was the primary architect in forming the district that brought Genoa and Kingston together with parts of Mayfield Township, closing the small country schools within its borders. He was married to Ruth Louderback, with whom he had four children. (Courtesy of Alice A. Paulson.)

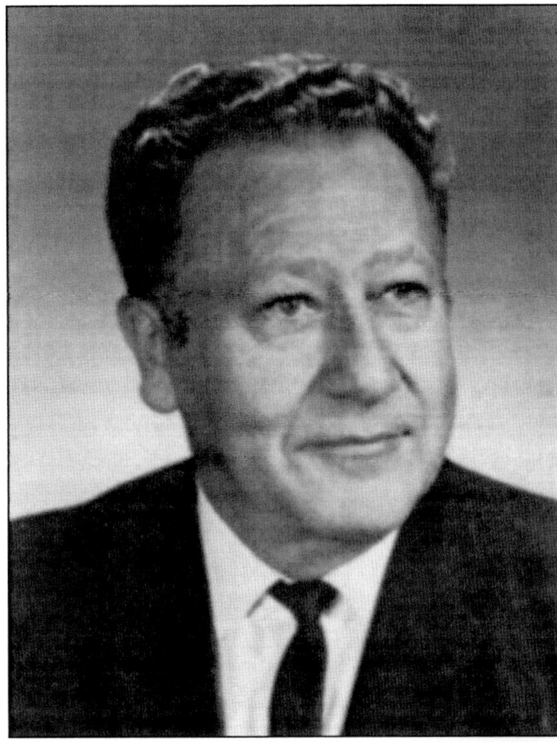

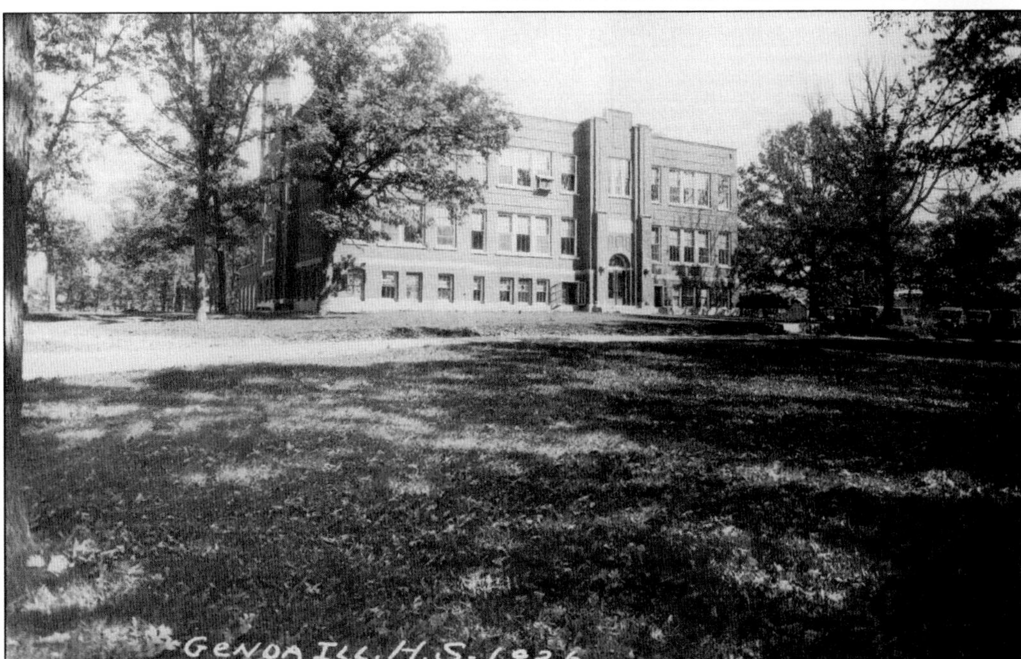

Tall trees shade the Genoa Township High School campus at 941 West Main Street in 1926. The school was completed in 1921 on what was known as the Oak Park site. Some residents at that time felt that the site was too far from town. The enrollment at the high school in 1919 was 70 students. (Courtesy of Joiner Room.)

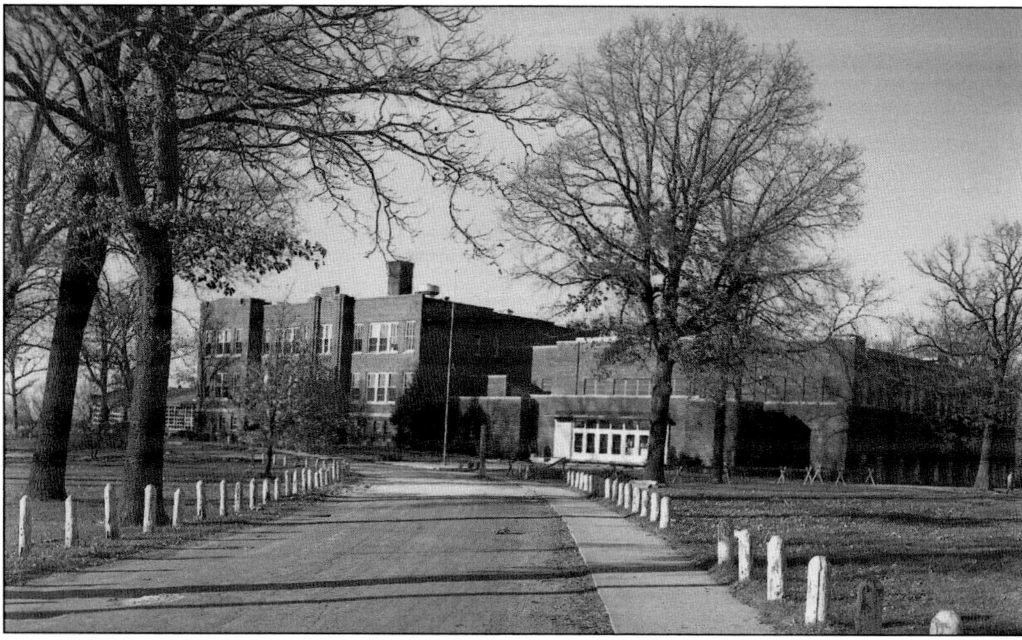

A road winds toward the entrance of Genoa Township High School at 941 West Main Street in 1949, the year Community Unit School District 424 was formed. Roy Hubbell marked his 21st year of teaching instrumental music at the high school in 1949. An industrial arts facility and gymnasium were added to the high school in 1948 and 1949. (Courtesy of Joiner Room.)

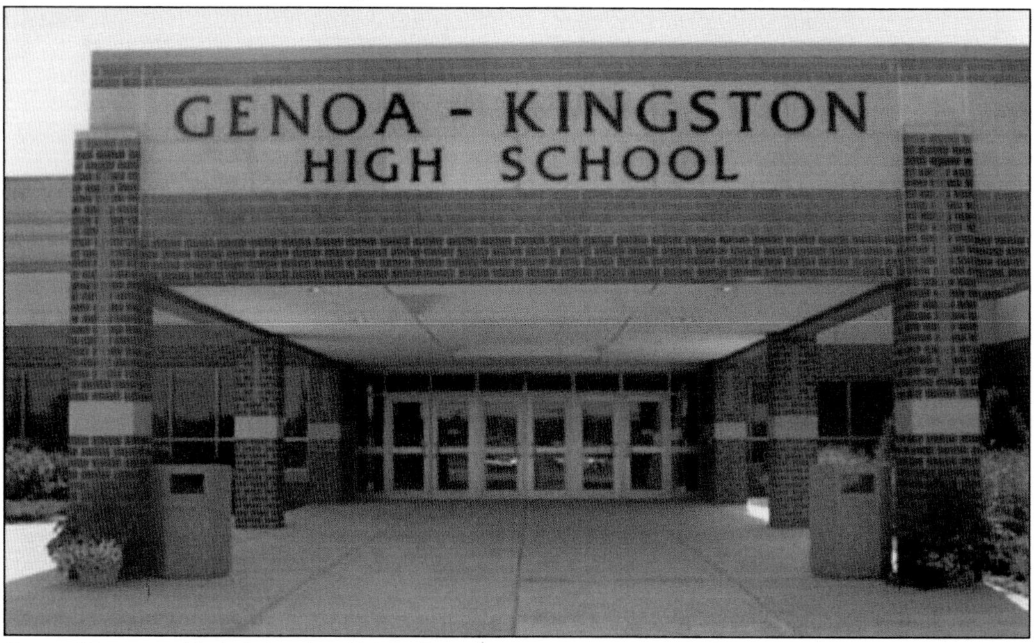

Genoa-Kingston High School at 980 Park Avenue in Genoa was dedicated on August 9, 2003. The former high school site at 941 West Main Street is now home to Genoa-Kingston Middle School. The new campus gave the high school its first athletic fields, track, and a 500-seat auditorium. In 2010, Don Billington is the school's principal, while Bill McCarty is the assistant principal. (Courtesy of Genoa-Kingston High School.)

Five

Community Churches

Churches traditionally have been the place to honor the most important times in life—namely, birth, marriage, and death. They also offer people a chance to socialize with others of similar beliefs. Every church in Kingston and Genoa has its own special history. Faith United Methodist Church has the oldest continually active congregation in Genoa. Kingston Methodist Church once had a guitar and mandolin club. In addition to being named after St. Catherine of Genoa in Italy, the church in Genoa, Illinois, is also named in honor of a church member's mother. St. Catherine of Genoa Church today holds some masses in Spanish. Peace United Church of Christ in Genoa, formerly known as Peace Evangelical and Reformed Church, once held services in German. CrossWind Community Church, formerly known as Foursquare Gospel Church, built its new facility in Genoa in November 2006. First Baptist Church in Genoa held its first services in 1954. The church's current facility on Sycamore Street was built in 1962, and the church is home to First Christian Academy. Trinity Lutheran Church's first services in Genoa were held in August Teyler's home. His great-grandson Richard Watson donated the land where the current church was built.

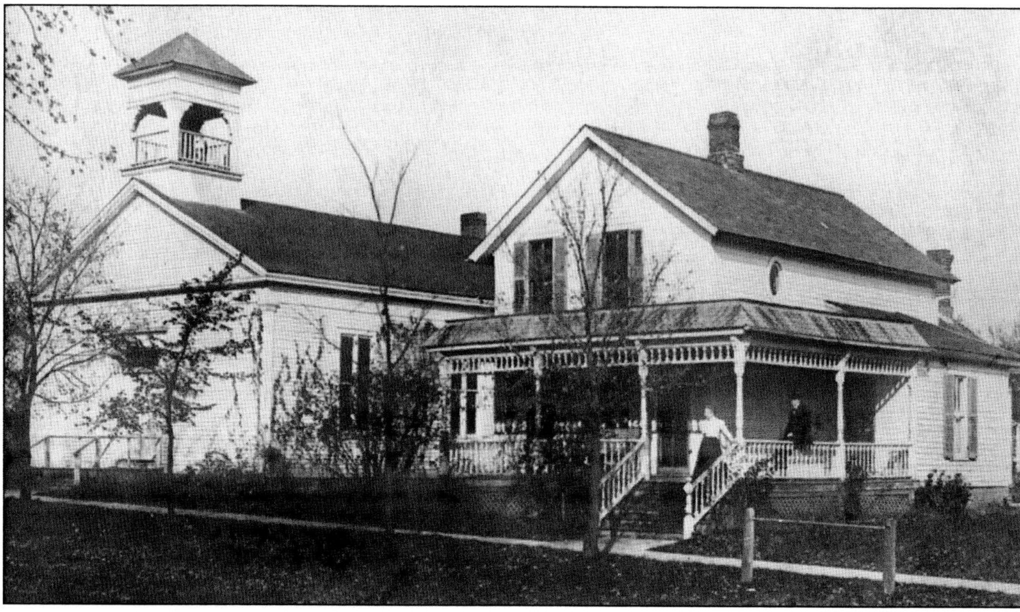

Levi Lee, a Methodist preacher and owner of Lee's Mill in Kingston, preached the first sermon in Sycamore in June 1836. Lee became Kingston's first postmaster in 1837. Prior to 1876, the Methodist church in Kingston was originally located on the south line of the township of Kingston. It was later built in the village so it would be more centrally located.

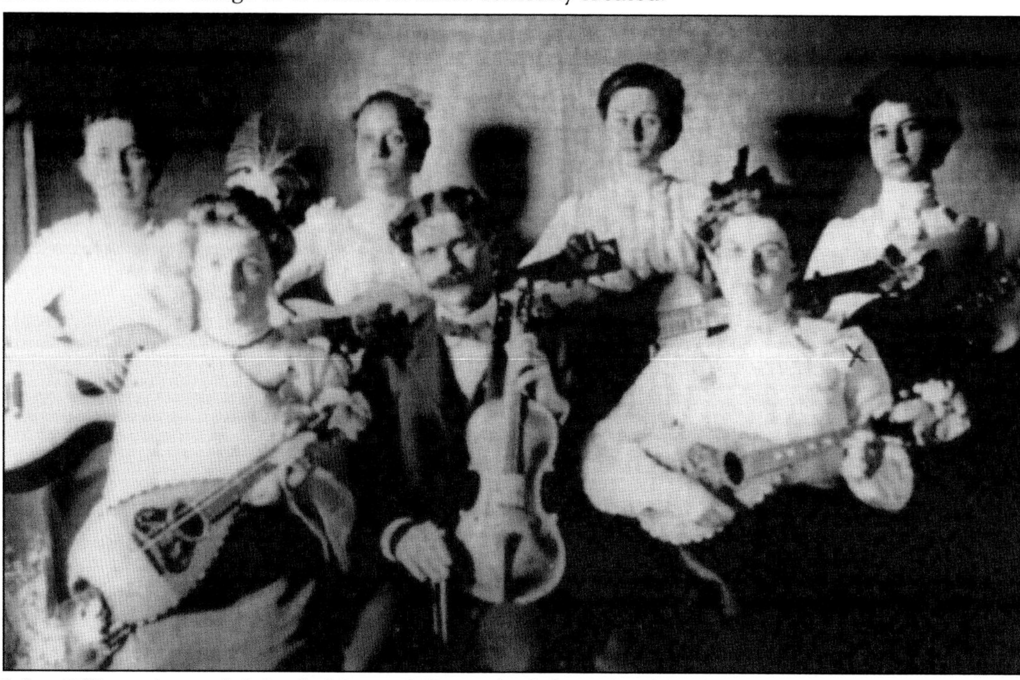

John O'Brien (center), Maude Moyer O'Brien (right), and Mildred Farrell Gibbs (left rear) make beautiful music together in 1902 with other musicians in Kingston Methodist Church's guitar and mandolin club. The mandolin became popular during the 1850s, along with the zither, mandola, ukulele, and other instruments. In 1897, the Montgomery Ward catalog noted, "The phenomenal growth in our mandolin trade."

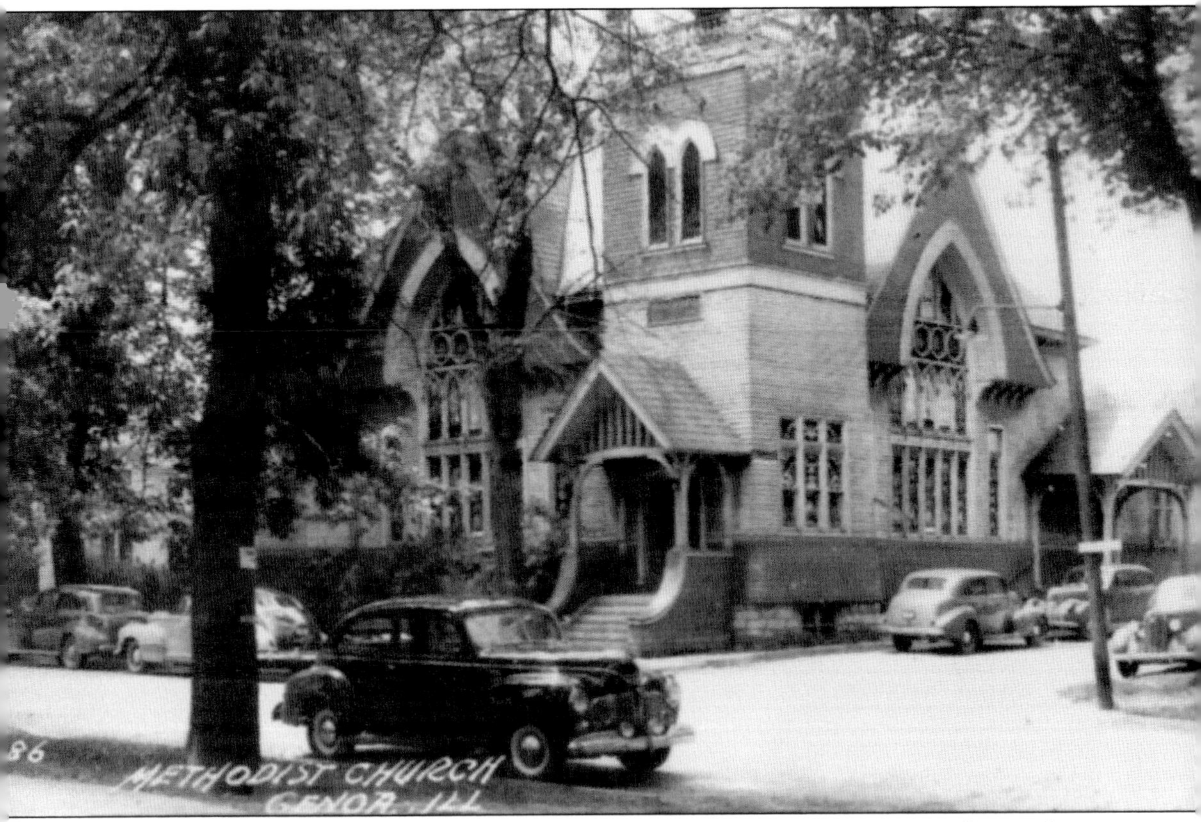

Faith United Methodist Church is the oldest continually active congregation in Genoa. It was part of the church-planting movement in the early 1800s. Rev. Ora Walker conducted the first religious services in Genoa in the home of Henry Perkins. From 1838 to 1854, services were held in Genoa's first schoolhouse. In 1852, Henry and Jane Durham deeded a half acre of land for $100 to the trustees of the church. The Durhams also supplied the lumber and the money for the construction of the church, which was built in 1854 (pictured). A parsonage was built across the street from the church in 1889. It was destroyed by fire in 1899. A new parsonage was built in 1973 at the corner of Brown and Hill Streets. Reverend Deming and his family were its first occupants. A new church was built in 1962 at 325 South Stott Street. The church changed its name in 1968 from First Methodist Church to Faith United Methodist Church.

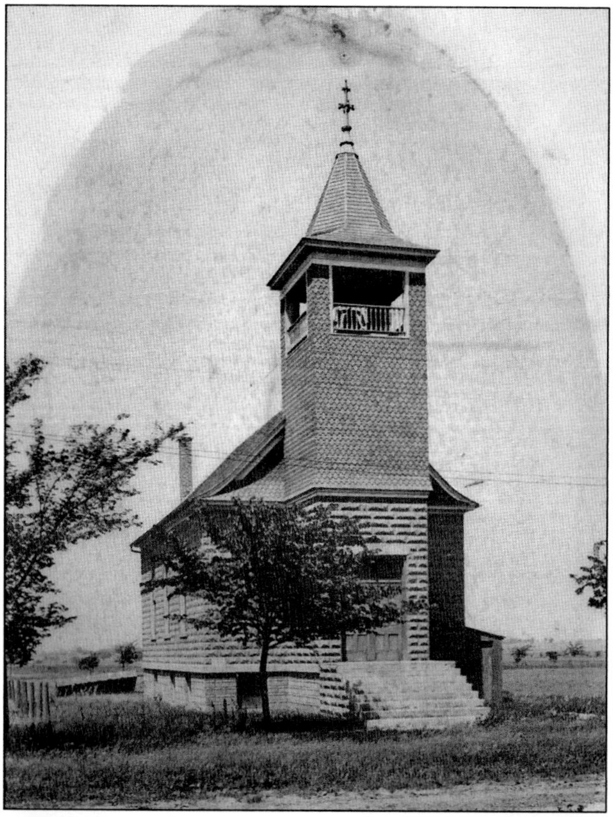

Peace Evangelical and Reformed Church in Genoa was built in 1909. Services were originally held in English and German, but the church discontinued holding services in German in 1921. The church, located at 301 East First Street in Genoa, changed its name to Peace United Church of Christ in 1961.

The Freewill Baptist Church of Kingston was organized in 1884 with 17 members. In 1892, the members built a church that cost $3,000. When the church disbanded, the building was sold for use as a grange hall. It later was used again for a house of worship when it became the Calvary Assembly of God Church.

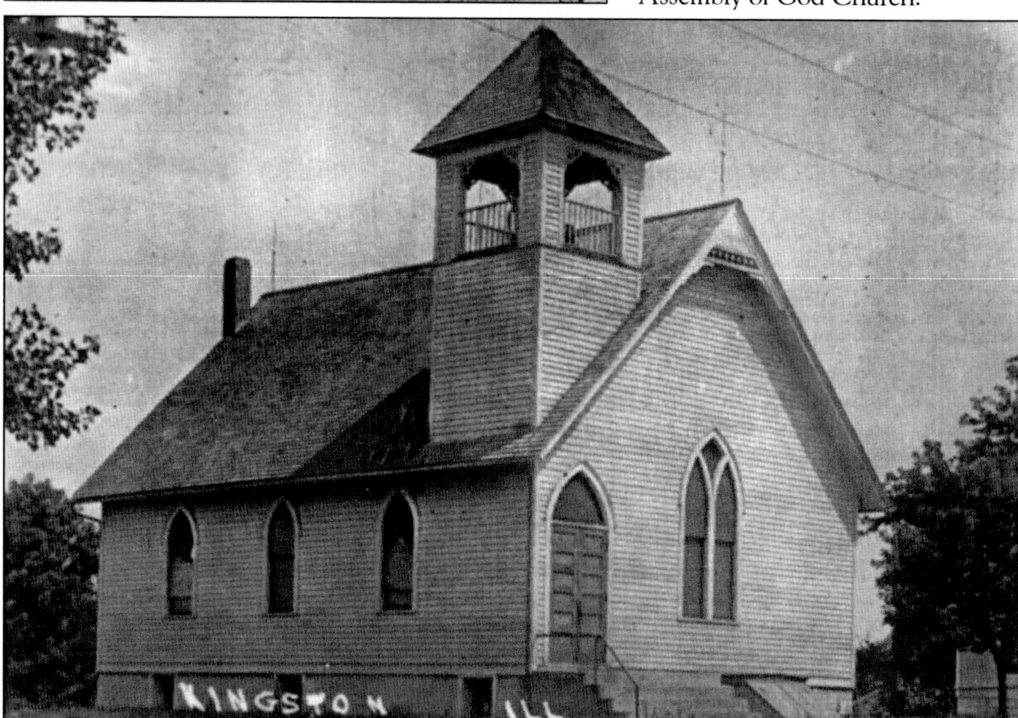

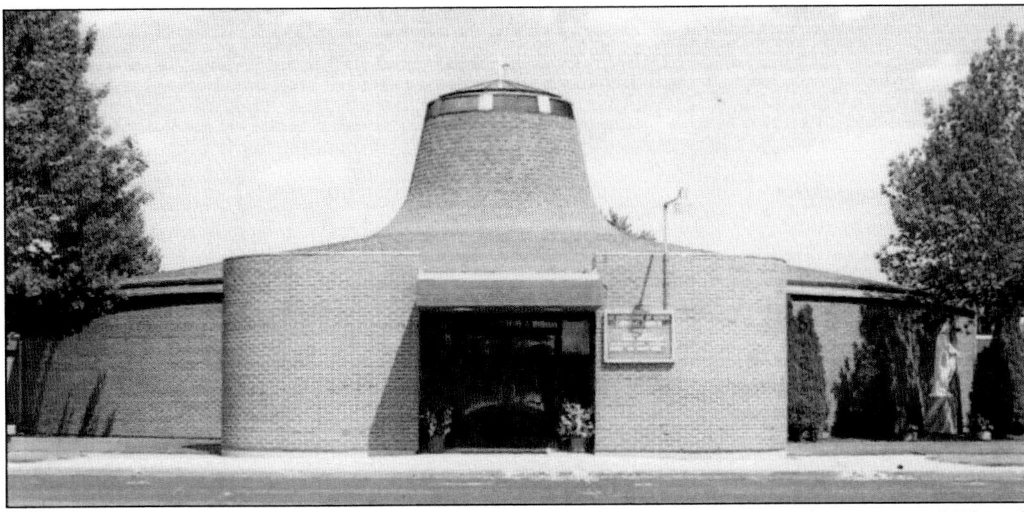

The original St. Catherine of Genoa Church was dedicated in 1912 at the corner of Church and South Emmett Streets with Fr. Thomas O'Brien as the church's first pastor. In 1967, the parish built a huge complex, including a church in the round, hall, classrooms, office space, and attached rectory, for approximately $1 million. It took 30 years to pay off the debt. (Courtesy of St. Catherine of Genoa Church.)

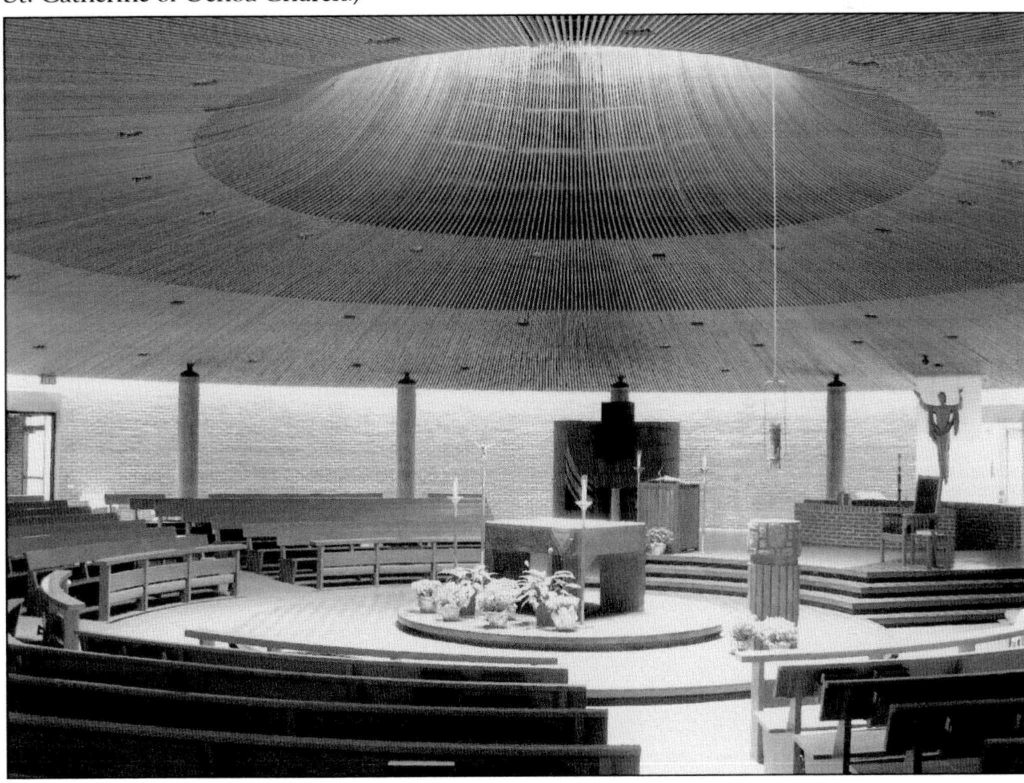

St. Catherine of Genoa Church won the award for outstanding religious edifice in 1968. The liturgical space is designed to seat 400. The seating is curved to bring parishioners in a close circle around the celebrant and the altar. A skylight over the altar provides natural lighting to bathe the outer brick walls in light. (Courtesy of St. Catherine of Genoa Church.)

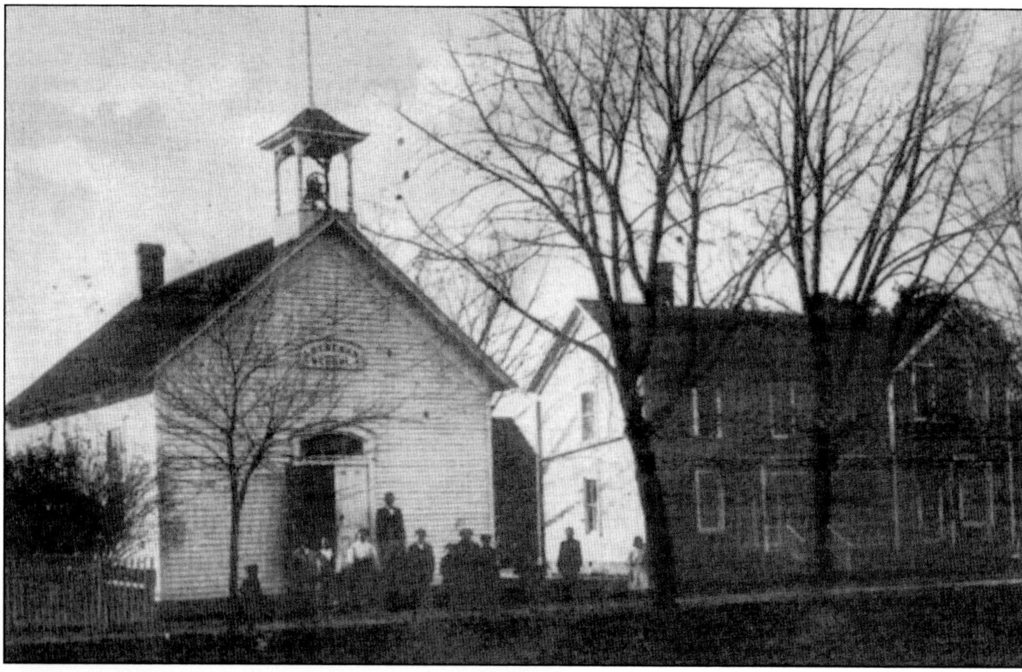

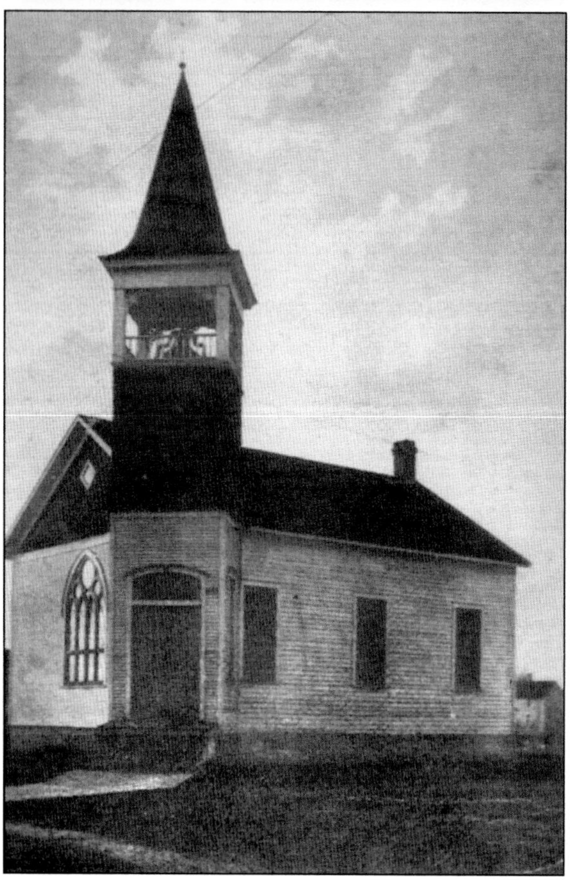

The first Lutheran services in Genoa were held in the home of August Teyler in 1878. In 1881, the congregation purchased two lots on North Washington Street. The house on one of the lots was used as a parsonage, while a small church (above) was built on the other lot and dedicated on March 5, 1882. The house has been in continuous use as a parsonage since 1881. In 1895, a larger church was built across the street from the parsonage on Second Street (left). The first church was then used for day school and Sunday school. Trinity Lutheran Church at 33930 North State Road was built on 5 acres donated by the family of Richard Watson, Teyler's great-grandson. It was dedicated in 1975.

Six

Merchants and Tigers

Kingston once had a baseball team known as the Kingston Tigers. Ralph Ortt, who played on the team, later served in the army during World War I. Chamberlain Park in Genoa was once the only lighted baseball field in northern Illinois. Genoa resident Sandy Lyon often watched her cousin Gary Joe Bloom play with the Genoa Merchants baseball team in Chamberlain Park. Bloom later became a Genoa-Kingston High School coach. Chamberlain Park was used for the playoffs and finals for the 1954 Illinois state amateur baseball title. The Genoa Merchants won the Illinois state semi-pro baseball championship in 1953 and 1954. The legendary player Satchel Paige once pitched a game at Chamberlain Park. During the early 1900s, black baseball players were not allowed to play on white professional baseball teams, but mixed games occurred when major-league white teams played against black teams in barnstorming (exhibition) games. In 1947, major-league teams began integrating players, and the Negro leagues finally folded in 1960. The Genoa-Kingston High School baseball team took over Chamberlain Park from the late 1950s until 2003. The field is now used by the Genoa-Kingston Baseball League, with players ranging from ages 6 to 18.

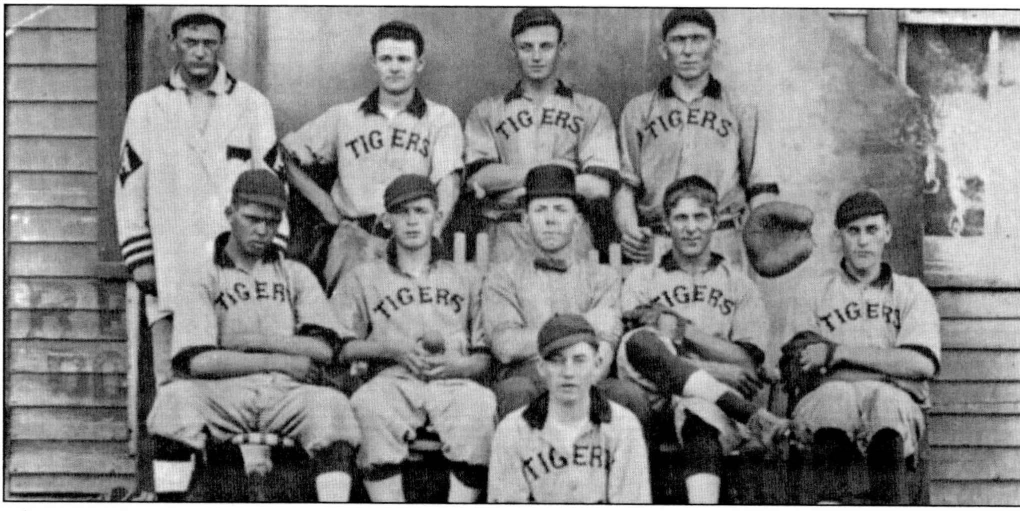

The Kingston Tigers baseball players band together in 1901 for a team photograph. Pictured from left to right are (first row) Clyde Ottman; (second row) "Nig" Patterson, Ralph Ortt, Homer Witler, Charlie Carlson, and William Sullivan; (third row) Roy McKee, Elmer Bell, Ray Helsdon, and George Winchester.

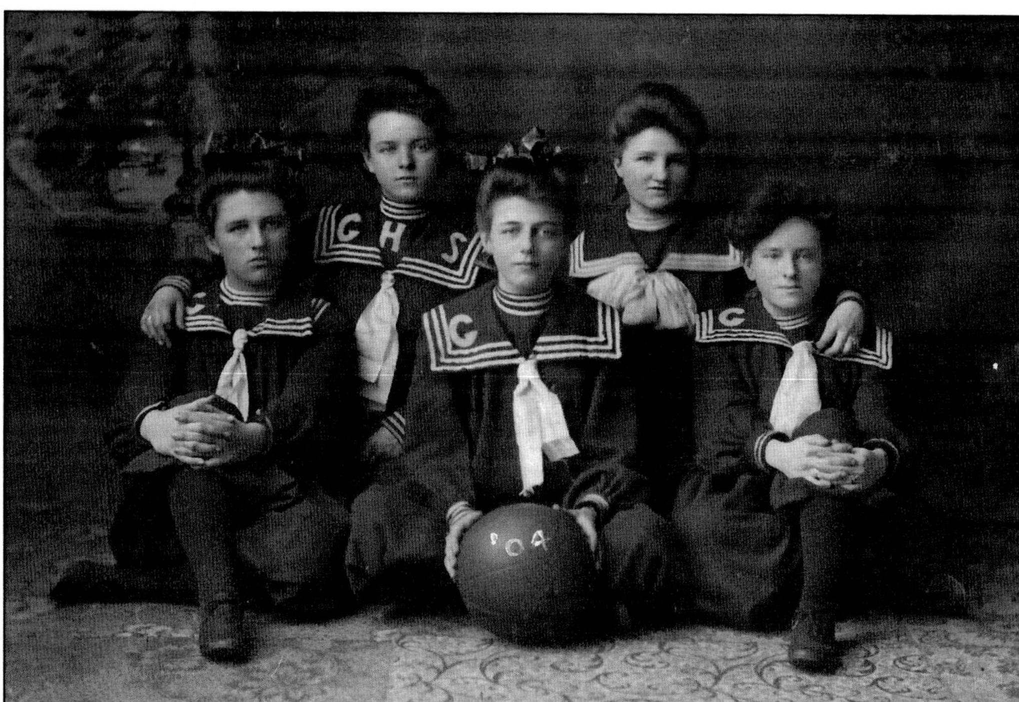

Members of the 1904 Genoa High School girls' basketball team pose for a picture. From left to right are Louise Stewart, Sabina Leonard, Margaret Hutchison, Hazel Robinson, and Eva Sager. In 1900, a high school newspaper in Indiana described basketball as "the only exercise that thus far has been found that most girls can indulge in."

The 1908 Genoa Baseball Club members pose with their mascot. Pictured from left to right are (first row) pitcher C. Senska, mascot "Jack," and catcher Crawford; (second row) pitcher Evans, shortstop Furr, third baseman McKee, and right fielder Miller; (third row) captain and second baseman Senska, right fielder Crawford, manager and first baseman Olmsted, left fielder Patterson, and center fielder Lietzow. The players' first names are unknown.

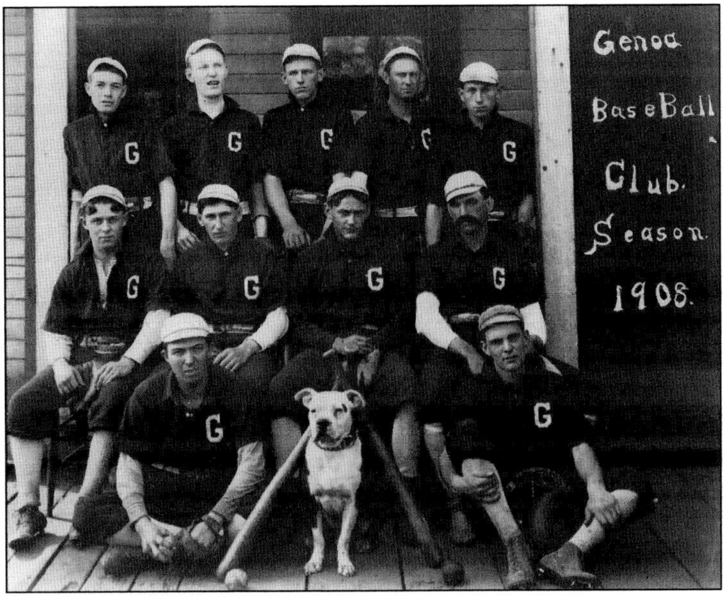

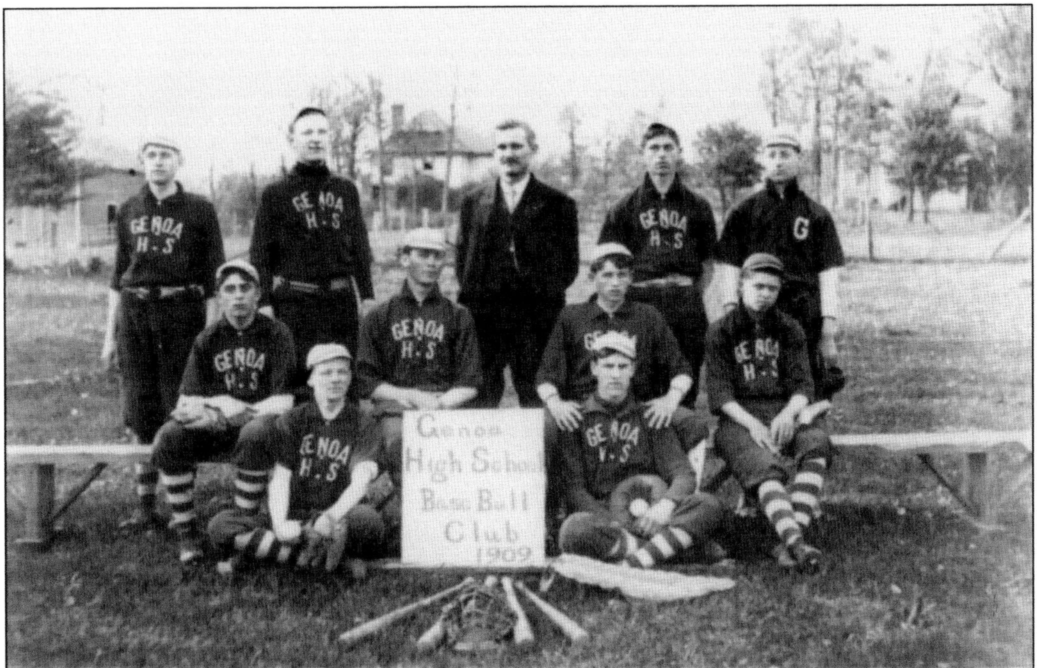

The 1909 Genoa High School Baseball Club members are shown wearing striped leggings, or stirrups, over white stockings called "sanitaries." The stirrups allowed players to show off their team colors. Baseball heroes in 1909 included Ty Cobb of the American League and Honus Wagner of the National League. (Courtesy of Kishwaukee Valley Heritage Society Museum.)

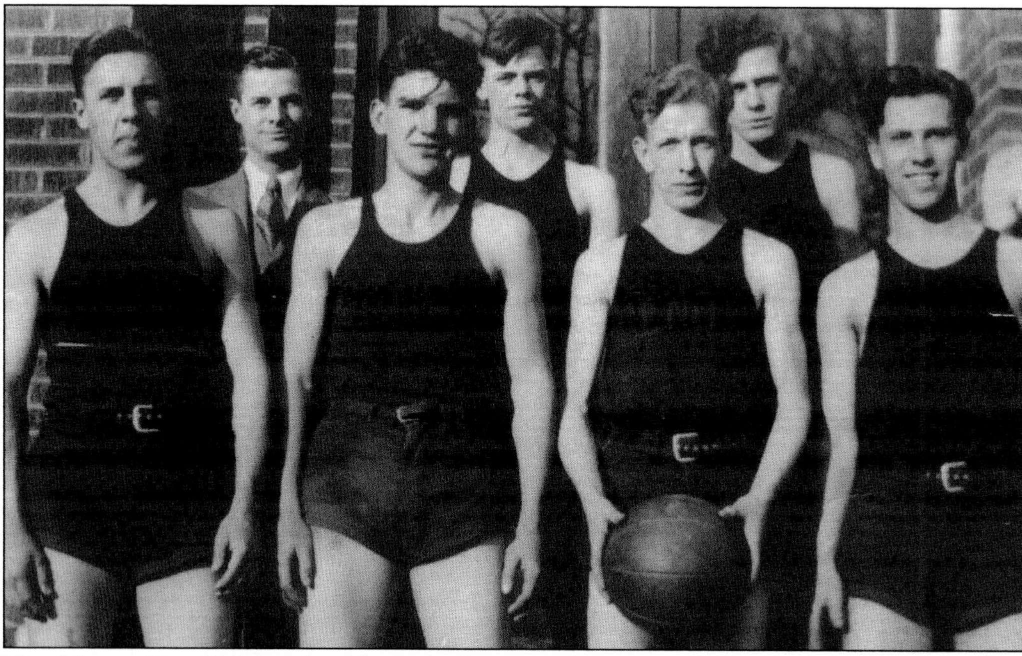

The "Genoa Blues" High School basketball team gathers for a photograph in 1929–1930. Their coach, Ivan Bennet, is shown in suit and tie and standing in the back row on the left. Ed Wahl is holding the basketball. In the back row next to the coach are Carroll Holly (center) and Al Rudolph. The names of the other players are unknown.

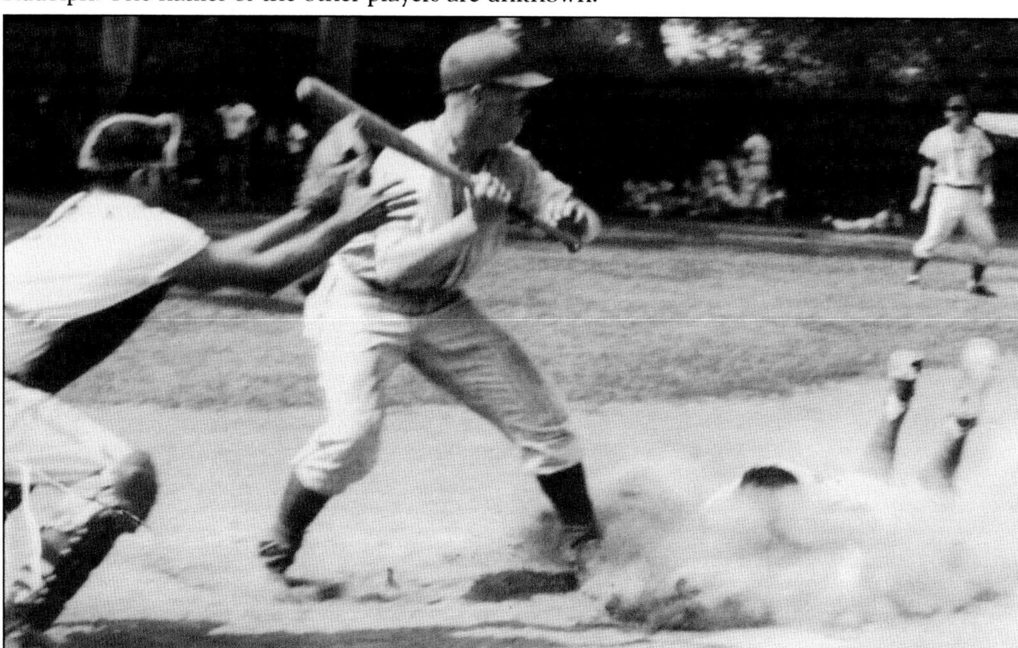

Genoa Merchants player Rex Freter is in the batter's box in 1958, while another player slides home amid a cloud of dust. The pitcher has delivered the pitch a little late to the catcher, whose hands are outstretched to receive it even though the run has already been scored.

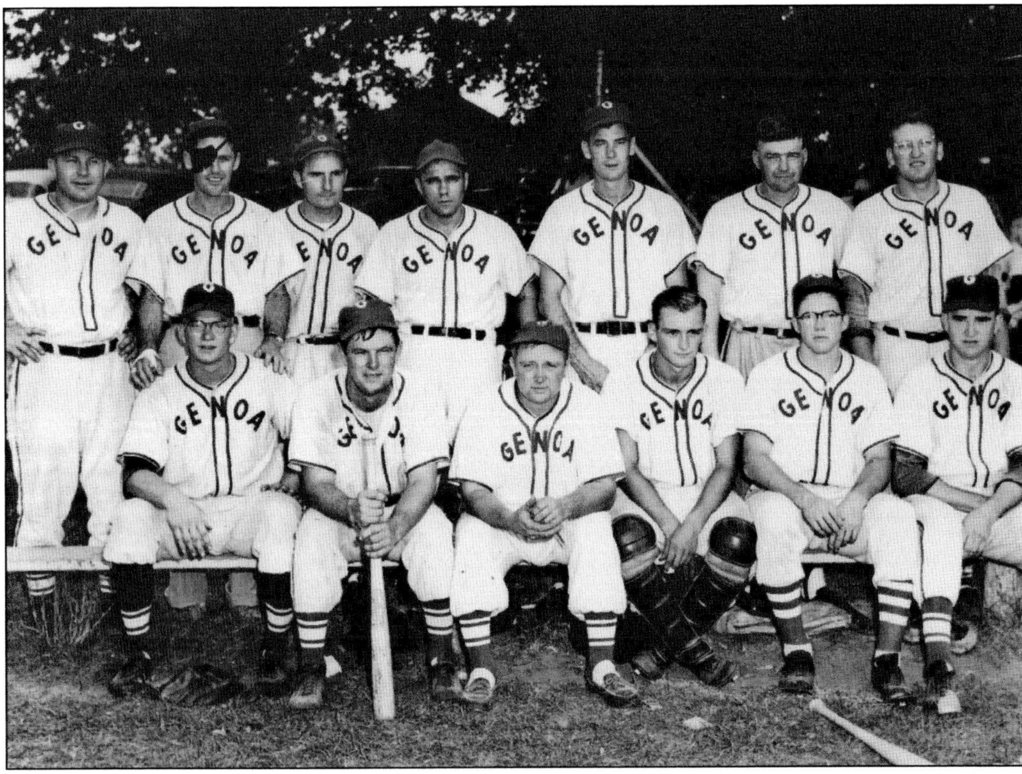

The Genoa Merchants baseball team won the Illinois state semi-pro baseball championship in 1953 and 1954. A group photograph in 1953 shows, from left to right, (first row) Chuck Westphal, Bob Maxwell, Fred Boettcher, Jerry Leber, Rodney Poppe, and Charlie Boxleitner; (second row) Jack Worden, Doc Mason, Ron Sadewater, Delbert Johnson, Dick Williams, Wally Westphal, and Rex Nelson.

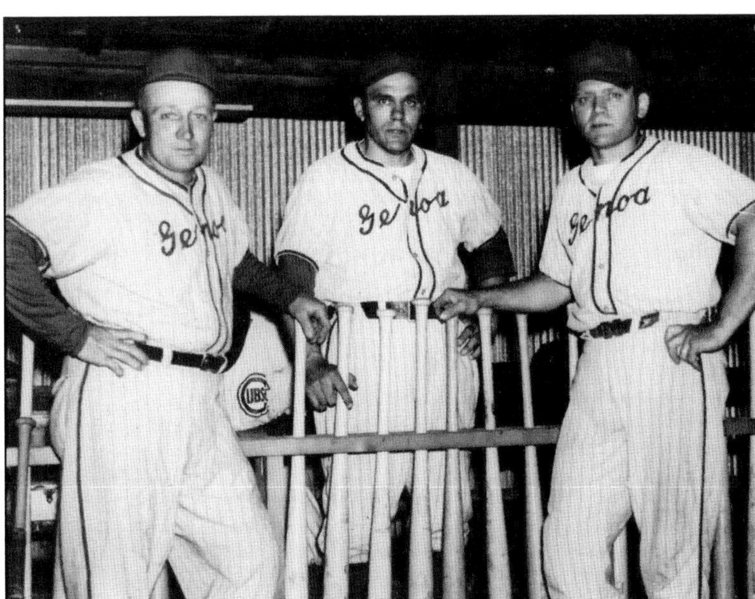

Genoa Merchants baseball players Fred Boettcher (left), Delbert Johnson (center), and Harold Johnson pose in the dugout in 1953. This was the year when the U.S. Congress officially credited Alexander Joy Cartwright Jr. with inventing the modern game of baseball, finally silencing an earlier myth that the game had been invented by Abner Doubleday.

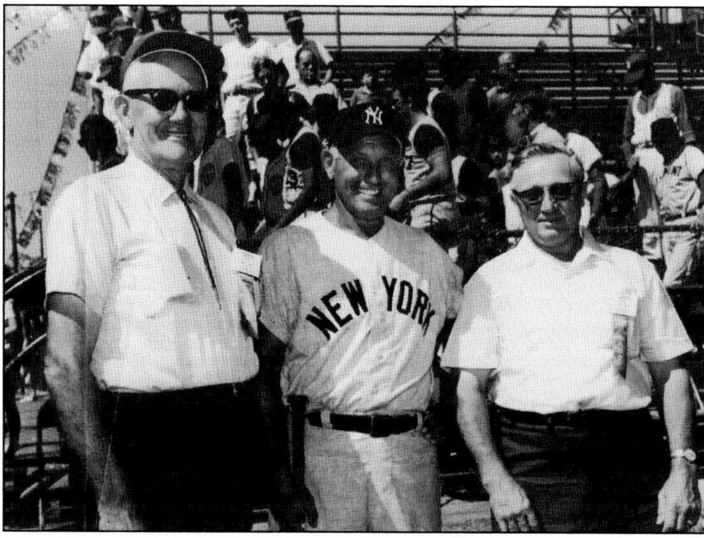

George Helman (left), Gene Woodling (center), and Fred Boettcher get together in 1978 in Farmington, New Mexico. Woodling played in the major leagues as an outfielder for the Cleveland Indians, Pittsburgh Pirates, New York Yankees, Baltimore Orioles, Washington Senators, and New York Mets. Boettcher played with the Genoa Merchants and later managed the team.

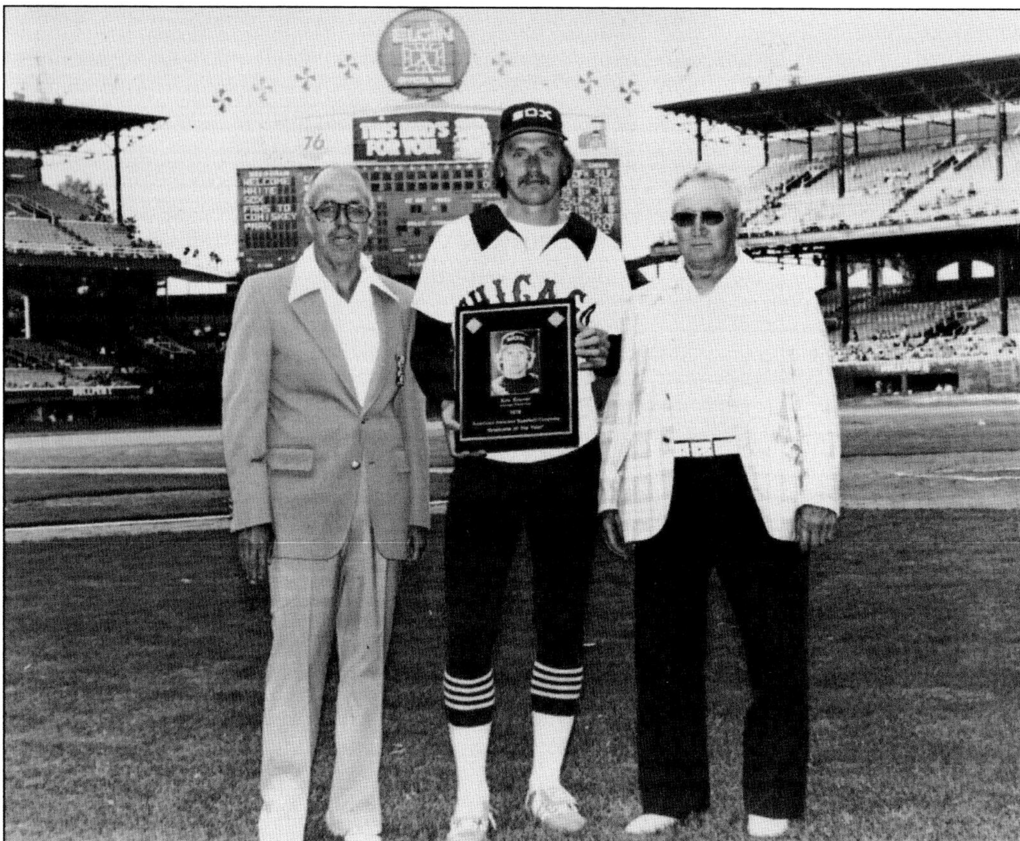

Fred Boettcher (right) presents a plaque to White Sox pitcher Ken Kravec at Comiskey Park in Chicago in 1979. Kravec led White Sox pitchers in strikeouts from 1977 to 1979. Boettcher managed the Genoa Merchants baseball team and was also the west central regional director for the American Amateur Baseball Congress. Notice the Elgin National Watch Company clock above the scoreboard.

Seven

Entertainment

There have been a number of clubs for Genoa and Kingston residents over the years. The Genoa Garden Club was started in 1928, and the Genoa Lions Club was chartered in 1953. Before Genoa could have city postal delivery, street signs and house numbers were needed. The Lions raised money for street signs and measured the streets so house numbers could be assigned. The Lions also donated $300 to the Genoa Rescue Squad toward the purchase of their first truck. In 2009, the Lions held their first Octoberfest at Chamberlain Park. In addition to clubs, there are opportunities for golf, dance, and other activities. The Oak Club of Genoa has an 18-hole course that was designed by golf architect Charles Maddox Sr. in 1971. The Beth Fowler School of Dance has been operating in Genoa for 27 years. The Genoa Township Park District offers programs such as preschool, Kids Klub, youth athletics, swimming at Chamberlain Park pool, and fitness classes at the Genoa/Kingston Fitness Center inside Genoa-Kingston High School. Educational programs are run by University of Illinois Extension staff at the Natural Resource Center in Russell Woods, which is owned by the DeKalb County Forest Preserve.

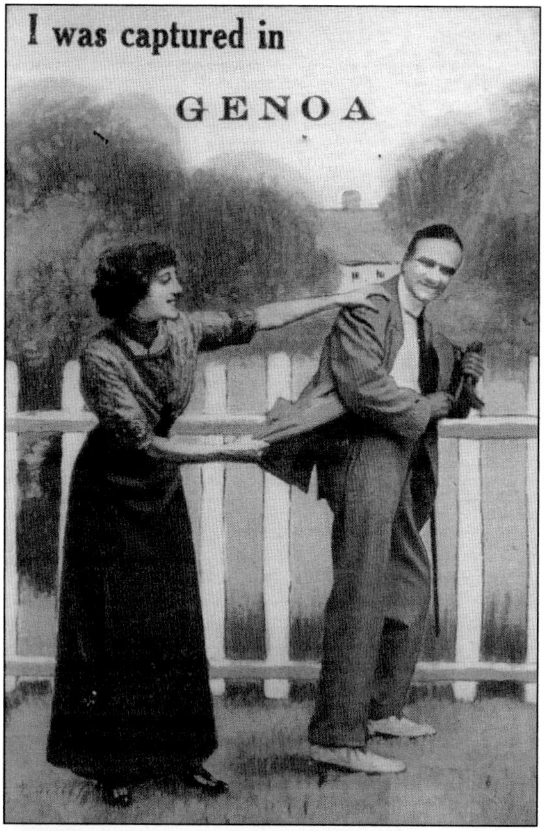

Before there were e-mails and texting on cell phones, postcards offered a fun way to send a short message to family and friends. The U.S. Postal Service produced its first picture postcards and commemorative stamp set in 1893 during the World's Colombian Exposition, which was also known as The Chicago World's Fair.

A group of women gather in Genoa to immerse themselves in Japanese culture and clothing around 1900. While some of the women donned kimonos and carried parasol umbrellas, others just preferred to wear a tag that featured the Japanese flag. During the early 20th century, over a million Japanese umbrellas were produced each year. The less expensive, Western-style umbrella later became more popular.

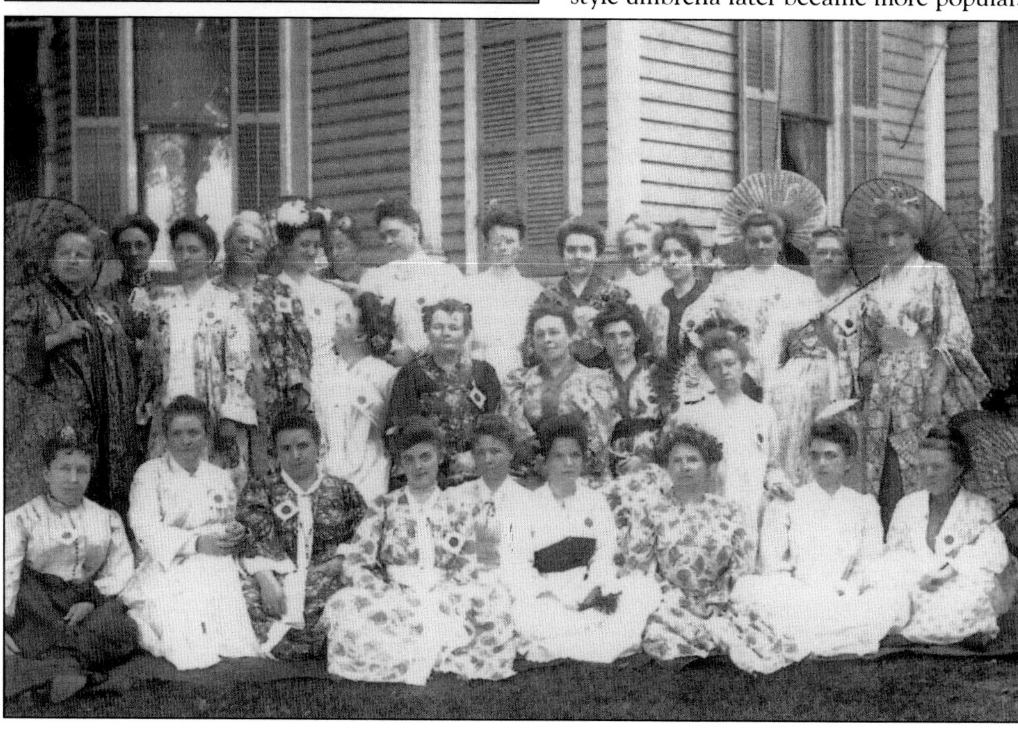

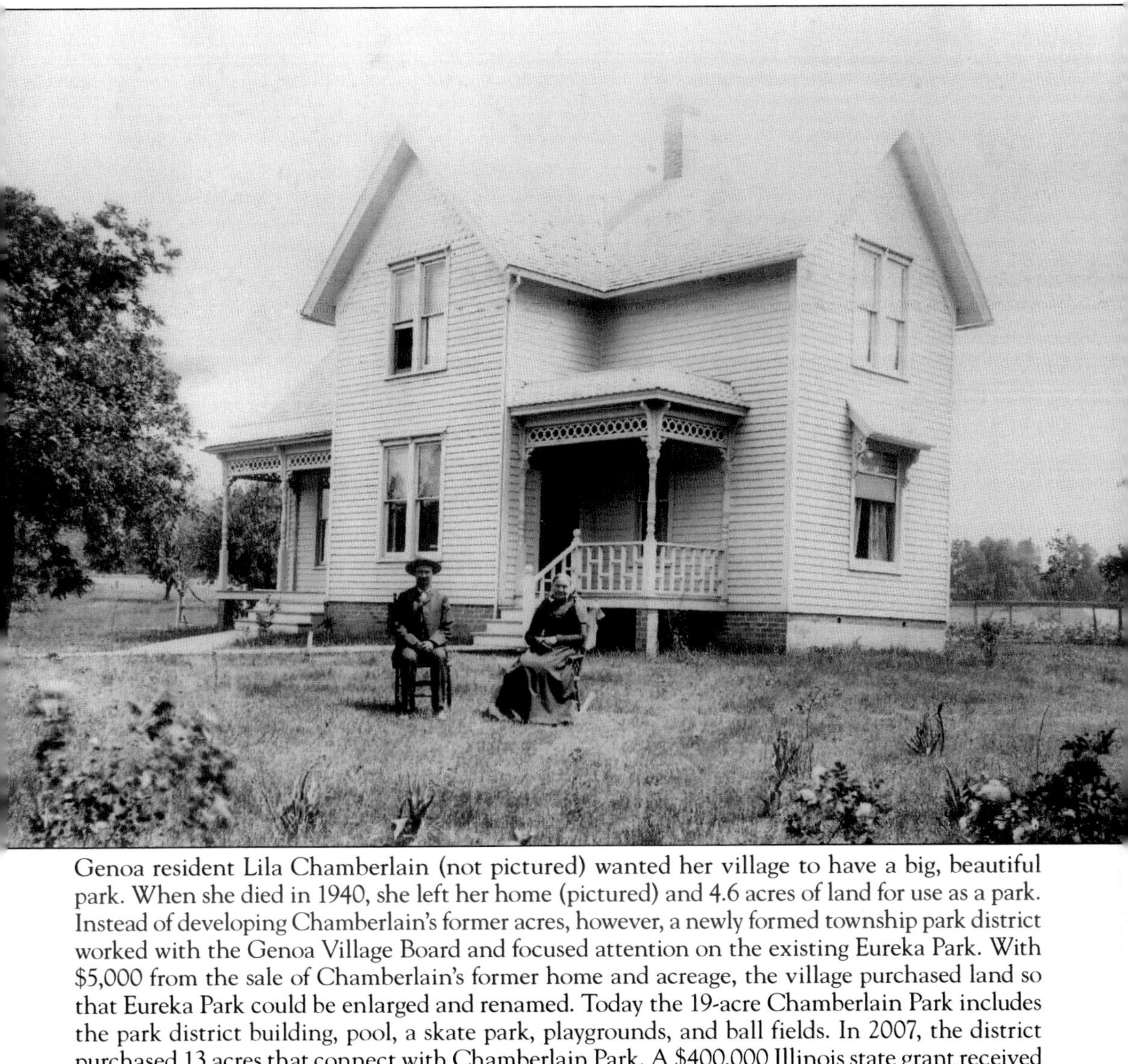

Genoa resident Lila Chamberlain (not pictured) wanted her village to have a big, beautiful park. When she died in 1940, she left her home (pictured) and 4.6 acres of land for use as a park. Instead of developing Chamberlain's former acres, however, a newly formed township park district worked with the Genoa Village Board and focused attention on the existing Eureka Park. With $5,000 from the sale of Chamberlain's former home and acreage, the village purchased land so that Eureka Park could be enlarged and renamed. Today the 19-acre Chamberlain Park includes the park district building, pool, a skate park, playgrounds, and ball fields. In 2007, the district purchased 13 acres that connect with Chamberlain Park. A $400,000 Illinois state grant received in 2010 will allow the district to develop the park and adjoining acres into two ball fields with two alternate ball fields, two soccer fields, a paved walkway with six fitness stations, a water-spray park, a basketball court, playground features and shelters, a stocked retention pond with a dock, and a sledding hill.

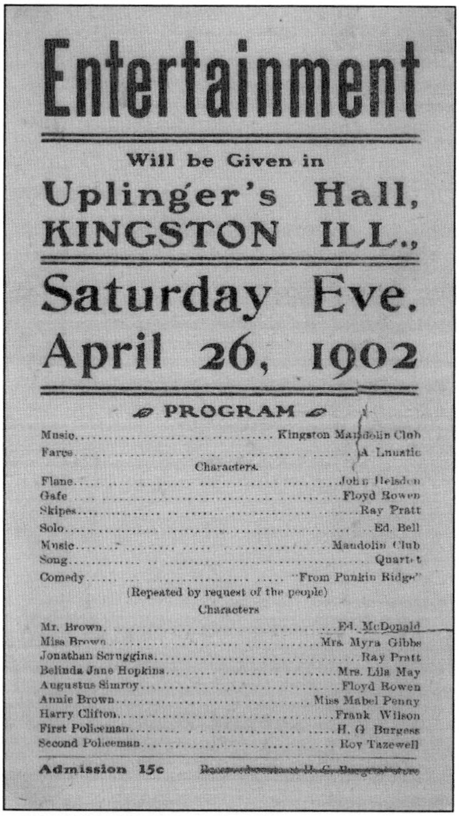
Entertainment

Will be Given in

Uplinger's Hall, KINGSTON ILL.,

Saturday Eve. April 26, 1902

PROGRAM

Music.......... Kingston Mandolin Club
Farce.......... A Lunatic

Characters.

Flane.......... John Helsden
Gafe.......... Floyd Rowen
Skipes.......... Ray Pratt
Solo.......... Ed. Bell
Music.......... Mandolin Club
Song.......... Quartet
Comedy.......... "From Punkin Ridge"

(Repeated by request of the people)

Characters

Mr. Brown.......... Ed. McDonald
Miss Brown.......... Mrs. Myra Gibbs
Jonathan Scruggins.......... Ray Pratt
Belinda Jane Hopkins.......... Mrs. Lila May
Augustus Simroy.......... Floyd Rowen
Annie Brown.......... Miss Mabel Penny
Harry Clifton.......... Frank Wilson
First Policeman.......... H. G Burgess
Second Policeman.......... Roy Tazewell

Admission 15c

On Saturday, April 26, 1902, people paid 15¢ apiece for admittance into Uplinger's Hall in Kingston. The entertainment lineup included music by members of the Mandolin Club and a performance by Ed McDonald, Myra Gibbs, Ray Pratt, Lila May, Floyd Rowen, Mabel Penay, Frank Wilson, H. G. Burgess, and Roy Tazwell.

Red Wood Billiard Parlor was located in the Crawford Building at the corner of North Emmett and Main Streets. Ralph Field became the owner in 1905 after he purchased the business from Elmer Sowers. Field is shown shooting pool at the second table from the front, while Fred Spansail (in a dark suit and hat) watches him play. Sowers is shooting pool at the front table.

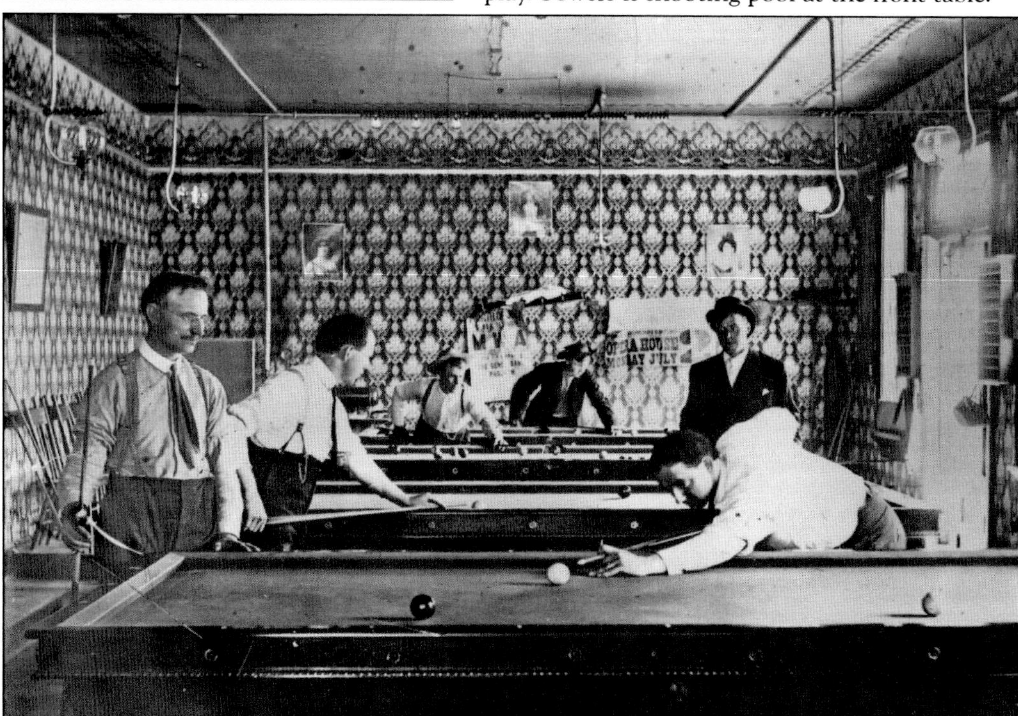

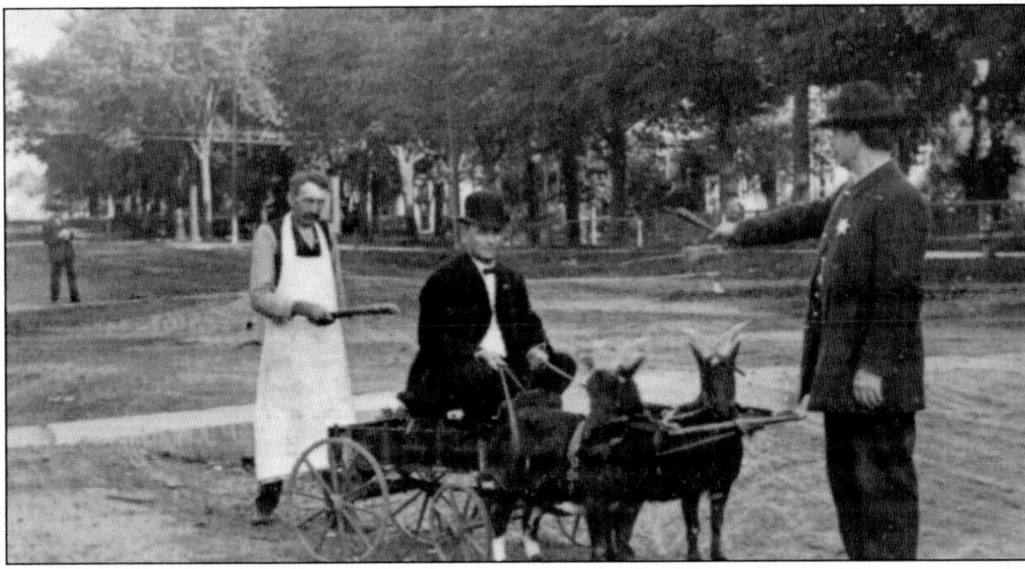

In the early 20th century, goat carts came in a variety of styles. They were used for transportation to and from church and school and also to carry garden produce. Children in goat carts were a popular subject for photographers at that time. In the image below, Mike Dander and his sister Dorothy are having fun riding in the Godding rig that is being pulled by goats. George Godding of Genoa, pictured above, takes his turn in the goat cart, while butcher Ed Pierce and policeman Bill Heed try to put a stop to his shenanigans.

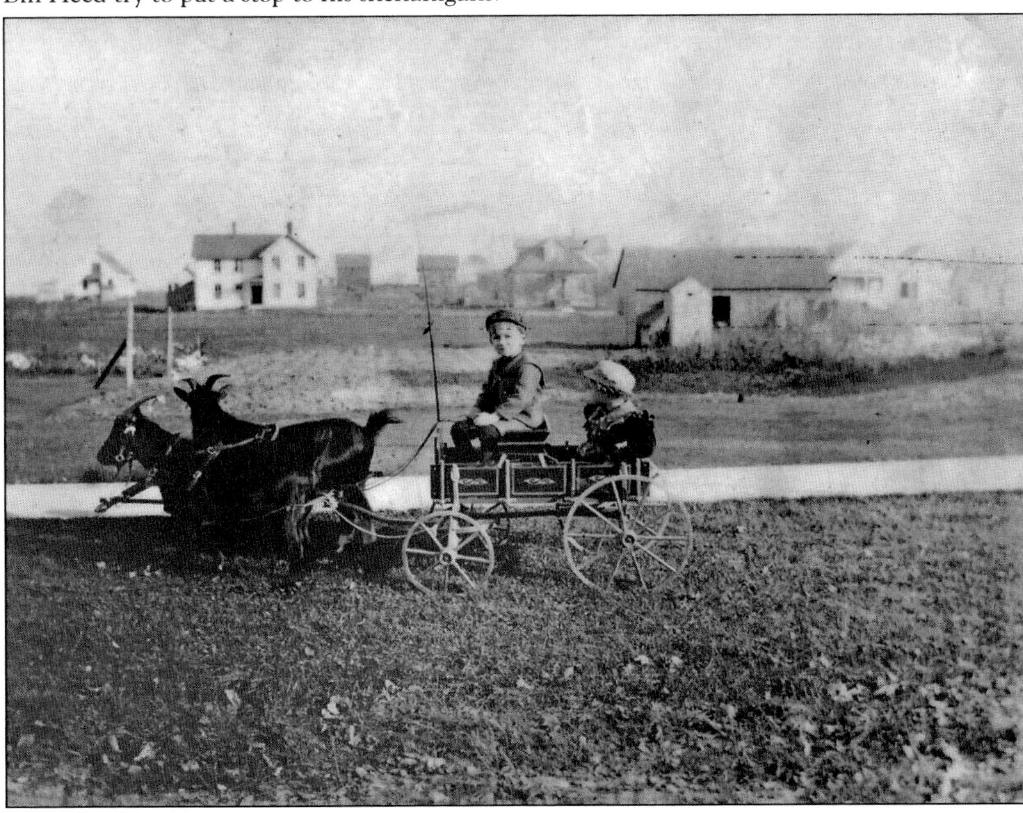

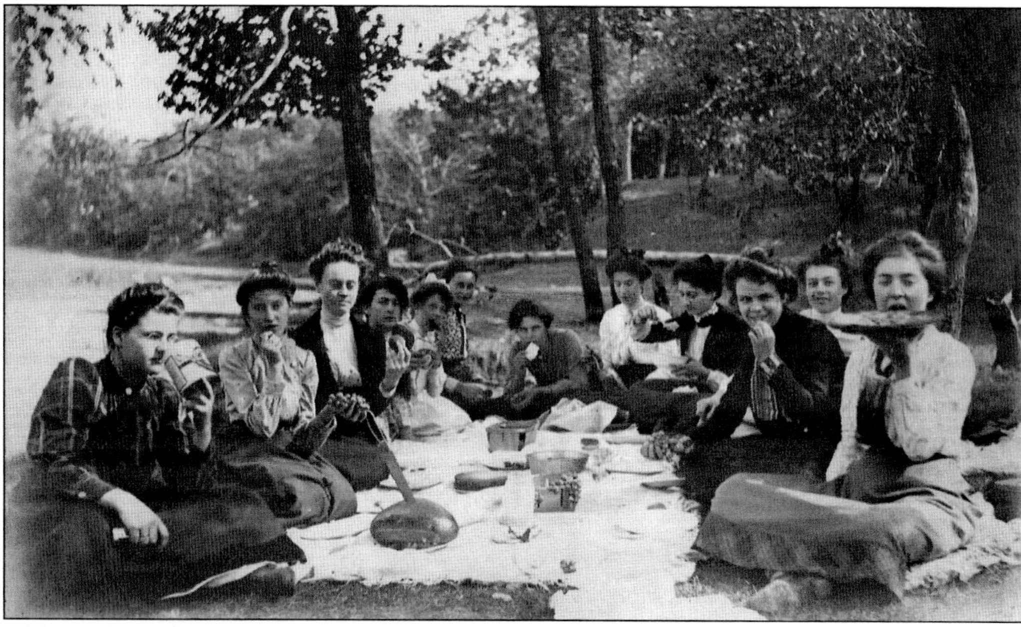

Old Maids Club members gather for a picnic. The members (above), from left to right, are Maude Bradford, Winnie Moore, Lizzie Sullivan, Bertha Ortt, Georgia Walker, Olive Moore, May Gibbs, Maude Benson, Katie Bassett, Ada Rubeck, Dorothy Dix, and Jennie Ortt. On July 20, 1900, the *Genoa Republican* newspaper stated, "The old maids of Kingston held their annual picnic last Saturday on the banks of the Kishwaukee. How awfully dull it must have been." The Independent Order of Odd Fellows Lodge No. 768 (below) poses for a photograph. The lodge was formed on October 31, 1899. Meetings were held on the second floor of the hardware store building in Genoa that was originally owned by Henry Perkins. Members continued to meet there until the building was sold in 1973. Genoa Lodge No. 768 then decided to consolidate with Sycamore Lodge No. 105.

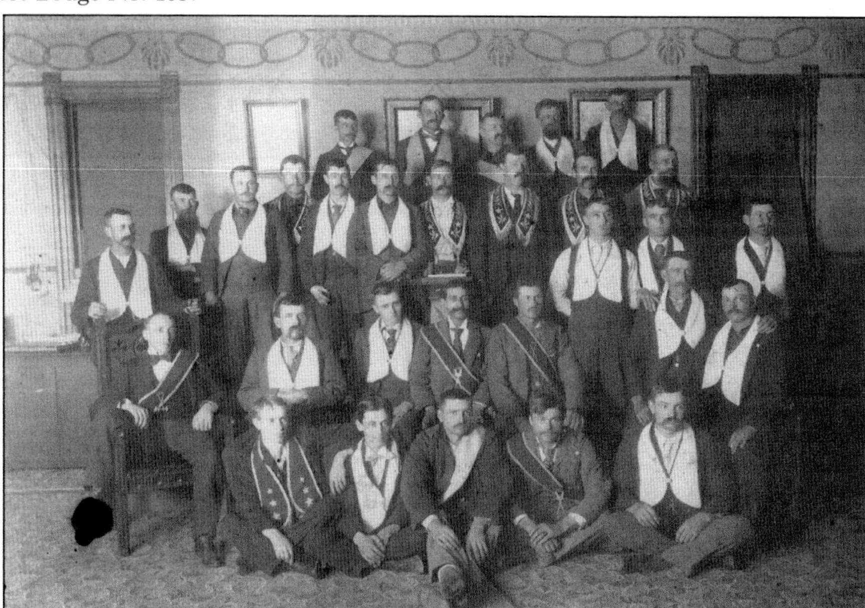

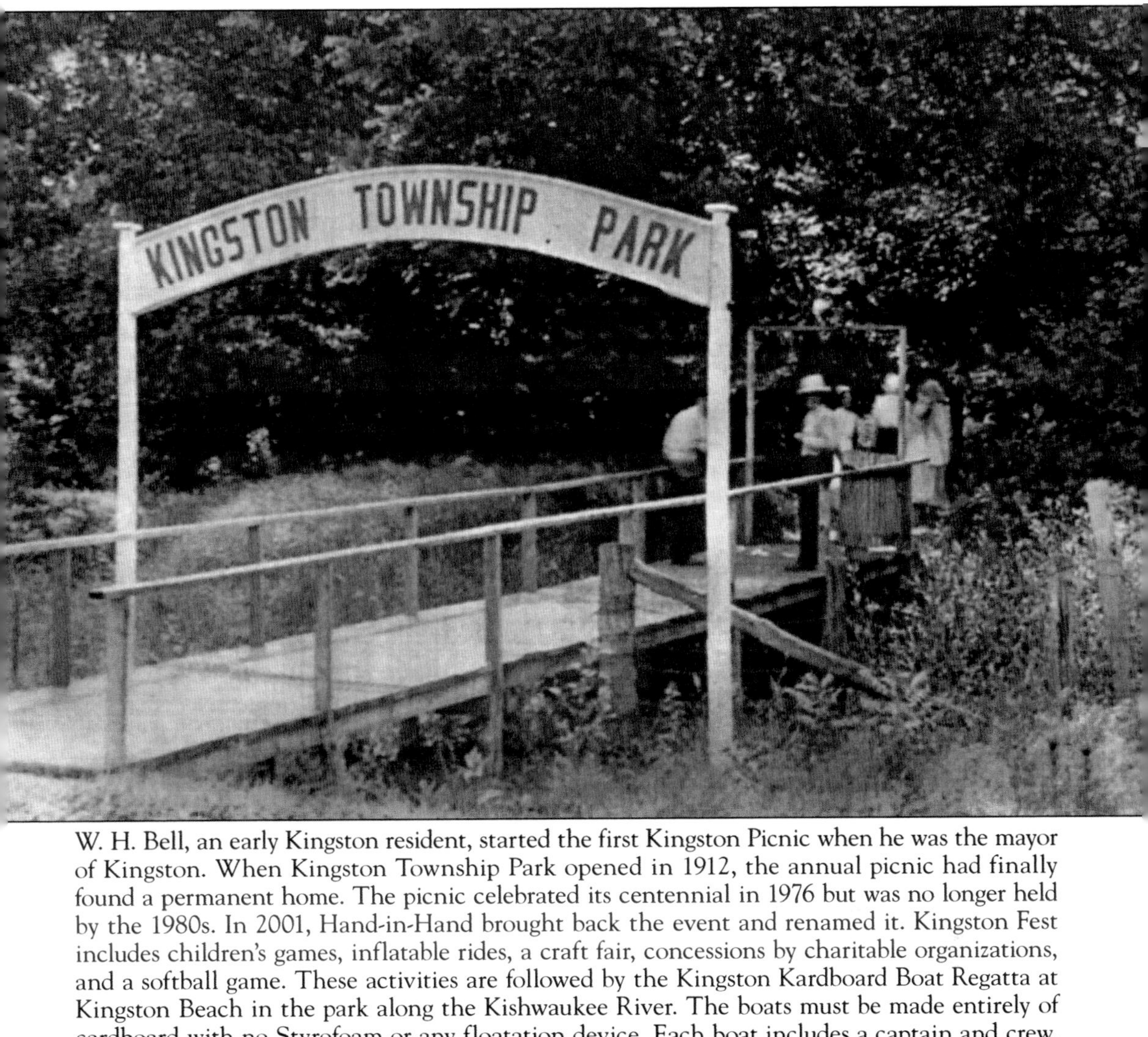

W. H. Bell, an early Kingston resident, started the first Kingston Picnic when he was the mayor of Kingston. When Kingston Township Park opened in 1912, the annual picnic had finally found a permanent home. The picnic celebrated its centennial in 1976 but was no longer held by the 1980s. In 2001, Hand-in-Hand brought back the event and renamed it. Kingston Fest includes children's games, inflatable rides, a craft fair, concessions by charitable organizations, and a softball game. These activities are followed by the Kingston Kardboard Boat Regatta at Kingston Beach in the park along the Kishwaukee River. The boats must be made entirely of cardboard with no Styrofoam or any floatation device. Each boat includes a captain and crew. Awards that have been given out to contestants include "Flamboyancy," the most outrageously decorated boat; "Pirates of Pizzaz," the crew/team with the most spirit; "Titanic," the boat with the most spectacular sinking; "Fleet-of-the-Fleet," the fastest boat in the race; and "Kishwaukee Ferry," for most crew in the boat.

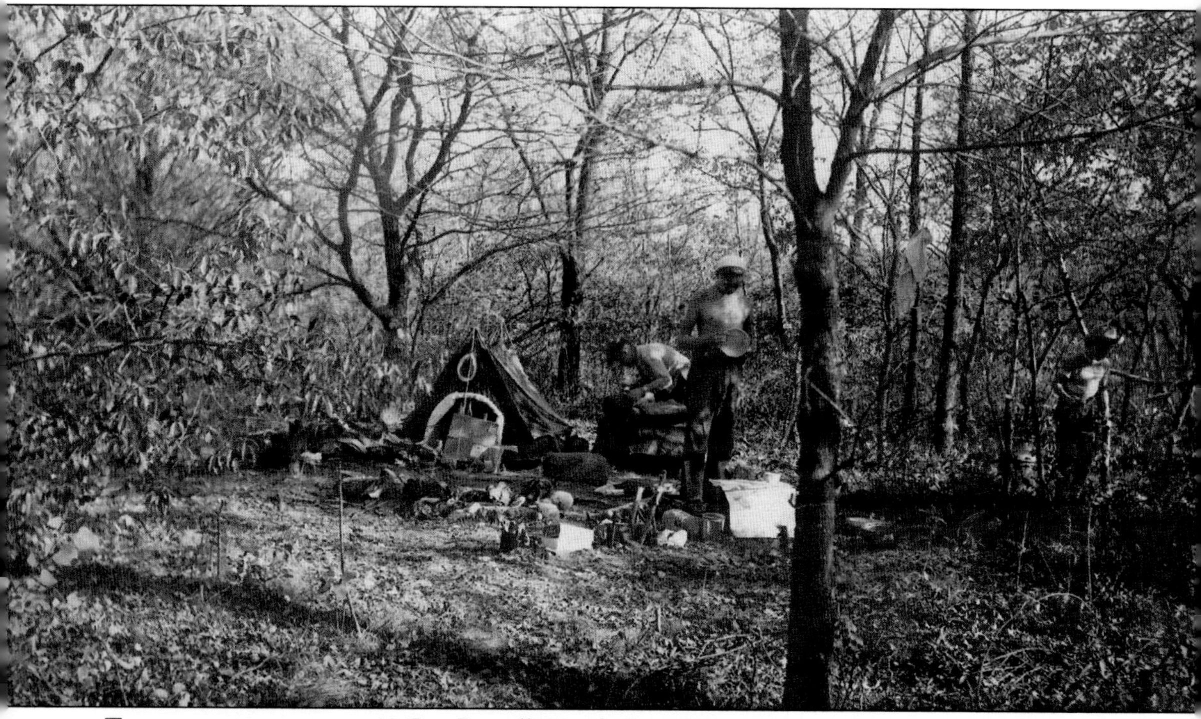

Two men set up camp in 1947 at Russell Woods Forest Preserve in Genoa. Russell Woods offers area residents a chance to enjoy the mature oaks and hickories of the forest, along with the wildlife found along the banks of the Kishwaukee River. During the winter, the hill at the preserve becomes a favorite place for sledding. The Natural Resources Education Center (NREC) at the preserve features both live and stuffed native wildlife. The University of Illinois Extension, along with four other county entities, created a joint natural resources education program in 1992. The groups include the DeKalb County Forest Preserve, DeKalb County Soil and Water Conservation District, Solid Waste Management of DeKalb County, and NREC. The center is owned by the DeKalb County Forest Preserve and maintained by University of Illinois Extension staff, which is headed by Natural Resources Educator Peggy Doty. The University of Illinois Extension teaches environmental education classes at the center to school groups, Cub Scouts, Girl Scouts, and other groups. They also teach students about recycling through the DeKalb County School Recycling Program. (Courtesy of Joiner Room.)

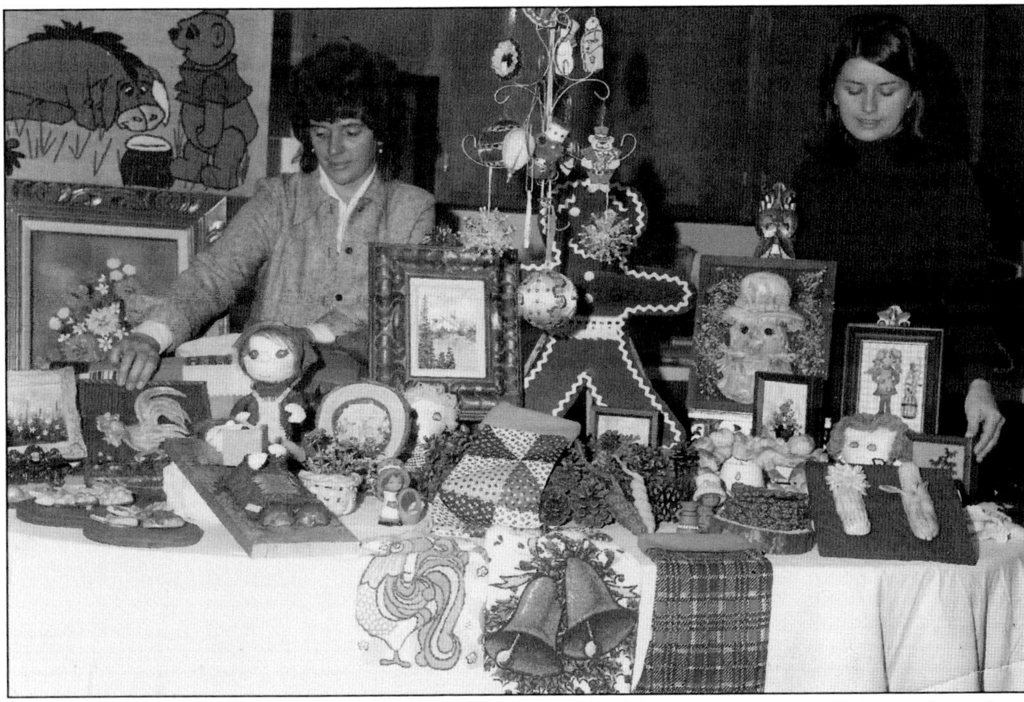

Genoa residents Marilyn Greenawalt (left) and Linda Mason arrange craft items for sale at Greenawalt's home during the first Ellen Oaks Christmas Open House in 1969. The annual event, now held at the Masonic Temple in Genoa, celebrated its 40th year in 2009. The craft show spurred the creation of the annual Christmas Craft Walk in Genoa and Kingston, which celebrated its 35th year in 2009. (Courtesy of Marilyn Greenawalt.)

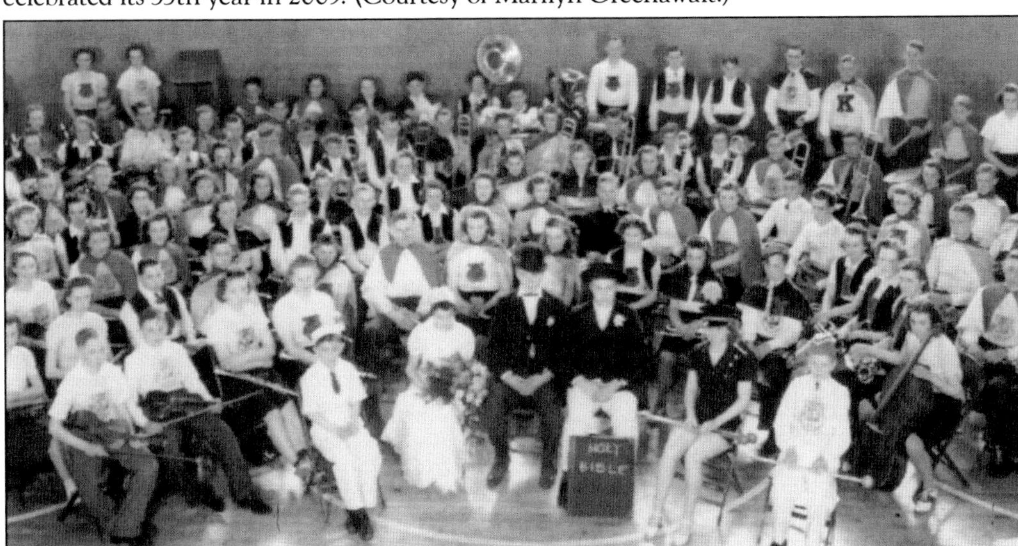

Kingston band members pose during a concert in this undated photograph. The children in the front row depict pioneers and members of the U.S. Armed Forces. Kingston Grade School, built in 1896, once housed a grade school and four-year high school. The last high school class from the school graduated in 1947.

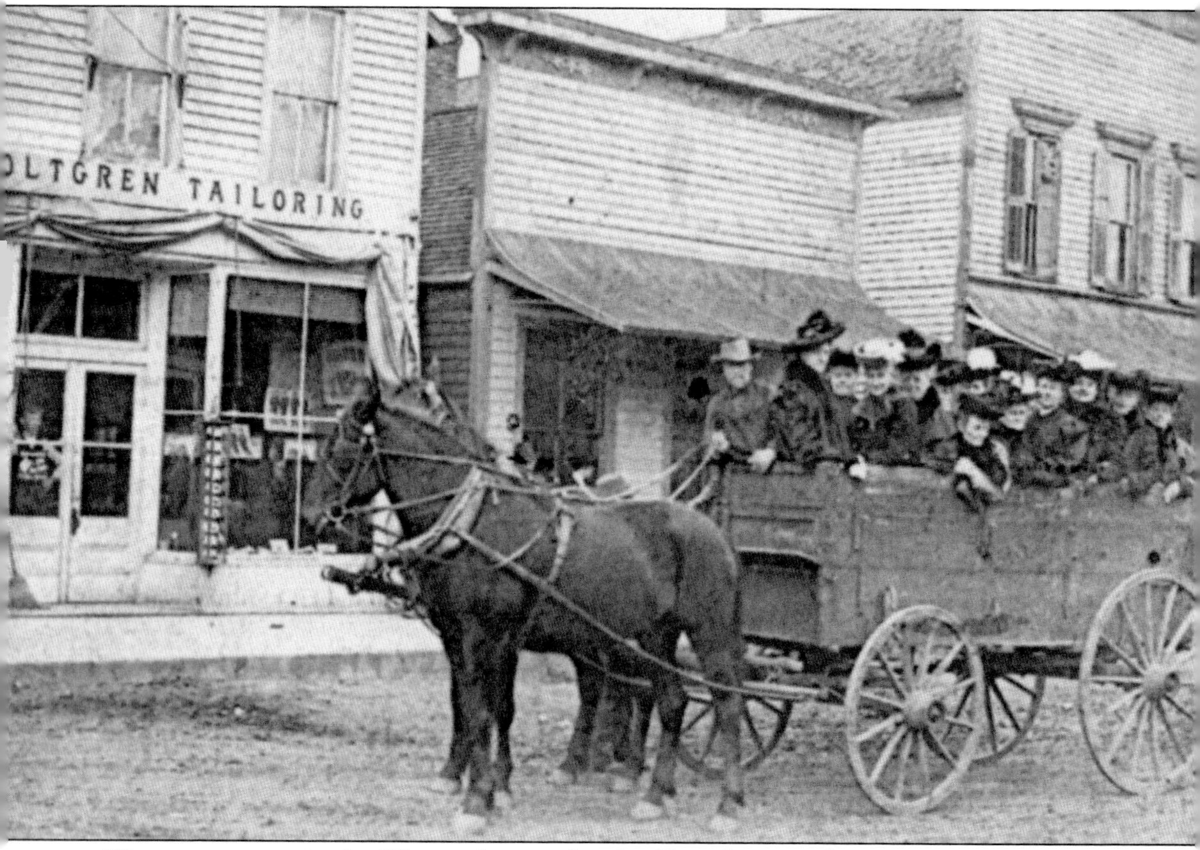

Women on an outing huddle together inside a buckboard wagon that stops along Main Street in Genoa around 1900. The "buckboard" is the front board on the wagon that served as both a footrest for the driver and protection for the driver in case the team of horses wanted to buck. The buckboard wagon was developed in the United States around the mid-1800s. It had four wheels and two axles mounted by a board of flexible wood and a front seat that could hold two people. It was usually drawn by one or two horses. The coach, a carriage with an enclosed cab, was used by the upper class. The buggy, also known as a "poor man's coach," had a roof but no sides. The buckboard and its passengers in Genoa are stopped in front of F. O. Holtgren's shop, which sold ready-made clothing and also ran a tailoring department.

Eight

Off to War

Many Genoa and Kingston residents have served their country over the years. Kingston gave 105 soldiers to the Union Army during the Civil War, while Genoa furnished them with 109 men. Genoan residents 2nd Lt. Bayard Brown and Pvts. Fred Niss, Tony Henry Muhr, and William Wolters lost their lives during World War I. Kingston resident Willard Aves was the first man to die from DeKalb County during World War II. On December 7, 1941, Aves was aboard the USS *Arizona* at Pearl Harbor. He was 1 of the 1,177 crewmen who are still entombed at the USS Arizona Memorial. Pictures of the people who have served can be found at the Genoa Veterans Home at 311 South Washington Street. The American Legion Bayard Brown Post 337 of Genoa was organized in 1920. The Veterans of Foreign Wars Post 8387 was formed in 1946. The two organizations joined forces in 1965 to form the Genoa Veterans Home. While the facility is a members-only club, there are public events such as bingo, fish fries, burger buffets, and breakfast buffets. The ballroom can also be rented by the public. The facility is also home to Bayard Brown American Legion Auxiliary 337 and Sons of the American Legion Squadron 337.

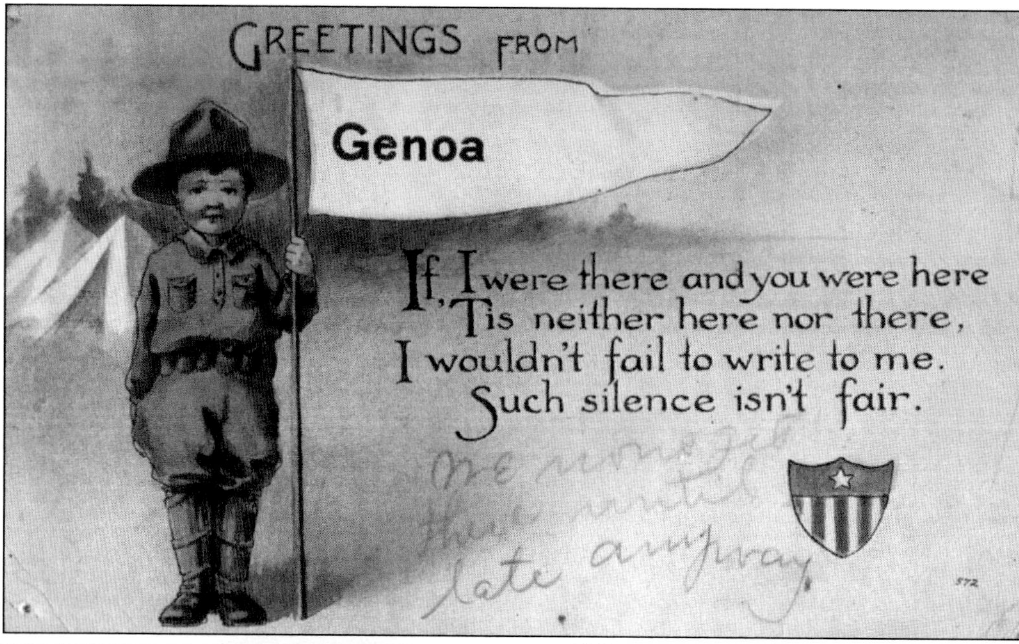

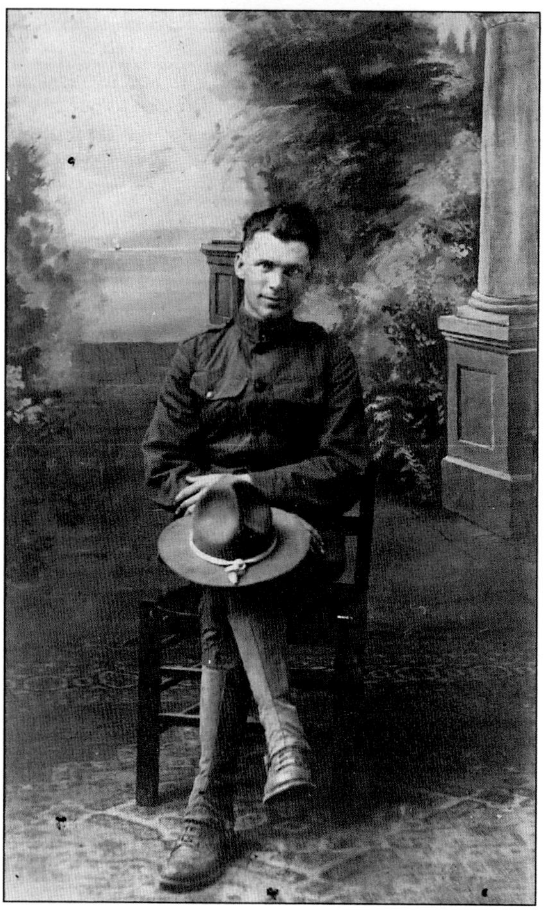

U.S. servicemen who were stationed overseas eagerly looked forward to receiving postcards and letters from family and friends back home. Dillon S. Brown paid for copies of the *Genoa Republican-Journal* to be sent to every Genoa man in the armed forces during World War I. Brown said, "You may be assured that the men will appreciate this."

Glen Charles Montgomery of Genoa, pictured here, served during World War I. Other Genoa residents who served at that time included Dr. John Ovitz, Charles Schoonmaker, John Duval, and Albert Awe. Ovitz ran the first and only hospital in Genoa before going off to war and earning the rank of lieutenant. Schoonmaker published the *Genoa Republican-Journal*. Duval and Awe operated Duval-Awe Garage in Genoa.

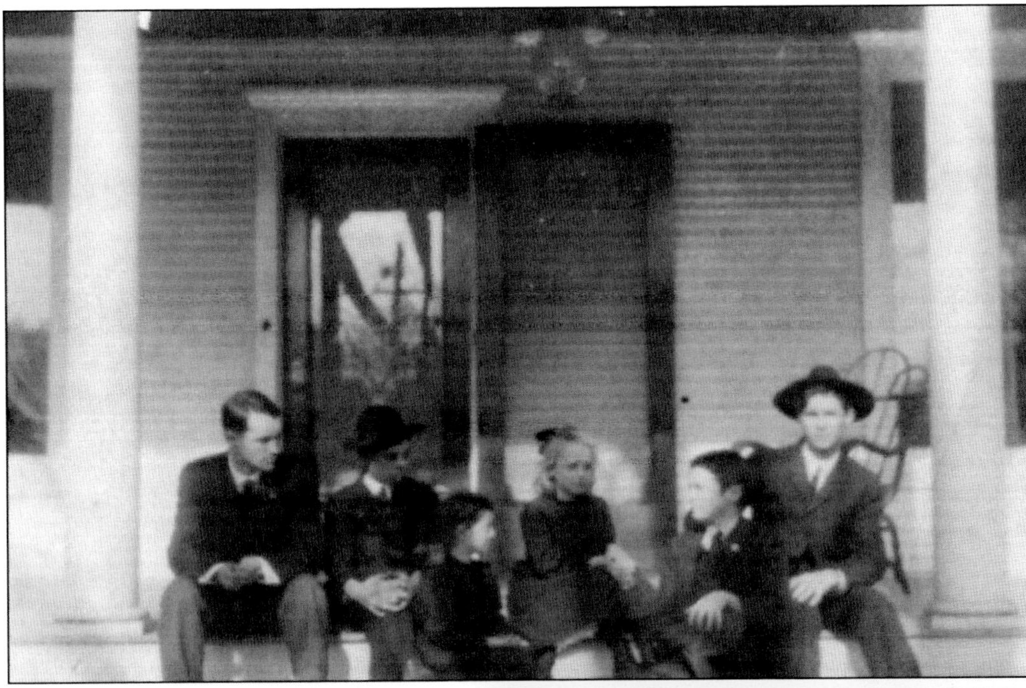

Two photographs portray Bayard Brown as a child and as a young man. In the above photograph, from left to right, Earl, Loyal, Lorene, Gladys, Bayard, and Roy Brown spend family time together seated on the front porch of their home. They are all smartly dressed as if they just came back from a wedding, a funeral, or some other formal event. In the photograph at right, Bayard is a young man with a starched white collar and fancy tie. His hair is left long on the top and short on the sides, which was a popular men's hairstyle at the time.

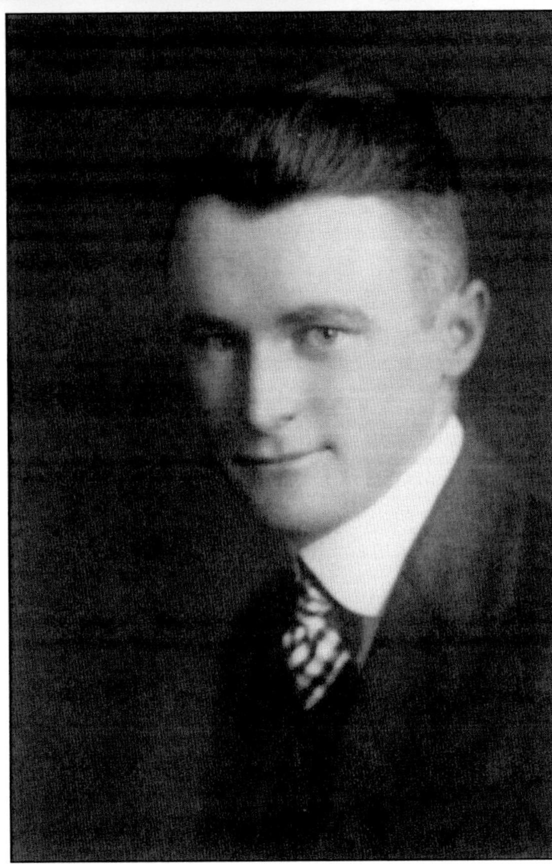

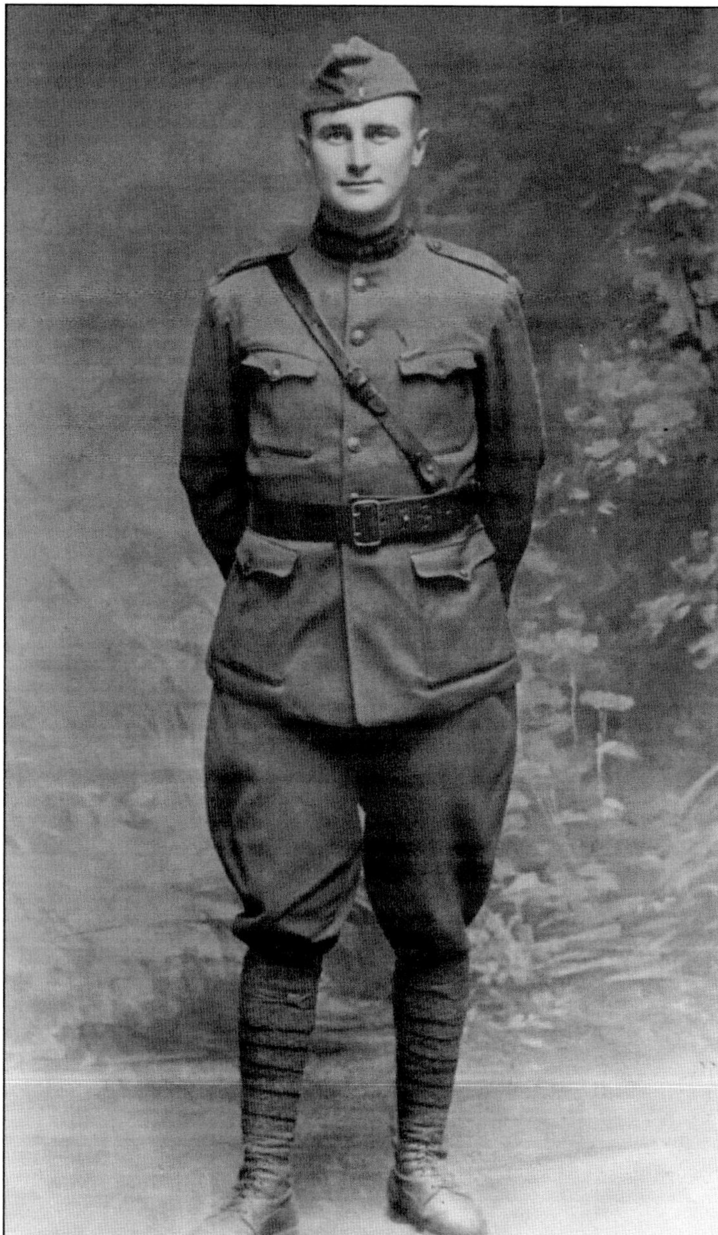

U.S. Army 2nd Lt. Bayard Brown of Genoa was awarded the Distinguished Service Cross for extraordinary heroism in action near Soissons, France, from July 2 to 22, and near Verdun, France, on October 9, 1918. Lieutenant Brown served with the 26th Infantry Regiment, 1st Division, AEF. He took command of his battalion at Soissons after all of his senior officers had been killed or wounded. He organized for a counterattack and held his command all day even though he had been dangerously wounded. In the fight for Hill 212 in the Argonne, he took command of his company after his commander had been killed. He led his company forward until he was mortally wounded within 50 yards of the enemy position. Bayard Brown American Legion Post 337 and Bayard Brown American Legion Auxiliary 337 at the Genoa Veterans Home, at 311 South Washington Street in Genoa, are named in his honor.

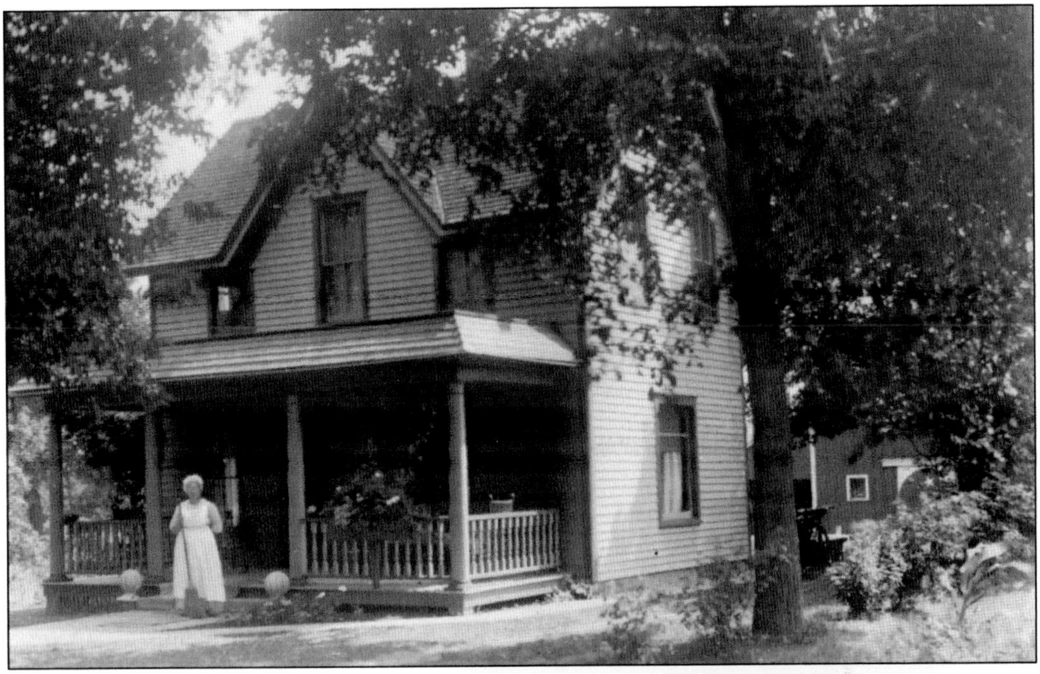

Olive Mary (Miller) Ortt finishes sweeping the front porch of her home on East Street in Kingston. She married John Pierson Ortt, a teamster, in 1884. Their children were Jennie, Bertha, Ralph, and Beatrice. Ralph was a World War I veteran who served in the army. He also played baseball as a Kingston Tiger and worked as a rural mail carrier.

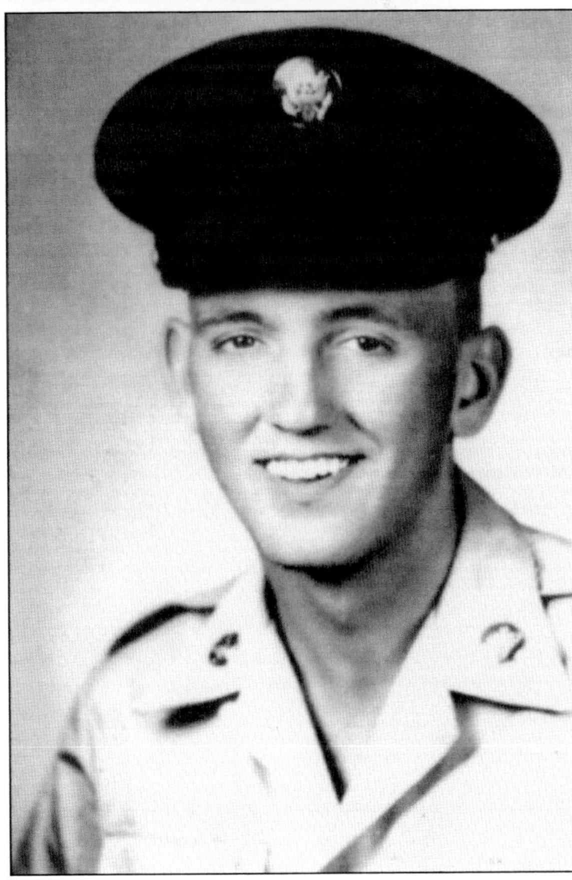

Sgt. Jessie Gerald Poe was a Kingston resident who was born on June 15, 1948. His army tour of duty in South Vietnam began on November 16, 1967. He was killed in Binh Dinh Province, South Vietnam, on June 2, 1968. In that year, there were 540,000 U.S. troops in Vietnam. Poe's name appears on the Vietnam Veterans Memorial Wall. (Courtesy of the Genoa Veterans Home.)

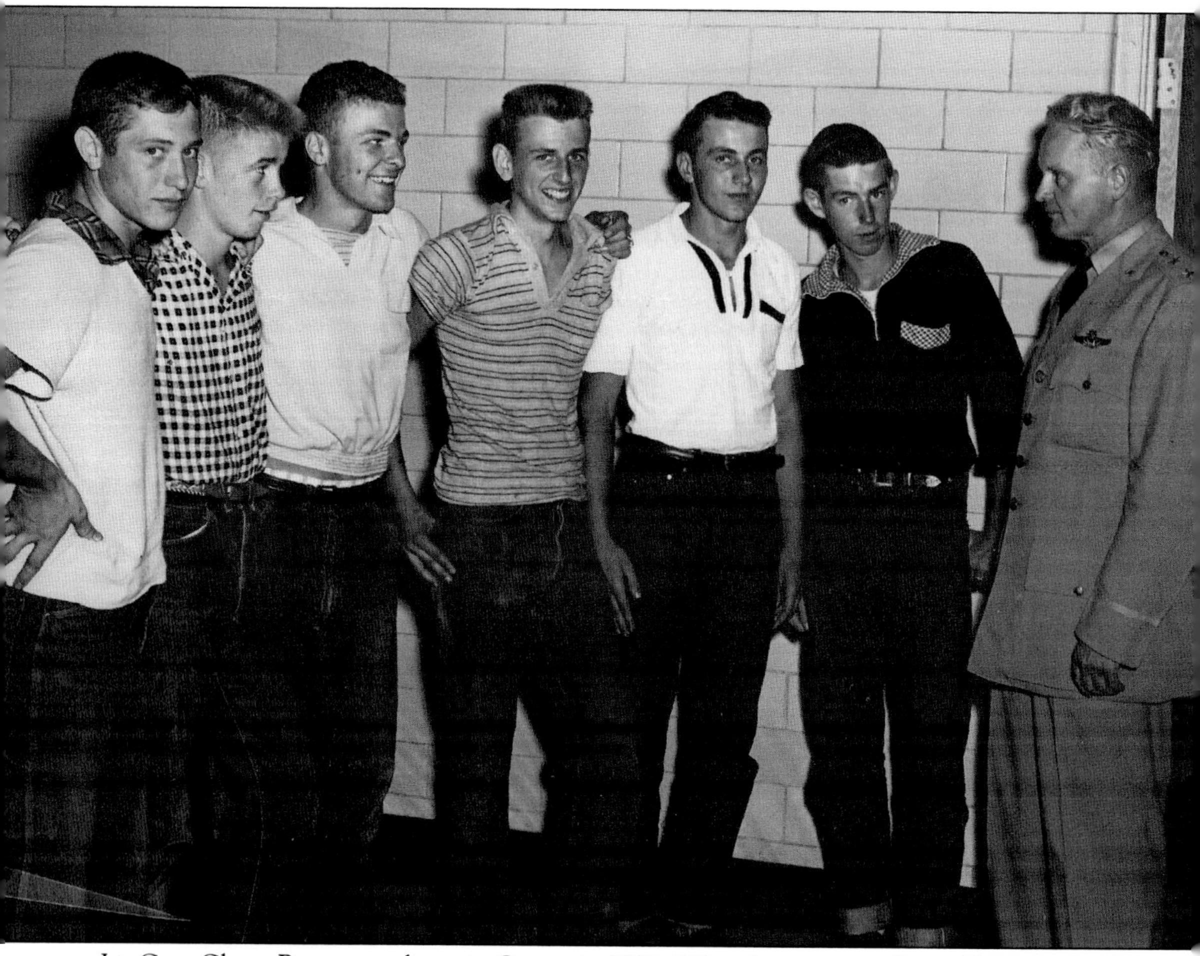

Lt. Gen. Glenn Barcus was born in Genoa in 1903. When he came to Genoa-Kingston High School during the 1950s, he was met with a parade and a banquet for over 400 people in the school's new gymnasium. He gave a speech about his experiences as commanding general of the Fifth Air Force in Korea. Students who posed with Barcus at the high school, from left to right, are Leroy Conro, Bob Holroyd, Don Coffey, Jack Fanning, Jack Fowler, and Jerry Rubeck. Some of the medals Barcus received in his lifetime included the Distinguished Service Medal, Legion of Merit, Distinguished Flying Cross, Bronze Star Medal, Air Medal, European-Mediterranean Campaign Medal, World War II Victory Medal, Army of Occupation/Japan, Korean Campaign, National Defense Service Medal, Air Force Longevity Service Award, French Croix de Guerre, British Companion of the Bath Order, Korean Order of Military Merit Taeguk, and United Nations Service Medal. His assignments took him to Hawaii, Puerto Rico, Trinidad, Washington D.C., Italy, France, Korea, and Newfoundland. He died on December 9, 1990, at the age of 87.

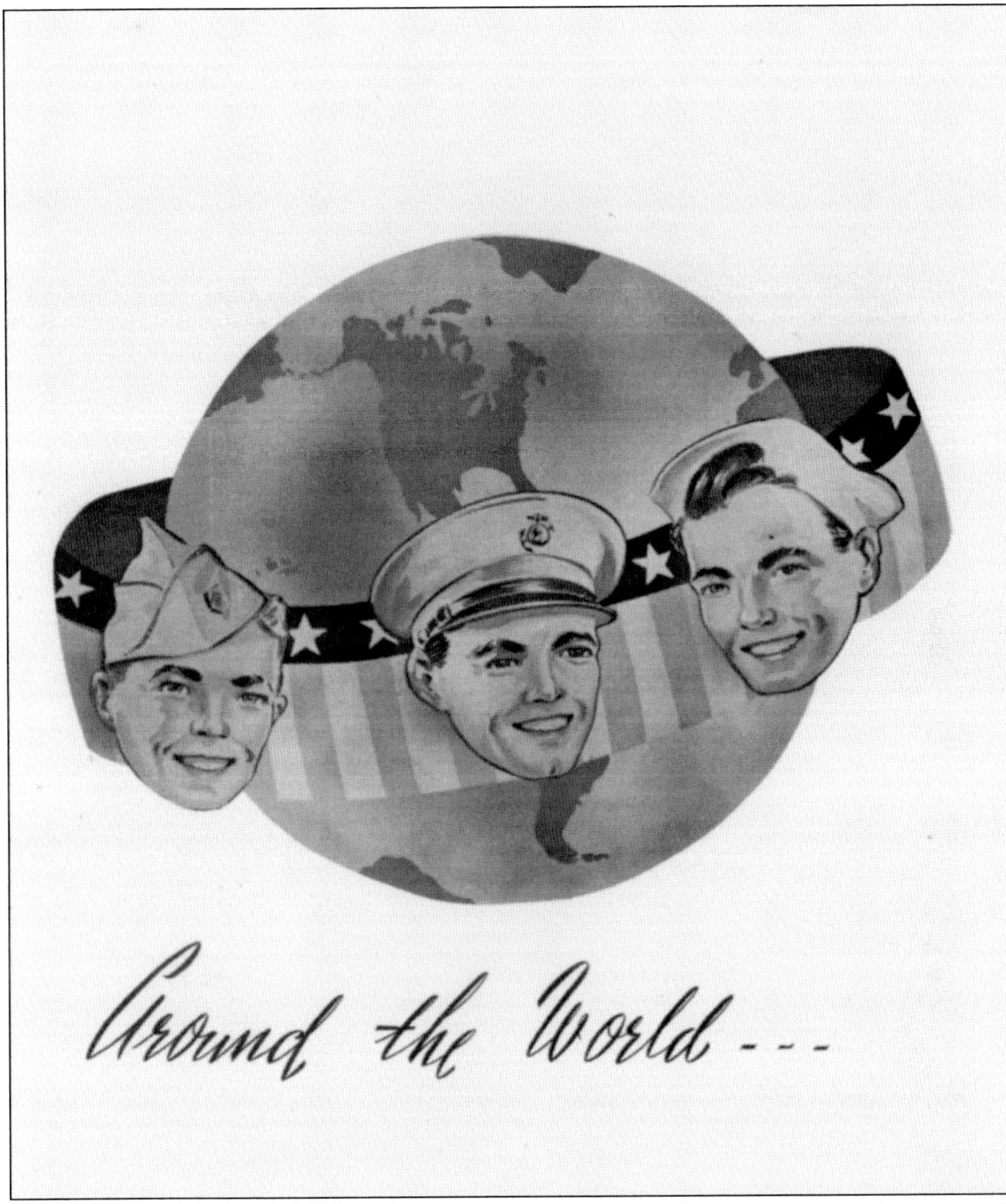

A picture taken from *World War II, Genoa, and Community Service Record* book shows U.S. military branches of service: The army, marines, and the navy. Two friends, Pvt. James Leonard Medine, 20, and Pfc. Henry Pinne, 24, were listed in the book as Gold Star Boys on Genoa Township's honor roll. Medine was born in Genoa, while Pinne was from Kirkland. Both men were employed by Leich Electric Company in Genoa. In 1942, Medine married Norma Smith, while Pinne married Marjorie Anderson. Medine and Pinne both entered the service on June 2, 1944, at Fort Sheridan. They were assigned to the 36th Infantry Division. They were together when they landed in France on Thanksgiving Day 1944. Medine was killed in action on December 12, 1944, and buried in France, while Pinne died on February 2, 1945, in France from wounds he received on January 9, 1945, during the Battle of the Bulge. A memorial was held for him at Genoa Evangelical Church. Both men posthumously received the Purple Heart.

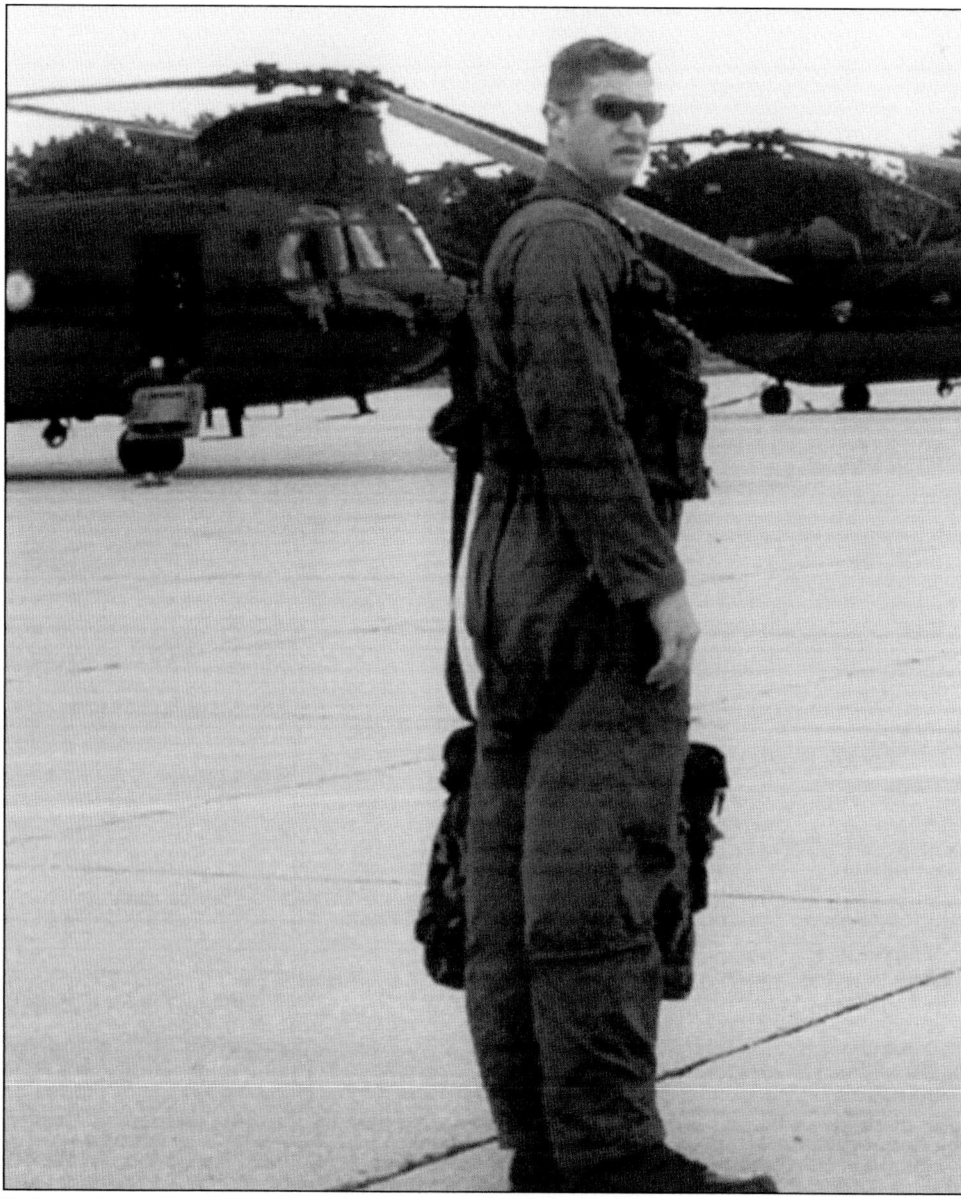

U.S. Army 1st Lt. Brian Donatus Slavenas, 30, of Genoa was flying a CH-47 Chinook helicopter on November 2, 2003, when it was downed in Al Fallujah, Iraq. An SA-7 missile took out the No. 2 engine. Brian was 1 of the 17 soldiers killed by the attack. He was assigned to F Company, 106th Aviation Battalion of the Army National Guard in Peoria, Illinois. He was an accomplished classical pianist, a 6-foot, 4-inch-tall body builder, and a recently graduated mechanical engineer. Like his paratrooper father, Ronald, and two older brothers, Eric and Marcus, Brian followed a path to the military. After high school graduation, he became an Army paratrooper and then joined the National Guard. He went on to officer school and became a helicopter pilot. He earned an engineering degree from the University of Illinois at Urbana-Champaign. The University of Illinois Department of Mechanical and Industrial Engineering has established the Brian Slavenas IIE Outstanding Member Award and Scholarship Fund in Brian's memory. The scholarships will be available to students enrolled in industrial engineering. (Courtesy of Genoa Veterans Home.)

Nine

DOWN ON MAIN STREET

Genoa and Kingston both have a Main Street that runs through their downtown areas. One side of Main Street in Genoa was developed before the other side. Ebenezer P. Gleason planted a row of maple trees on the south side of the street in the spring of 1838. The trees were later removed to make way for new businesses. In 1914, according to the *Genoa Republican-Journal*, Genoa residents celebrated the installation of new streetlights on Main Street. An automobile parade, cash prizes for decorated cars, a dance at Slater's Hall and Opera House, and bands from Burlington and Kirkland were planned for the event. The newspaper stated, "There were 200 autos and 2,000 people in Genoa to celebrate the new lighting system. Few autos entered because they were afraid of having their lamps bumped by the occasional stopping and starting. First prize went to Miss Lorene Brown; second prize to Mrs. W. A. Geithman, and third prize to Mrs. F. W. Olmstead." In 1958, $3,500 was appropriated for street lighting in Genoa. In 1989, the cost was $16,036. The cost in 2010 for street lighting was $81,500.

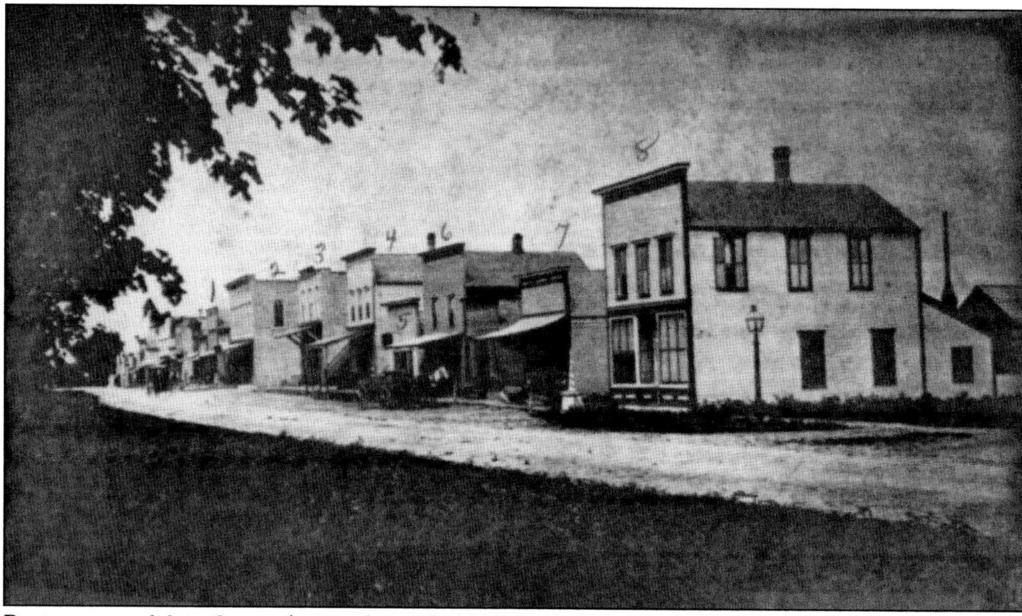

Businesses on Main Street during the early 1900s included, from right to left, Geo. Johnson Barber Shop at 201 Main, Jack Godding Saloon at 207 Main, a meat market at 209 Main, Wylde Cigar Store at 213 Main, a saloon at 217 Main, Slater-Douglass General Store at 233 Main, Red Wood Billiards and barbershop at 301 Main, and Sager's Hardware at 305 Main.

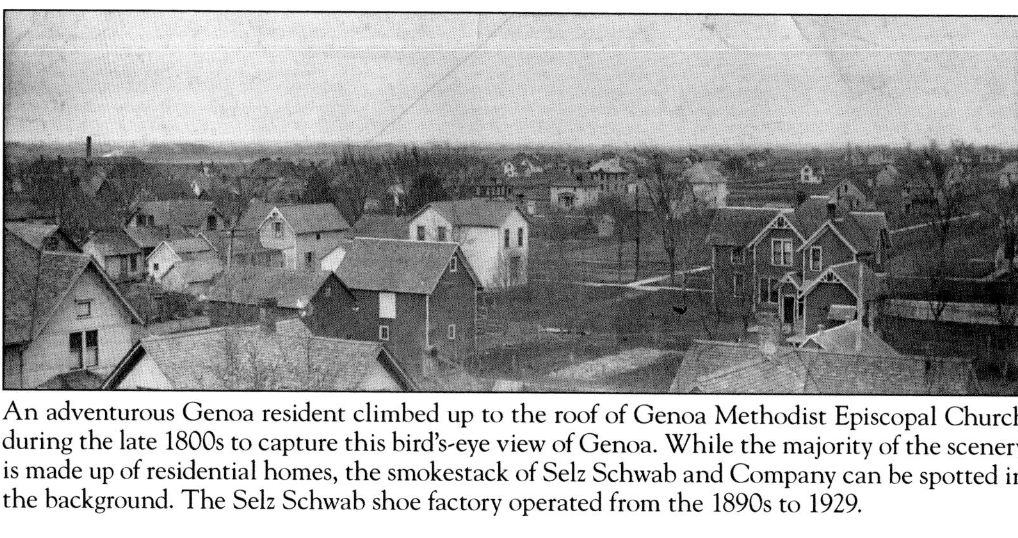

An adventurous Genoa resident climbed up to the roof of Genoa Methodist Episcopal Church during the late 1800s to capture this bird's-eye view of Genoa. While the majority of the scenery is made up of residential homes, the smokestack of Selz Schwab and Company can be spotted in the background. The Selz Schwab shoe factory operated from the 1890s to 1929.

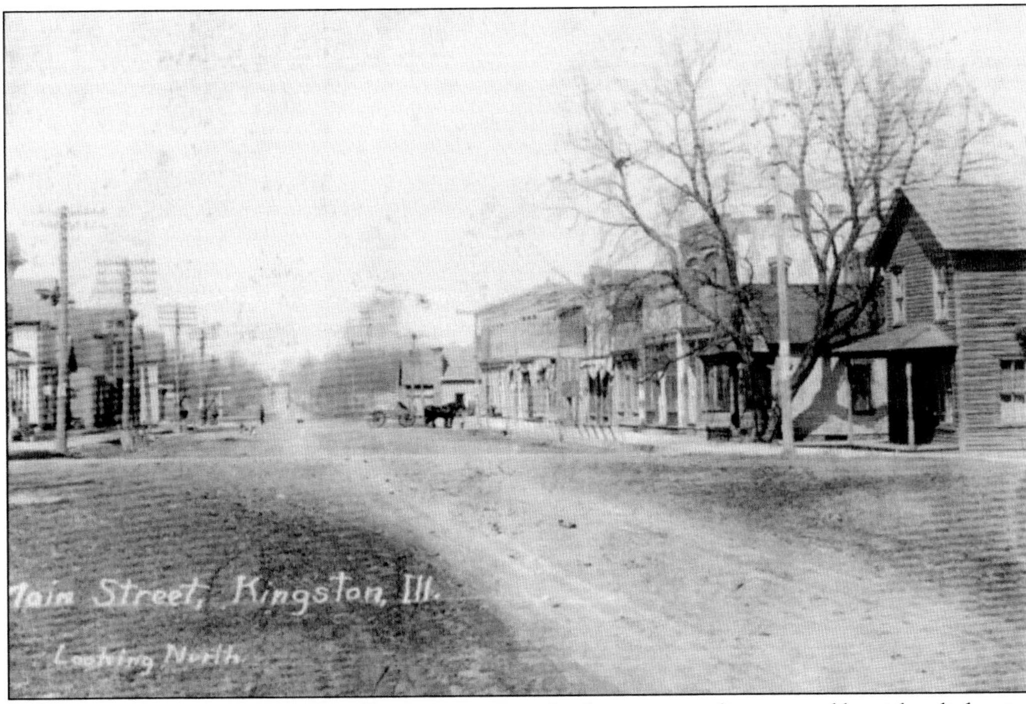

When the Midwest was mostly tall grass prairie and oak savannas, fires started by either lightning or Native Americans cleared dead brush and allowed new plants to grow. Early settlers moving into the Midwest were often plagued by fire. Like the mythical phoenix, however, pioneers would construct new buildings that would arise from the ashes. Kingston around 1900 (above) had many businesses. A fire on July 8, 1908, burned down a large part of the town on the west side of Main Street (below). Kingston residents looking at the ruins might have recalled the great Chicago fire of 1871, one of the largest U.S. disasters of the 19th century, and been spurred to begin rebuilding just as Chicagoans did almost immediately after their huge fire.

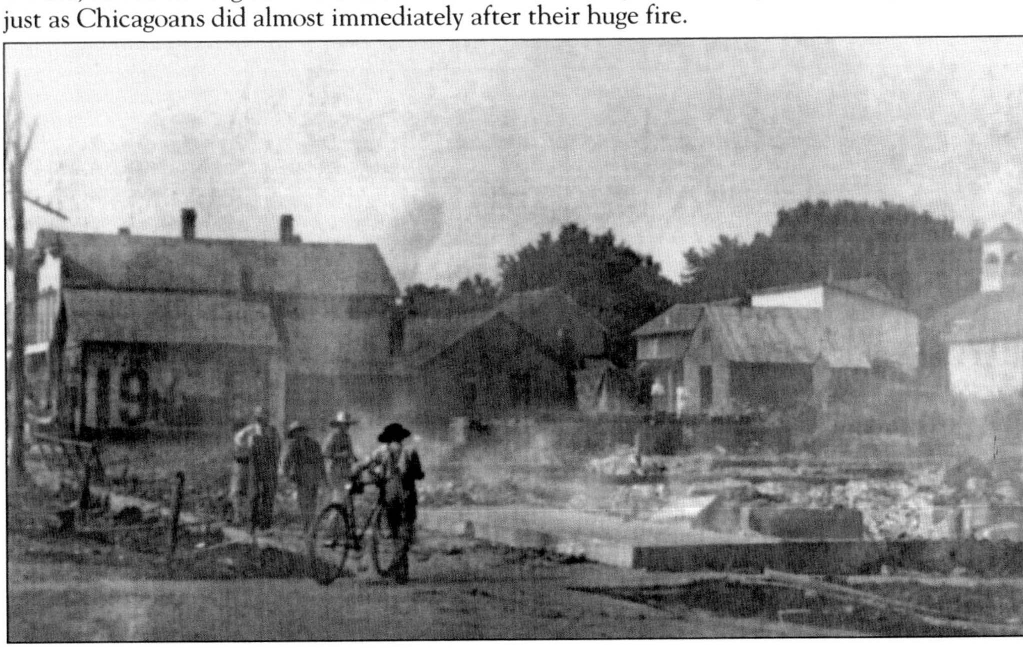

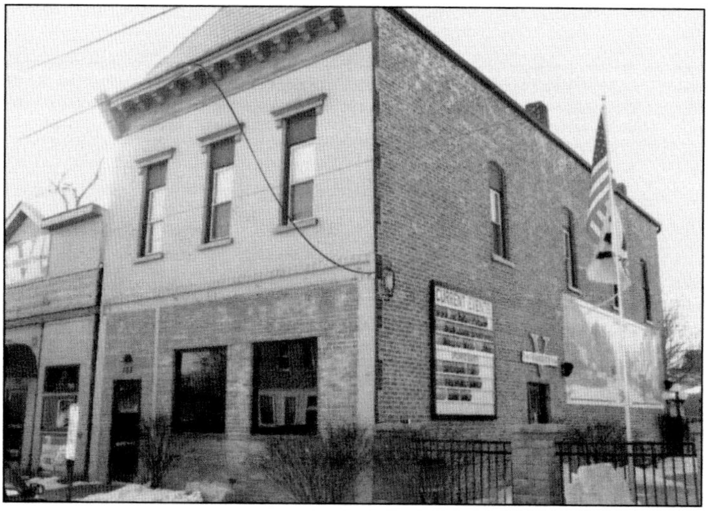

The Kingston fire of 1908 destroyed many businesses, including two buildings at the corner of Illinois Route 72 and Main Street. One of the buildings had been a bar. In 1918, two new 2,500-square-foot buildings were built. These buildings, at 103–105 South Main Street, have been combined to house The Varsity Pub, owned by Jerry Kline, for the past four years. A mural of Kingston decorates an outside wall. (Courtesy of Jerry Kline.)

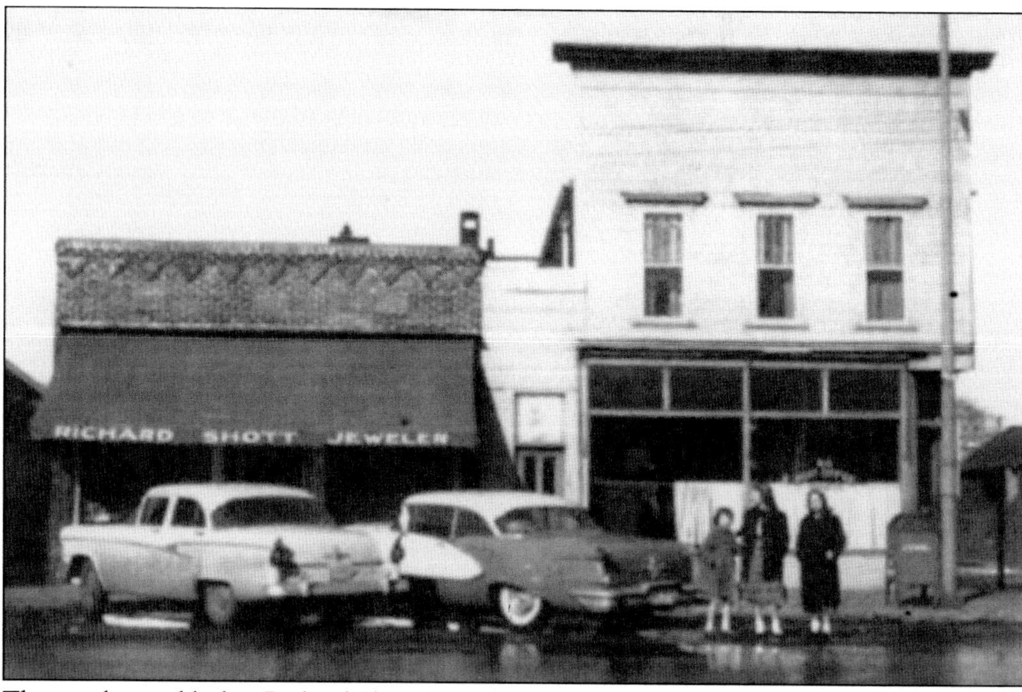

Three girls stand before Richard Shott Jeweler and the Genoa Post Office in 1954. Long coats, bobby socks, and saddle shoes were popular at that time. The Genoa Post Office was located at 415 West Main Street, and the postmaster in 1954 was Joe Sester. The former post office now houses Laughing Cat Antiques.

Ten

Celebrations

Genoa and Kingston celebrations have been known to draw crowds. Genoa held one of the first Fourth of July events in northern Illinois in 1838. George H. Hill delivered an oration to over 1,000 people. The year 2010 was chosen as the time to honor the 175th anniversary of the founding of Genoa, the 75th anniversary of the Genoa-Kingston Fire Protection District, and the 75th anniversary of Genoa Days. The annual Kingston Fest with the Kingston Cardboard Boat Regatta is held at Kingston Township Park every summer. Genoa is the site for the annual Pioneer Day, Red Hats Day, Dinner and a Movie, Harvest Moon Festival and Back Roads Tractor Run, and Celebrate the Season. During the first tractor run in 2008, Genoa mayor Todd Walker drove his father's tractor and pulled a hay wagon full of people. In 2009, the Guinness World Record for the largest pie fight was achieved in Genoa. The event took place at Derby Line Farm on June 13 and involved 242 people. The record was held for three months and four days until it was broken on September 17, 2009, during the *Live! With Regis and Kelly* television show.

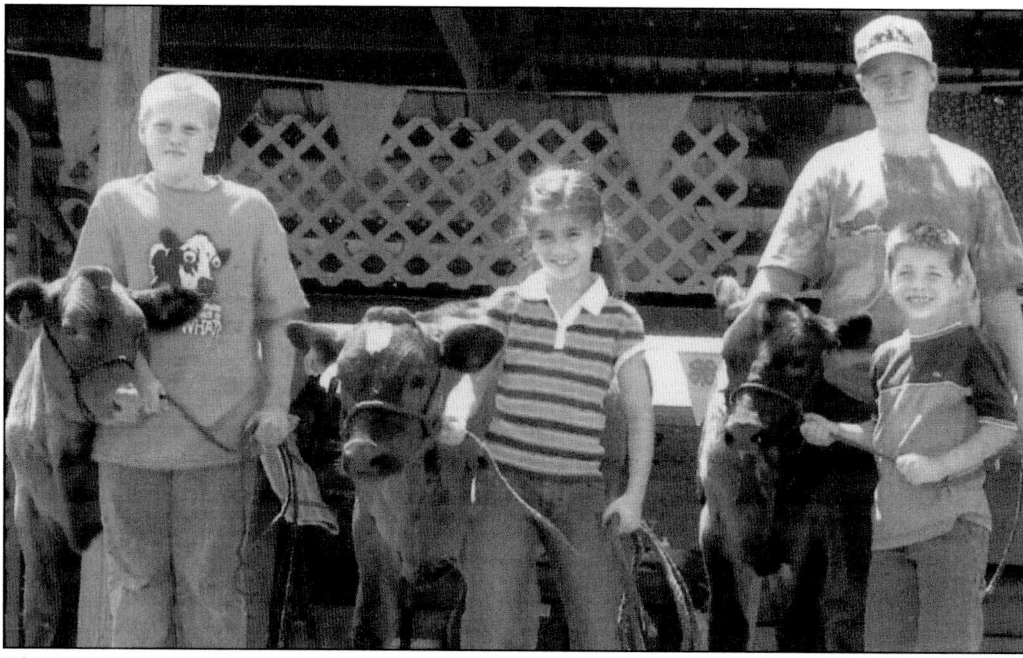

The Kingston Juniors 4-H Club has provided area youth with fun activities for many years. Kingston Juniors with their bucket calves (above), from left to right, are Matt Paulsen, Jamie Hall, Bart Hall, and Chris Paulsen. A bucket calf is an orphan or newborn calf that is purchased when it is 1 to 10 days old. The calf can be male or female as well as dairy or beef, and it is initially fed from a bucket or bottle. A 50th anniversary celebration held by Kingston Juniors in 1994 is pictured below. The members display the cans they collected for a food drive. The club is for youths from ages 9 to 18. The club's motto is "To make the best better." (Courtesy of Betty Fewell.)

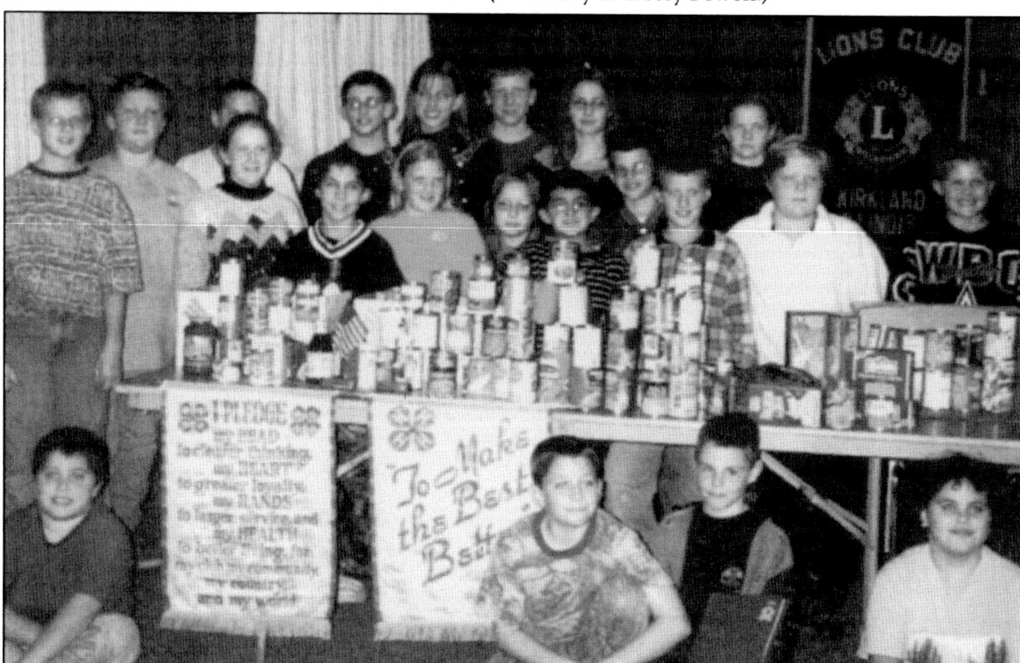

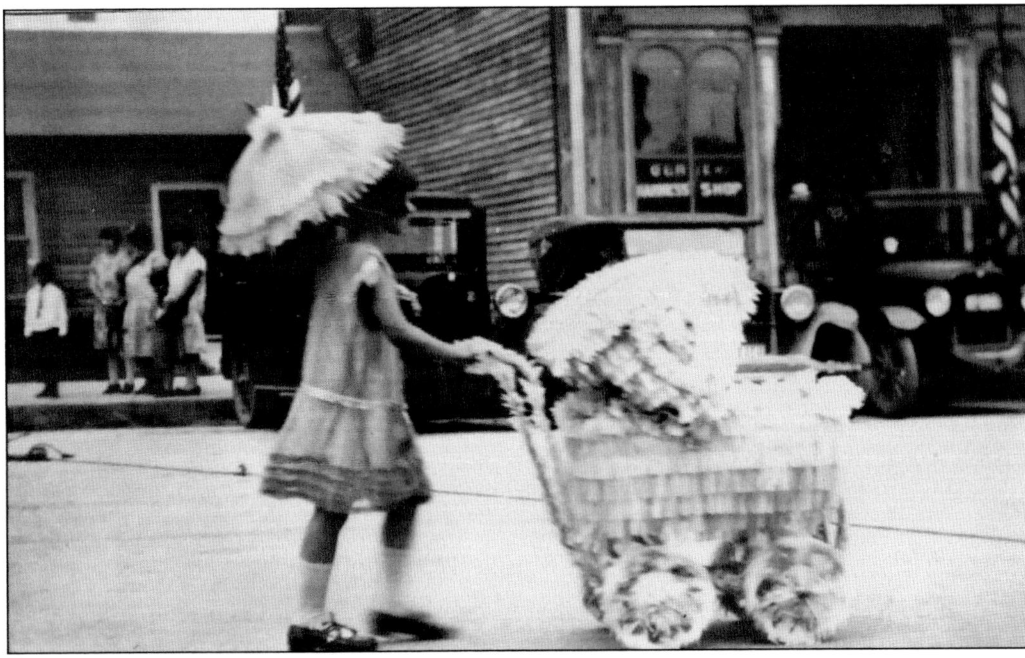

Peggy Hadsall pushes a baby carriage down Main Street in Genoa during the 1927 Memorial Day parade. Memorial Day, originally called Decoration Day, was first held to honor those who died during the Civil War. Today it commemorates all American men and women who have died while serving their country. (Courtesy of Kishwaukee Valley Heritage Society Museum)

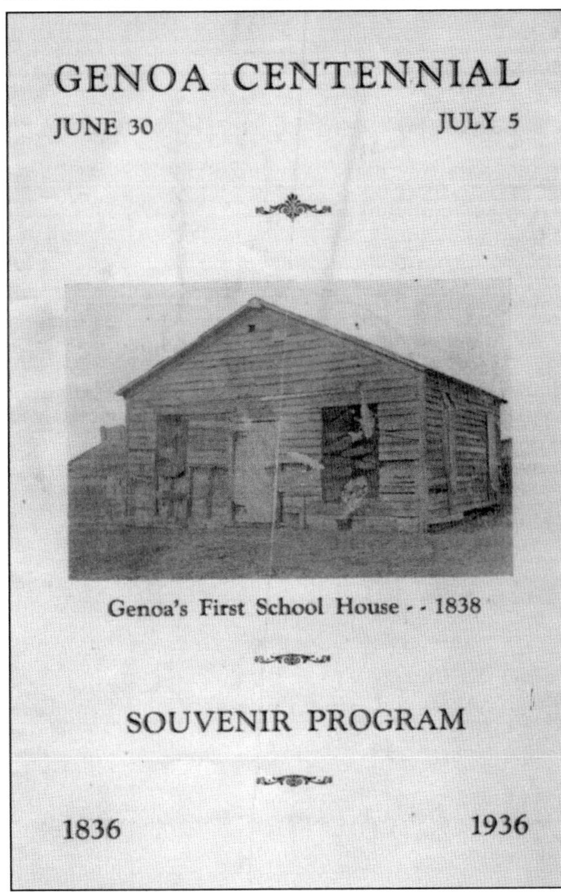

GENOA CENTENNIAL

JUNE 30 JULY 5

Genoa's First School House - - 1838

SOUVENIR PROGRAM

1836 1936

Genoa's centennial celebration was held June 30–July 5, 1936. The mayor of Genoa at that time was W. A. Lankton. W. A. Skinner was the fire marshal, and E. E. Crawford served as Genoa's police chief. Mary Ann Hill, daughter of Judge Hill from Kingston, was the first teacher at Genoa's first schoolhouse in 1838. The second teacher at the school was Josephine Colton.

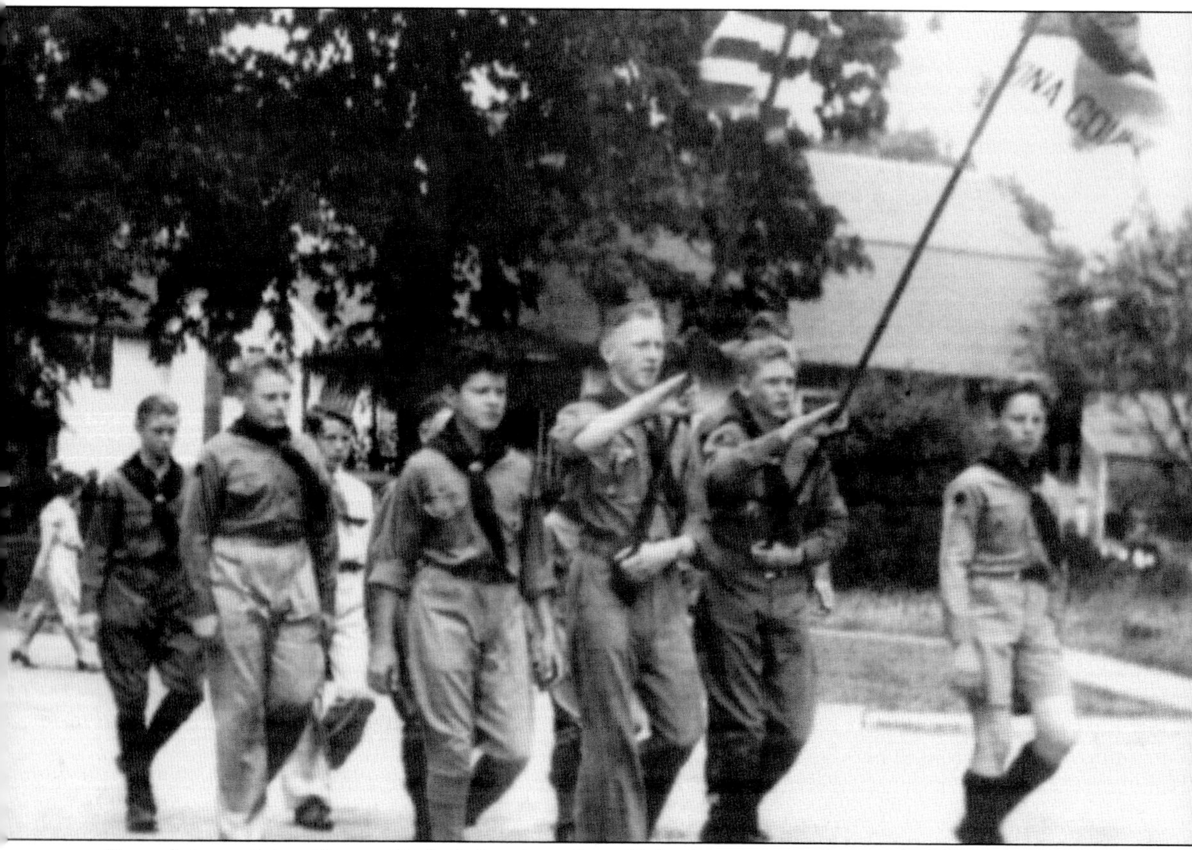

From left to right, Genoa High School student Dale Barcus marches with fellow students Gil Memmen, Leroy Merritt, Jon Holroyd, and Neil Giselson down Main Street in Genoa in 1947. The principal of the high school at the time was Ralph Elliott, and the assistant principal was I. H. Bennett. Barcus wrote the 1947 class song entitled "Thanks for the Memories." The opening lines were: "Yes, we've traveled far and wide together / Did we travel too fast? / Now I reminisce and wonder / whether any good things ever last / but our school days are past." Only two years earlier, the class of 1945 saw many of its students enter the military during World War II. The dedication of the 1945 yearbook stated, "We, the seniors of '45, dedicate our yearbook to all the members of our class who are in the Armed Forces and are not able to be here to enjoy the last of our high school days."

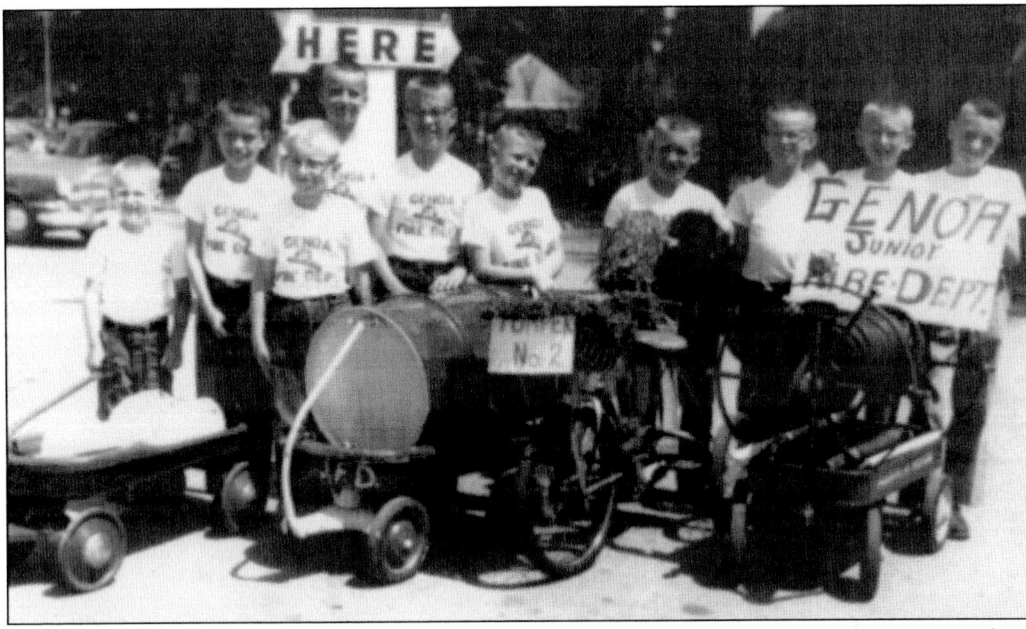

Genoa Days is sponsored annually by the Genoa-Kingston Fire Protection District. Proceeds go toward buying equipment for the district. Genoa Junior Fire Department members pose beside Pumper No. 2 and their trusty wagons in 1957. The boys, from left to right, are Tommy Duval, Rick Lewis, Gerry Euhus, Orrin Merritt, Tom Merritt, David Merritt, Bob Tischler, John Duval, John Tischler, and Gene Bradford.

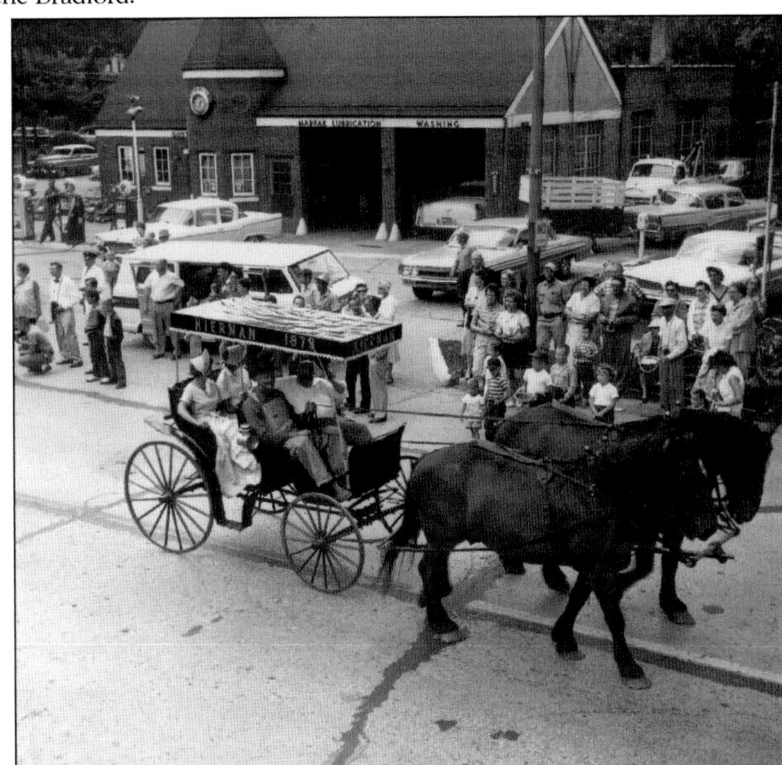

The Kiernan family's 1961 Genoa Days parade entry, a carriage pulled by two horses, passes Gustafson's Texaco gasoline station on 104 West Main Street. Kiernan sold agricultural implements, pumps, steam-fitting equipment, buggies, and wagons at his shop along Main Street in Genoa. Before the first St. Catherine of Genoa church in Genoa was built, services were held in Kiernan's building.

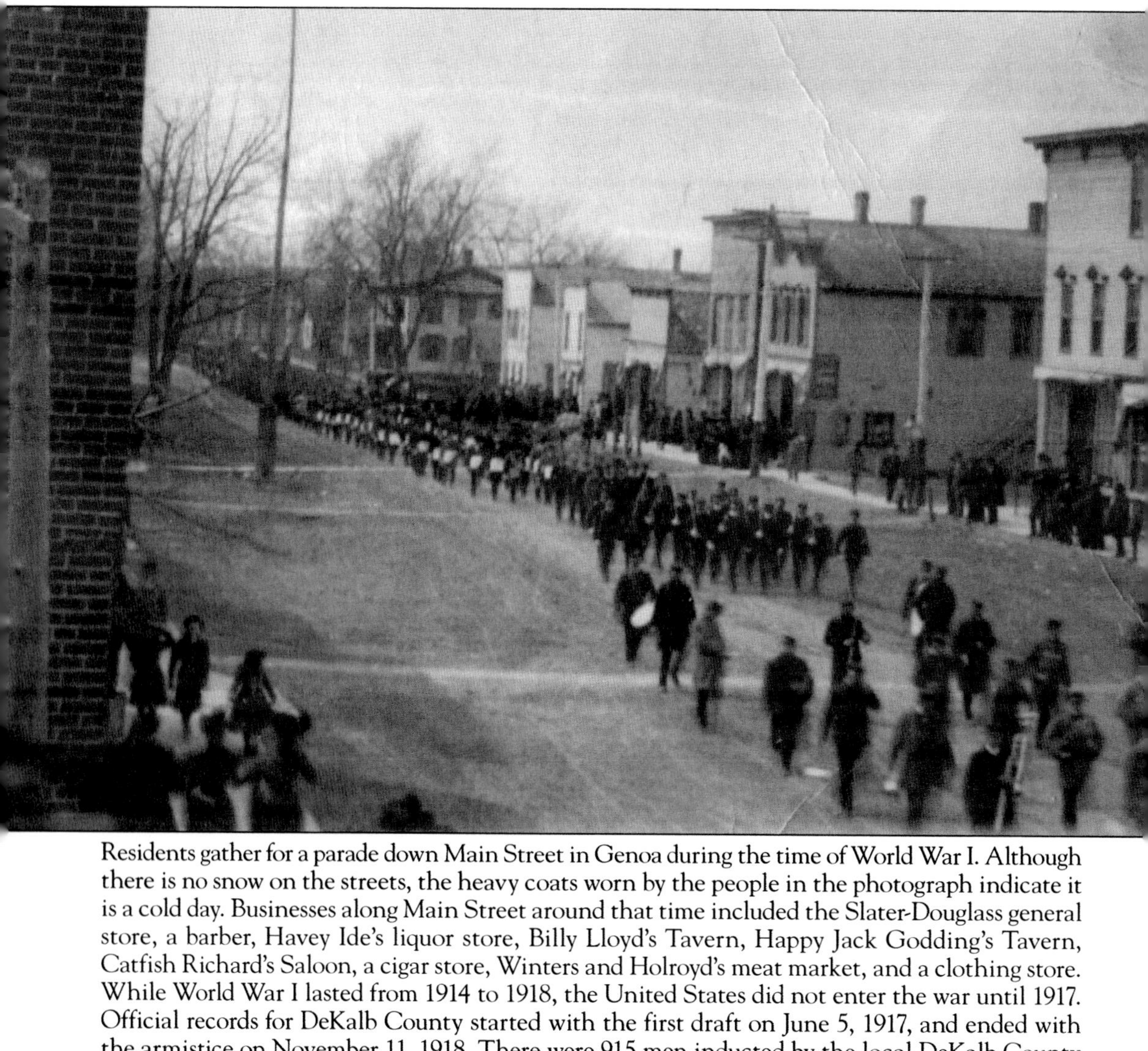

Residents gather for a parade down Main Street in Genoa during the time of World War I. Although there is no snow on the streets, the heavy coats worn by the people in the photograph indicate it is a cold day. Businesses along Main Street around that time included the Slater-Douglass general store, a barber, Havey Ide's liquor store, Billy Lloyd's Tavern, Happy Jack Godding's Tavern, Catfish Richard's Saloon, a cigar store, Winters and Holroyd's meat market, and a clothing store. While World War I lasted from 1914 to 1918, the United States did not enter the war until 1917. Official records for DeKalb County started with the first draft on June 5, 1917, and ended with the armistice on November 11, 1918. There were 915 men inducted by the local DeKalb County Board, with some 69 men rejected for different physical reasons at the various camps.

Genoa held its 125th anniversary in 1961. The event included water fights between the fire departments of Genoa, Kirkland, Boone County, Marengo, Pingree Grove, Burlington, Rochelle, Kingston, and Hampshire. There was also a beard-judging contest, an anniversary pageant, and the annual parade.

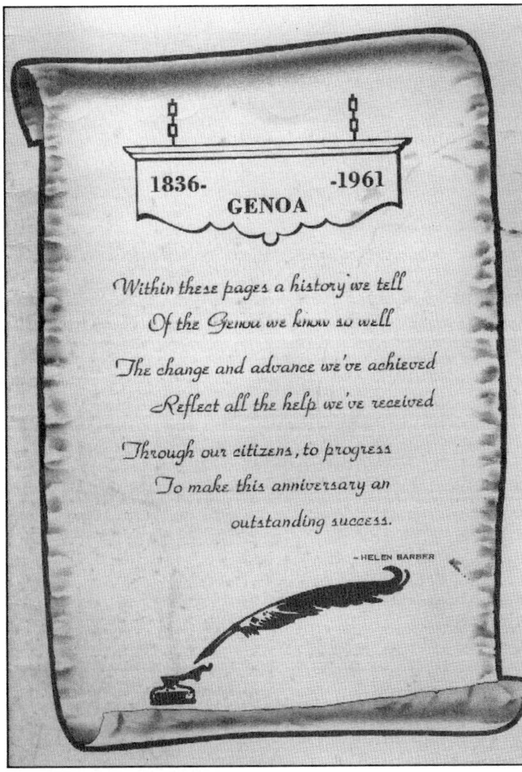

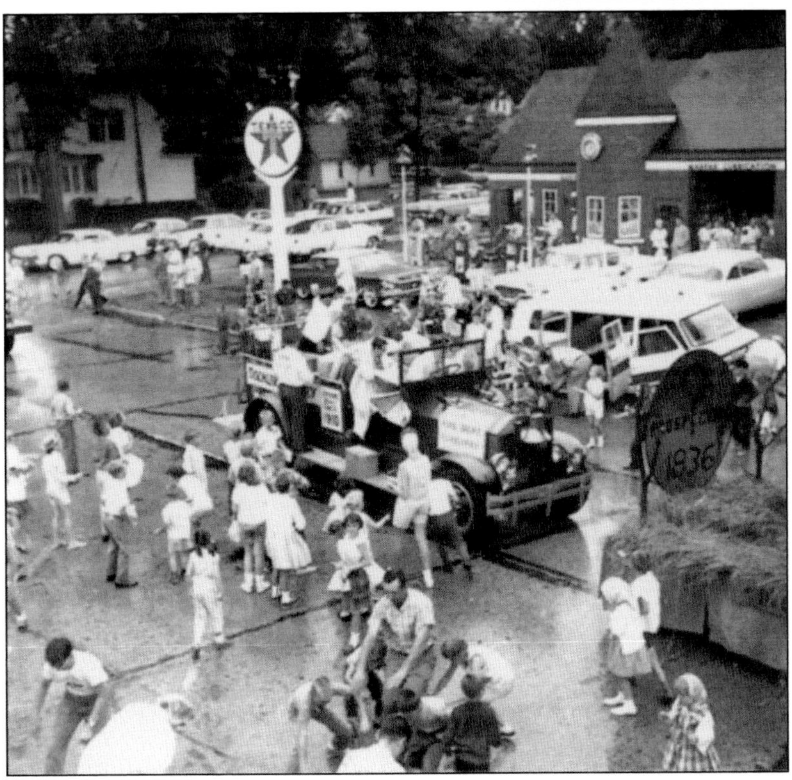

Everyone loves a parade, especially when free candy is thrown from the different floats to parade watchers. A crowd gathers to collect candy in front of Gustafson's Texaco station at 104 West Main Street during the 1961 Genoa Days parade. Notice some of the girls wearing scarves, bobby socks, and dresses. Parked cars include Buicks, Chevys, and Studebakers.

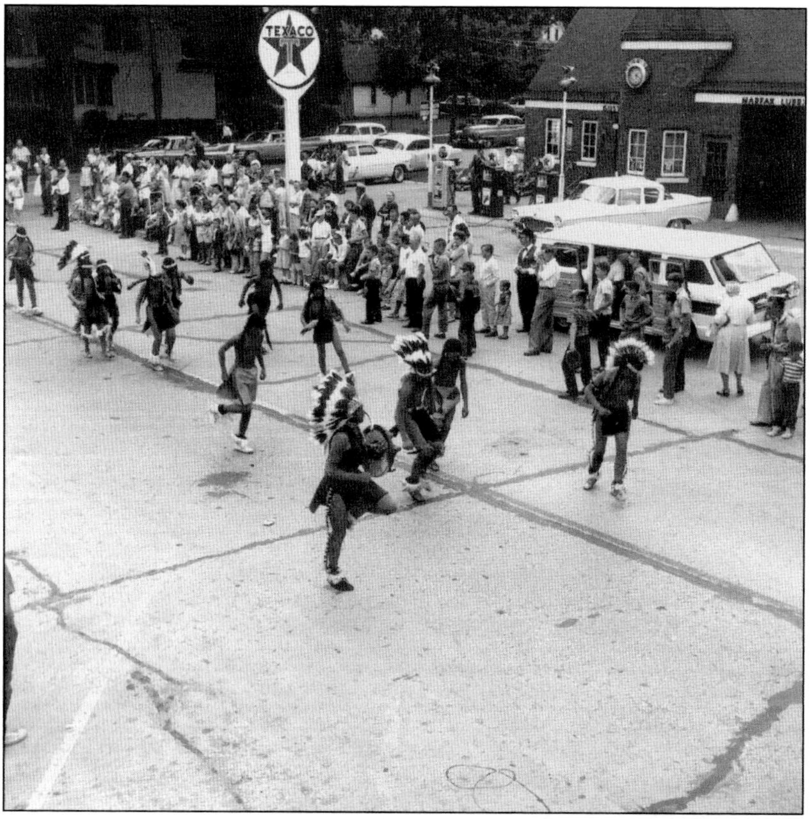

Native American dancers were a part of the 1961 Genoa Days parade. Before settlers from Europe and the Eastern United States came to the Genoa-Kingston area, the land was home to the Potawatomi until 1835. Early settler James Harrington Moore said, "They were kindly to us pale faces, as they called us in pioneer days."

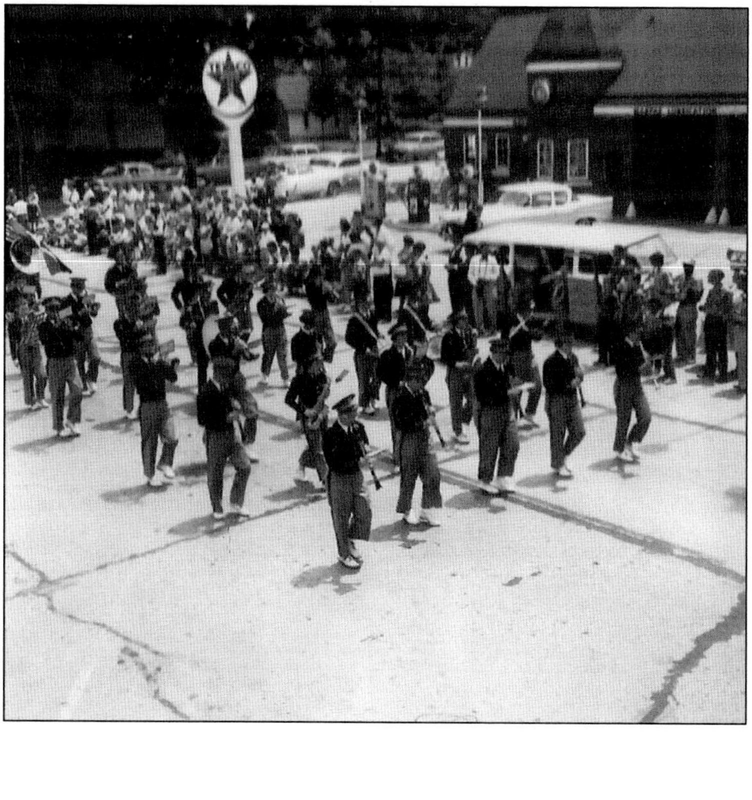

The Genoa Township High School Band, led by band teacher Roy Hubbell, marches during the 1961 Genoa Days parade. The Genoa-Kingston High School music department (concert band, marching band, jazz ensemble, concert choir, and chamber choir) traveled to the Cedar Point Amusement Park in Sandusky, Ohio, for the Music in the Parks Festival in May 2010.

At right, outgoing Genoa Days queen Dorothy Wahl crowns Jackie Hodgson, the Genoa Days queen in 1961. Below, the queen and her court ride aboard a float during the 1961 Genoa Days parade. The 50th annual Genoa Days king and queen contest, sponsored by the Genoa Area Chamber of Commerce, took place in 2009. Genoa residents T. C. Holterhaus and Kristin Orozco were crowned as king and queen. Genoa had a queen reside over Genoa Days until 1998. Josef Wills was the first Genoa Days king. The royal couple every year receives monetary awards as well as donations from local businesses, such as gift certificates, baseball caps, and T-shirts. In addition to presiding over Genoa Days, the king and queen also attend the annual Fourth of July parade in Kirkland.

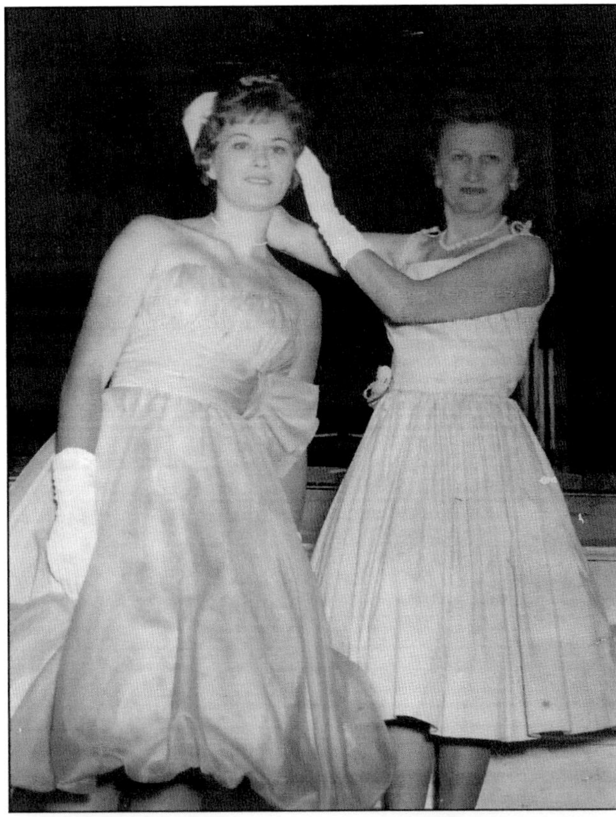

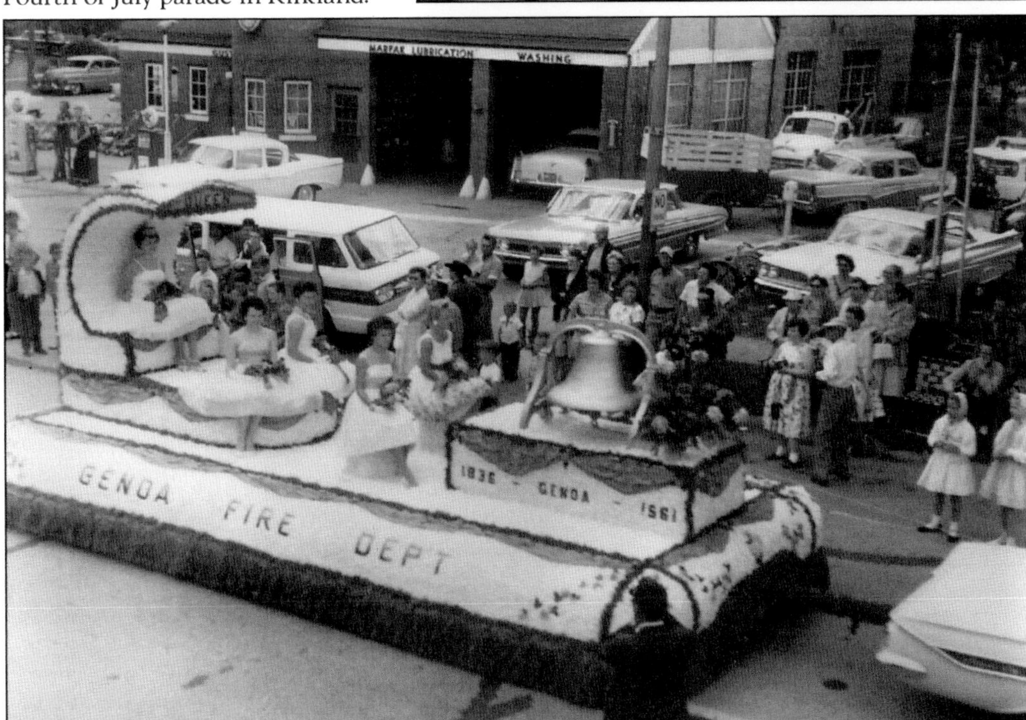

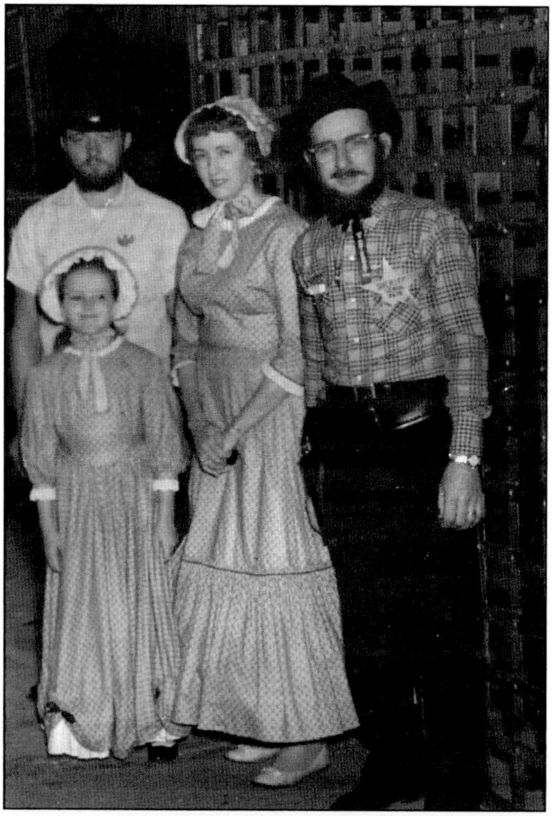

Russell Melton (left), Patty Hughes (front left), Jean Hughes, and "Sheriff" Elmer T. Hughes (far right) pose together during the 1961 Genoa Days celebration. Elmer and Russell are sporting beards for the beard-growing contest, while Patty and Jean are dressed as pioneer women. Elmer is a trustee with the Genoa-Kingston Fire Protection District.

Shown from left to right, Ralph Becker, Wilbur Knight, Rollie Erwin, Floyd Carlson, Glenn Bell, and Horace H. P. "Horsepower" Williams pose after winning awards for the beard-growing contest during Genoa Days in 1961. Featured facial hair included a moustache, muttonchops, goatee, and three beards. Horsepower Williams was the top winner of the contest. William A. Skinner (not pictured) served as mayor of Genoa at that time.

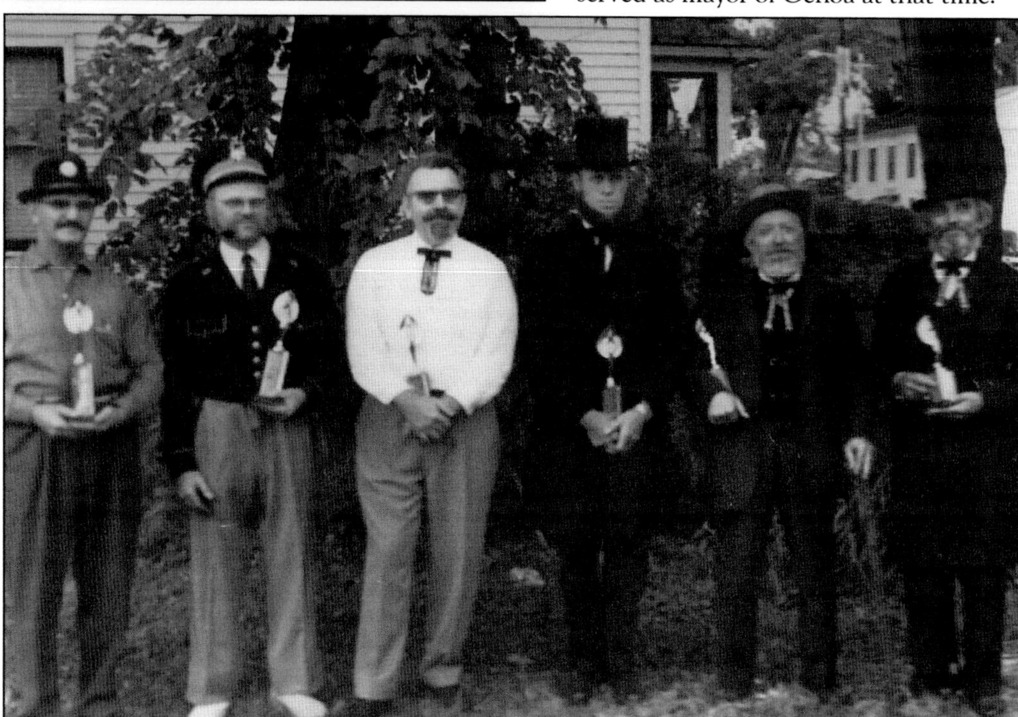

Genoa resident Molly Smith, a junior at Genoa-Kingston High School (at right, center), portrays the Snow Queen in the Beth Fowler School of Dance Company's 2009 production of *The Nutcracker* at the Egyptian Theatre in DeKalb, Illinois. Below, Susan Belles of Rockford takes center stage as the Rose Queen during the "Waltz of the Flowers." Fowler established the Beth Fowler School of Dance in 1983 and the Beth Fowler Dance Company in 1994. In addition to her dance studio at 303 West Main Street in Genoa, Fowler opened a second studio at 3720 Illinois Avenue in St. Charles. The studios teach ballet, jazz, hip-hop, tap, creative, lyrical, and modern dance. *The Nutcracker* was performed at the historic Egyptian Theatre, a 1929 Art Deco movie palace that celebrated its 80th anniversary in 2009.

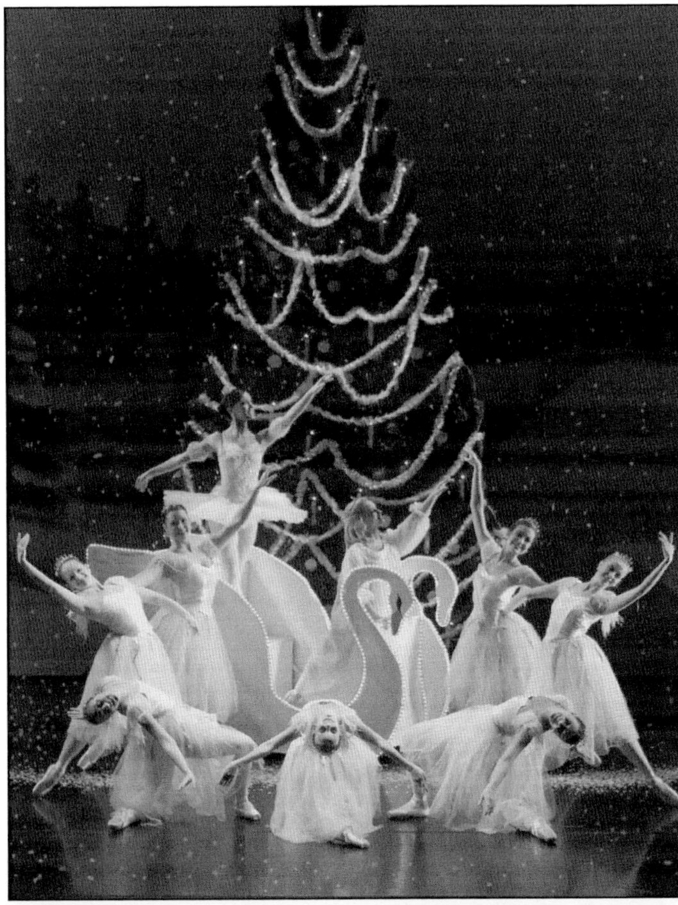

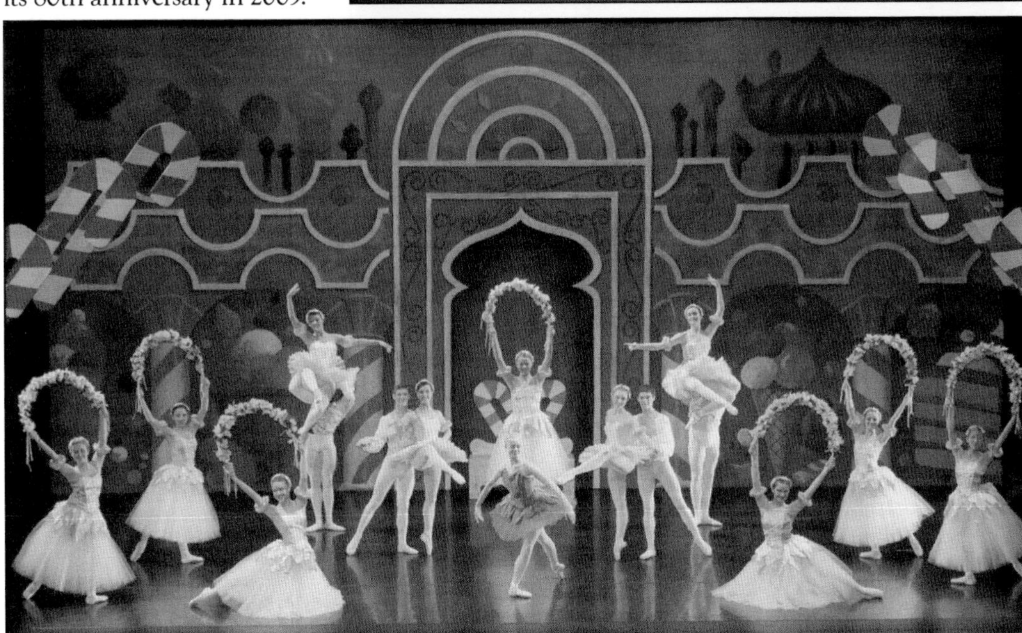

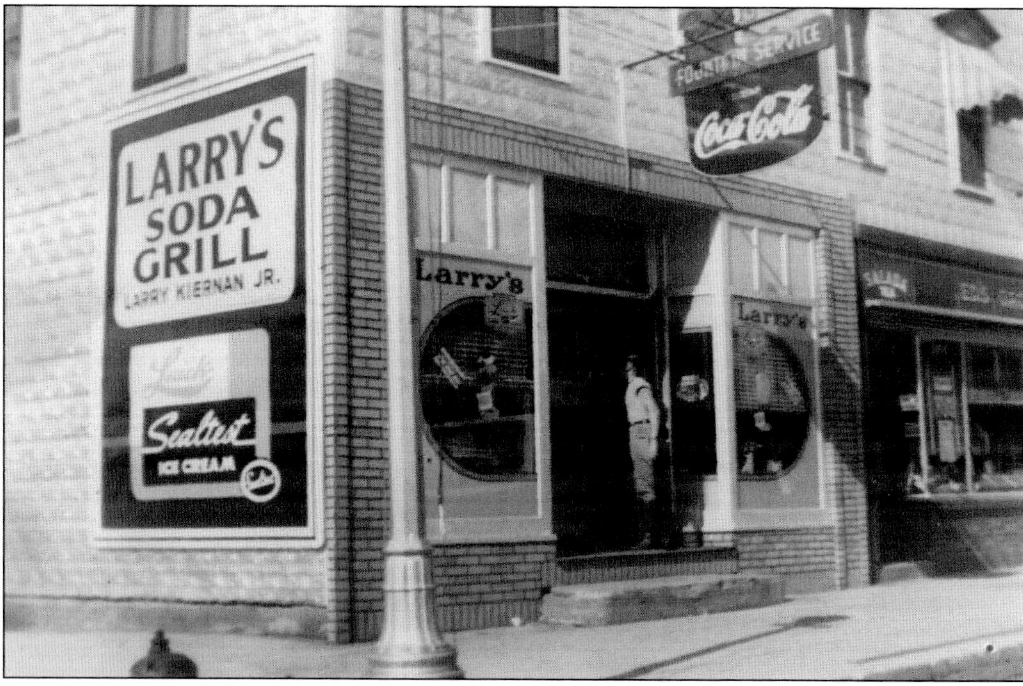

People who attended Genoa Days during the 1940s and 1950s might have stopped by Larry's Soda Grill along Main Street. Larry Kiernan Jr. started the business in 1941. A tall fir tree next to Citizens First National Bank now marks the spot where the building once stood. The fir is the city's official Christmas tree and is lit by Santa every year.

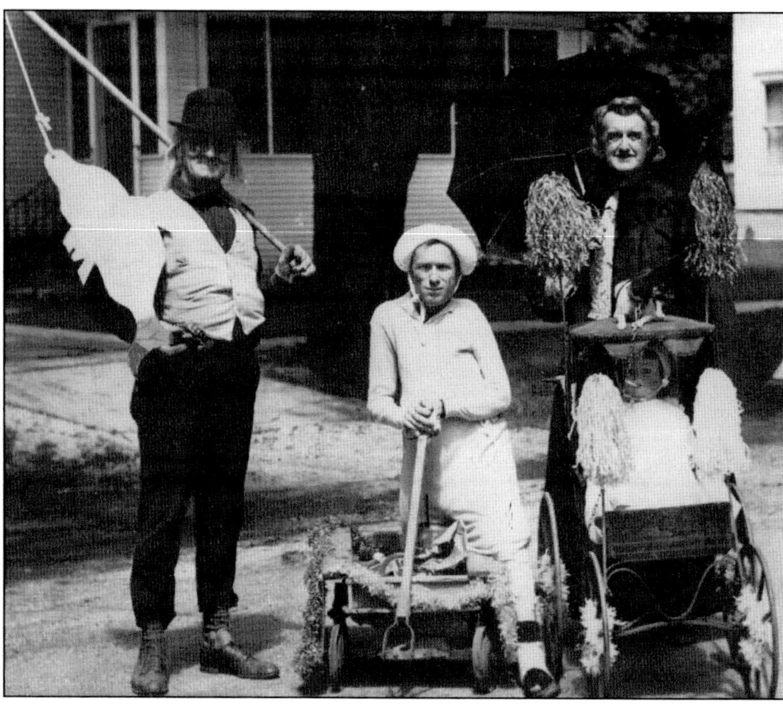

John Sell (fisherman), Roy Hartman (center), and John Duval pose in their costumes during Genoa Days in 1961. Duval started Duval Brothers Garage at 112 North Emmett Street in Genoa with his brother Fred in 1924. The business was a local agent for Dodge and Plymouth cars and trucks and was later an agent for Chrysler vehicles.

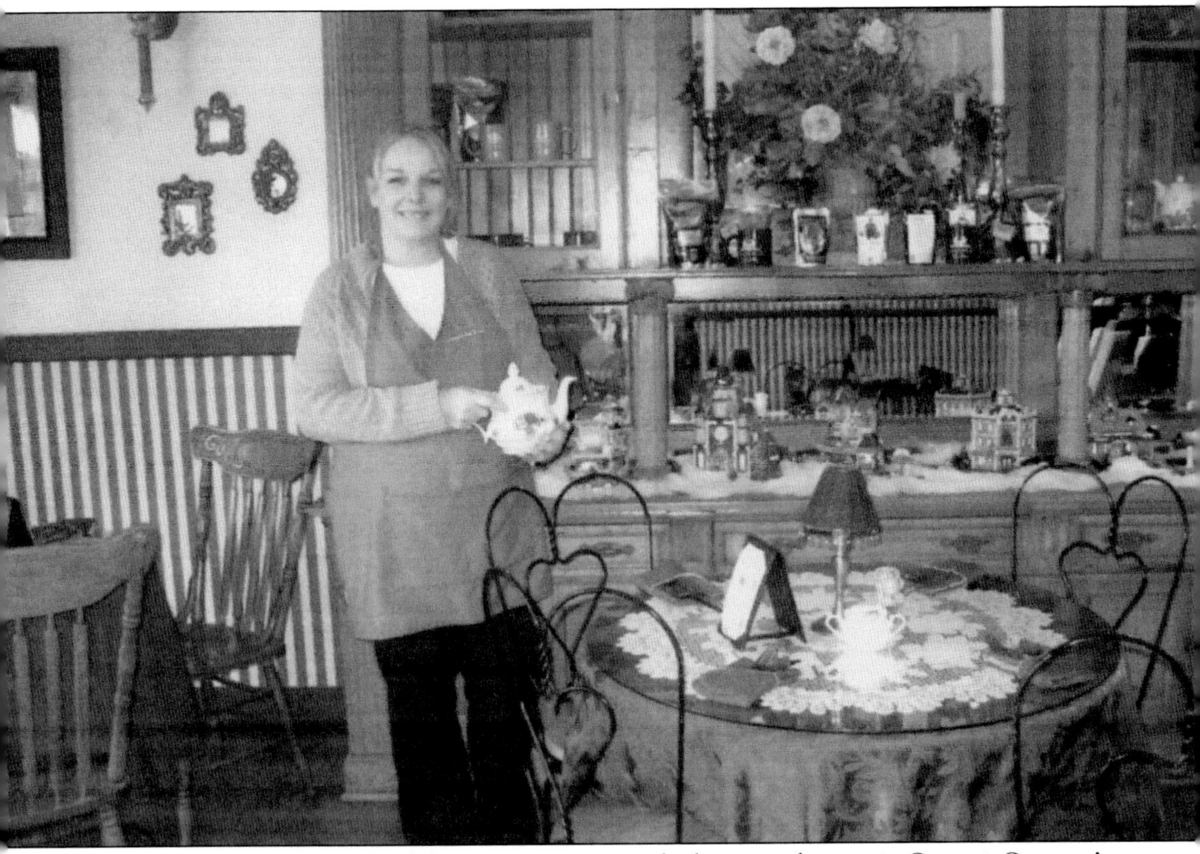

A favorite place to celebrate birthdays, anniversaries, and other special events in Genoa is Crumpet's Tea Room at 221 West Main Street. The building was originally constructed in 1894 by Merritt and Hadsall for $6,000. Over the years, the building has served as Billy Lloyd's Saloon (1895–1926), Tischler's Grocery (1926–1964), Doug Carr Furniture and Appliance (1964–1965), Ken's Klothes Kloset (1965–1985), Guys and Dolls Fashion Theater (1985–1988), Robert Michael's (1988–1994), and Barbara Ann's Antiques (1994–1996). George and Barbara Daugherty, owners of Victoria's Crossing at 220 West Main Street in Genoa, purchased the building on May 4, 1996. A major renovation took place before the building reopened as Crumpet's in October 1996. John and Ann Seisser bought the business in 1999. Edward and Sheree Weskerna ran it starting in 2004. Pamela (pictured) and Gerald Semro Jr. purchased the business in October 2009. The authentic English tearoom has a restored tin ceiling and wood floors. (Courtesy of Crumpet's Tea Room.)

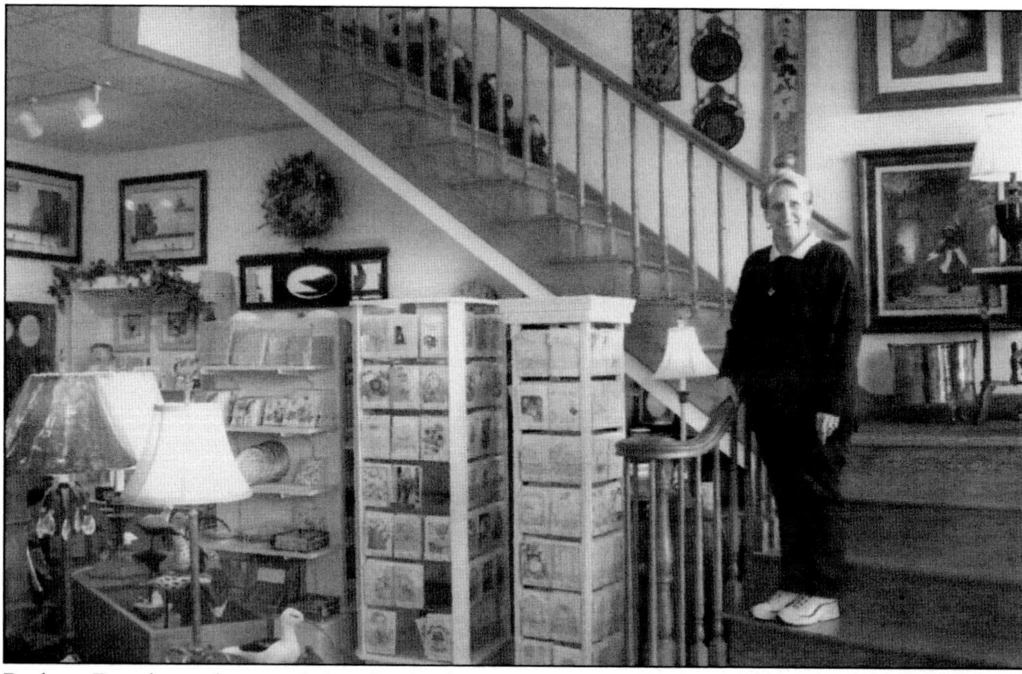

Barbara Daugherty (pictured above), who has owned Victoria's Crossing at 220 West Main Street in Genoa since 1993 with her husband, George, poses on the staircase inside the store. Victoria's Crossing sells gifts, home furnishings and accessories, antiques, and collectibles. In 1993, the Daughertys purchased the former Farmers State Bank building, which was constructed in 1901. They bought the building next door in 1996 and turned the two buildings into one. The site has also been used by Genoa Telephone Exchange, Western Auto, a restaurant, an arcade, a jewelry store, and a pizzeria. George designed a courtyard behind Victoria's Crossing with bricks from a street in West Chicago. During summer nights, a crowd gathers in the municipal parking lot for Dinner and a Movie, sponsored by Genoa Main Street, Inc. Films are shown on Victoria's Crossing's outer brick wall. (Courtesy of Victoria's Crossing.)

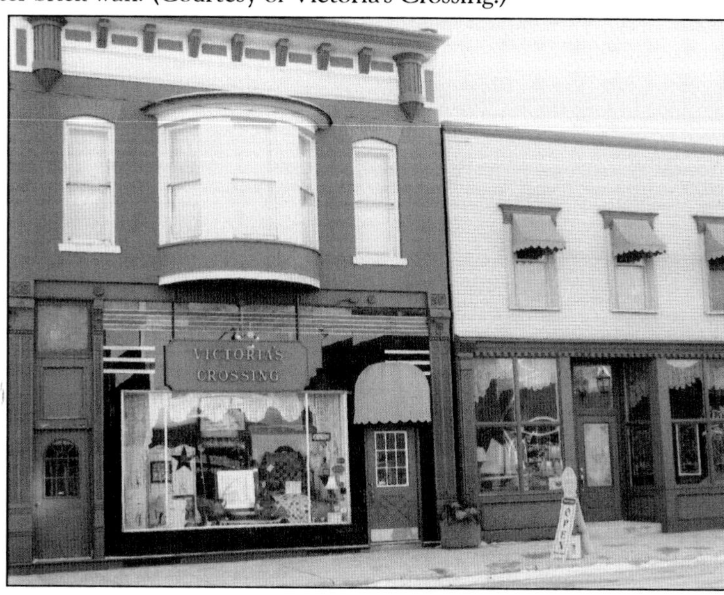

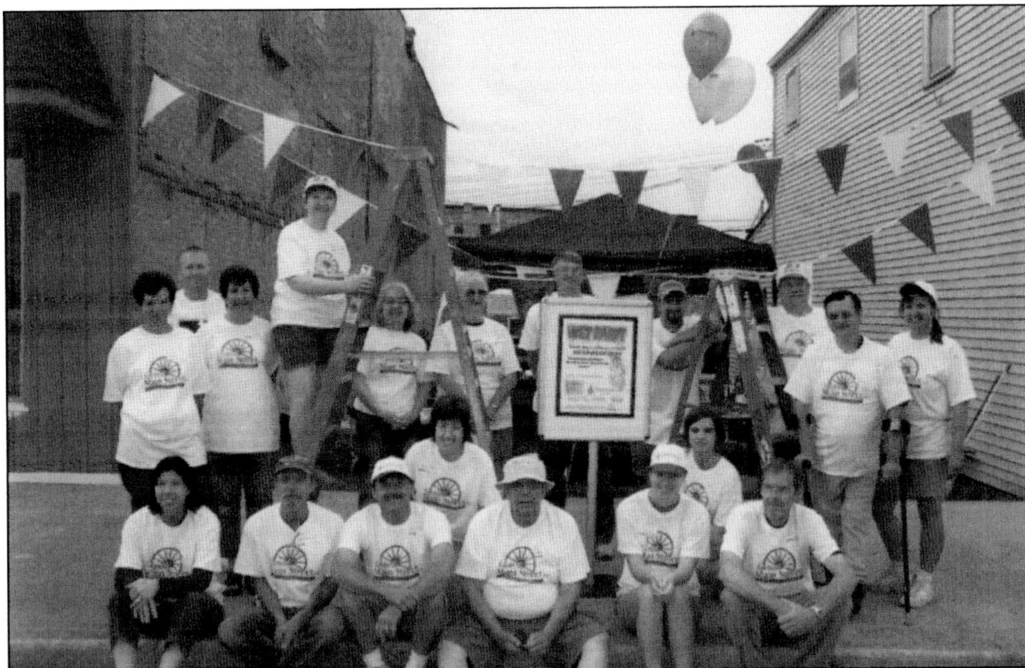

Genoa Main Street, Inc. volunteers for the Wet Paint Project in 2008 pose for a group shot. The goal was to improve the city's downtown curb appeal. After securing the support of a local developer and the Genoa city government headed by Mayor Todd Walker, volunteers painted a total of 13 facades, along with benches, trash cans, planters, and signposts, in just one day. (Courtesy of Genoa Main Street, Inc.)

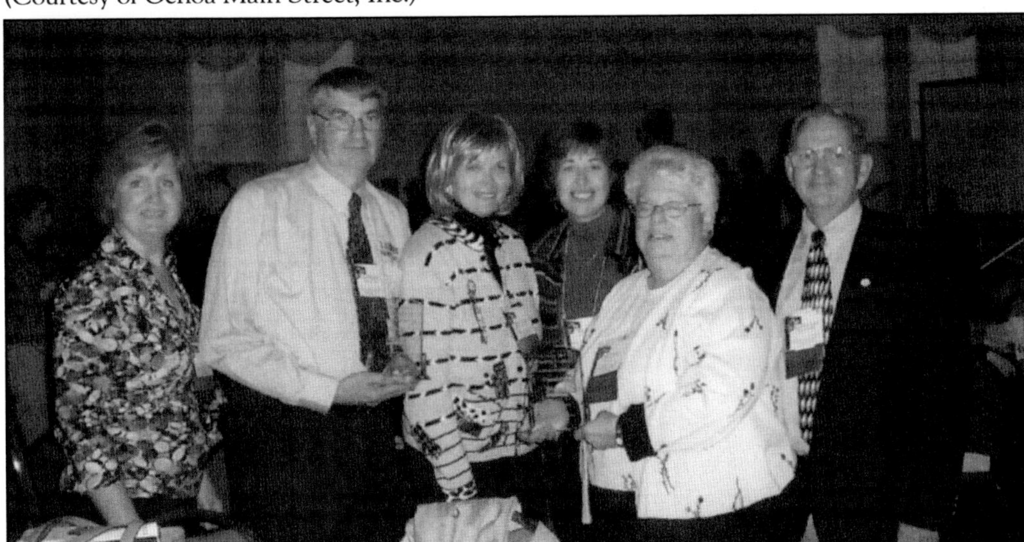

Genoa Main Street, Inc. won two awards during the 2008 Lieutenant Governor's Awards for Excellence in Downtown Revitalization. The awards were for Genoa Main Street's Wet Paint Project and Dinner and a Movie. Accepting the awards were Genoa Main Street volunteers, shown from left to right, Leslie Sanderson (treasurer), Gene Bradford (director and organization chair), Arlene Erickson (secretary), Mim Evans (executive director), Pattie Marx (president), and Gordon Jones (vice president). (Courtesy of Genoa Main Street, Inc.)

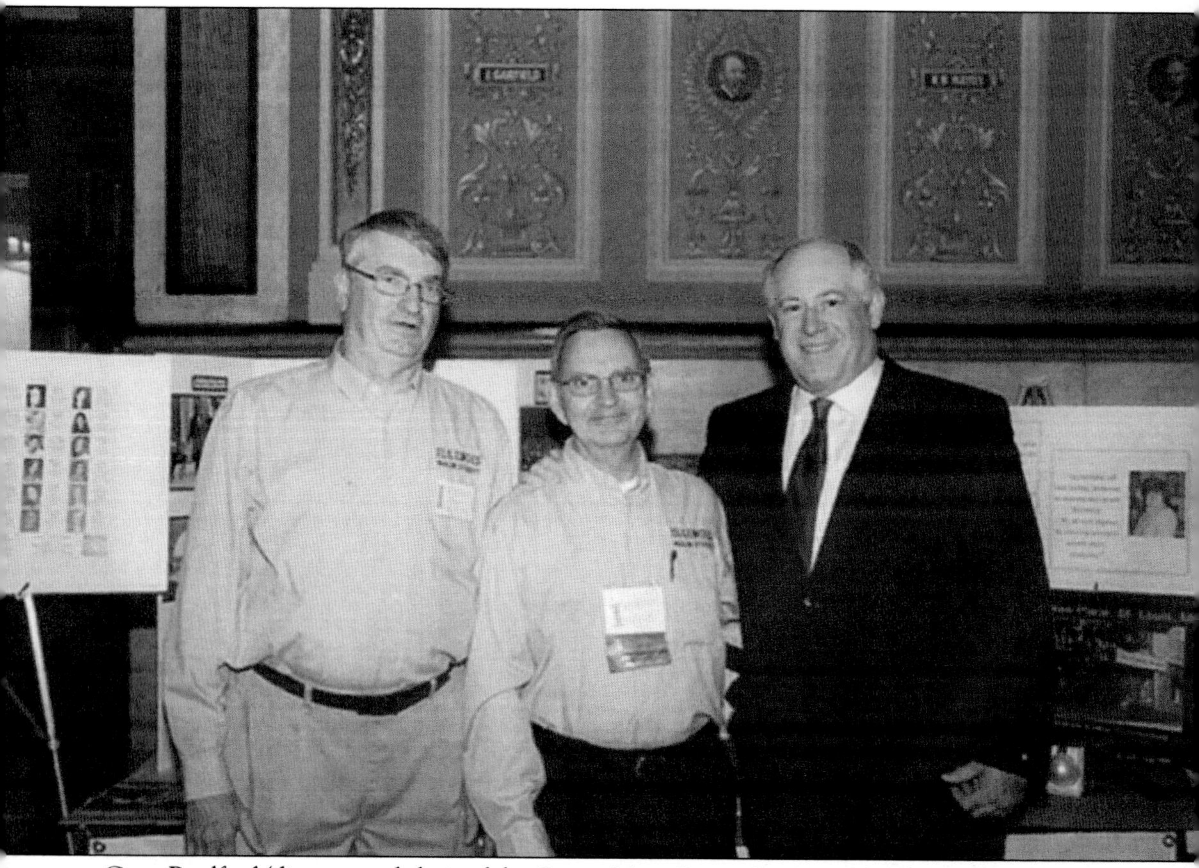

Gene Bradford (director and chair of the Genoa Main Street, Inc.'s membership and development committee, at left) and Gordon Jones (Genoa Main Street, Inc.'s vice president, center) stand with Illinois governor Pat Quinn during the largest ever Main Street Day rally in Springfield, Illinois, in April 2009. At the rally, Quinn commended communities for their assistance in hosting the 2009 National Main Streets Conference in Chicago in March 2009. More than 1,600 people attended the conference from across the nation and six countries. Illinois has the fourth-largest Main Street program in the United States. Since its inception, Main Street communities have reported net gains of more than 1,600 downtown businesses and the creation of more than 6,000 new full- and part-time jobs. Genoa became a member of the Illinois Main Street Program in 1996. Its first president was Terry Strain. The mayor of Genoa at that time was Gene Lawrence. (Courtesy of Genoa Main Street, Inc.)

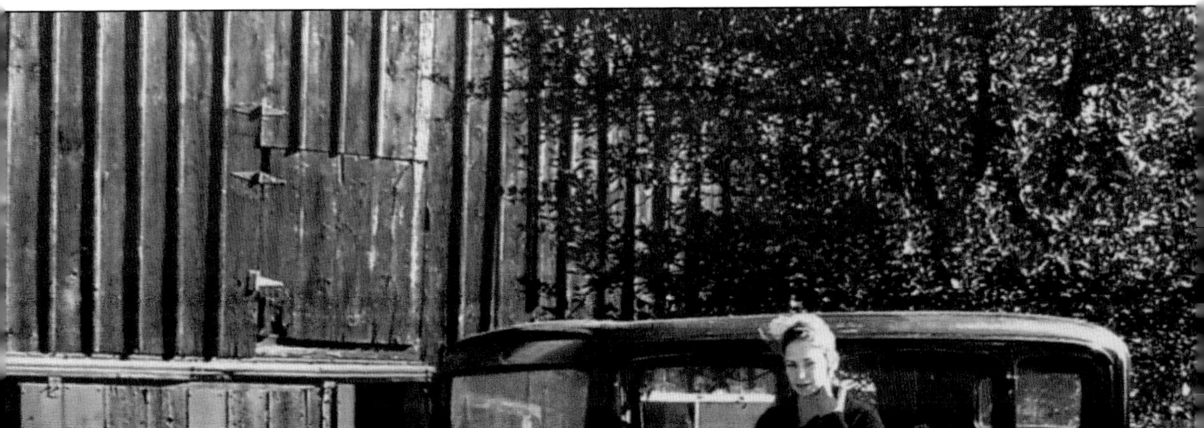

Molly Holbrook poses with her children, Herman, 4, and Olive, 1, by a 1931 Dodge Brothers car on their farm in Genoa. Derby Line Farm is estimated to be over 150 years old. The car is owned by Molly's husband, Josh, who is a member of the Bare Bones Car Club. The farm was the scene for a record-breaking pie fight on June 13, 2009, which was attended by 242 people. In addition to flinging traditional apple and pumpkin pies, people also tossed mashed potato pies, hot dog pies, and even pies with peas, whipped cream, sloppy Joe filling, and chocolate syrup. The Genoa event achieved the Guinness World Record for the largest pie fight and held it for three months and four days. The record was broken on September 17, 2009, on the *Live! With Regis and Kelly* television show by a pie fight with 269 participants. (Courtesy of Molly Holbrook.)

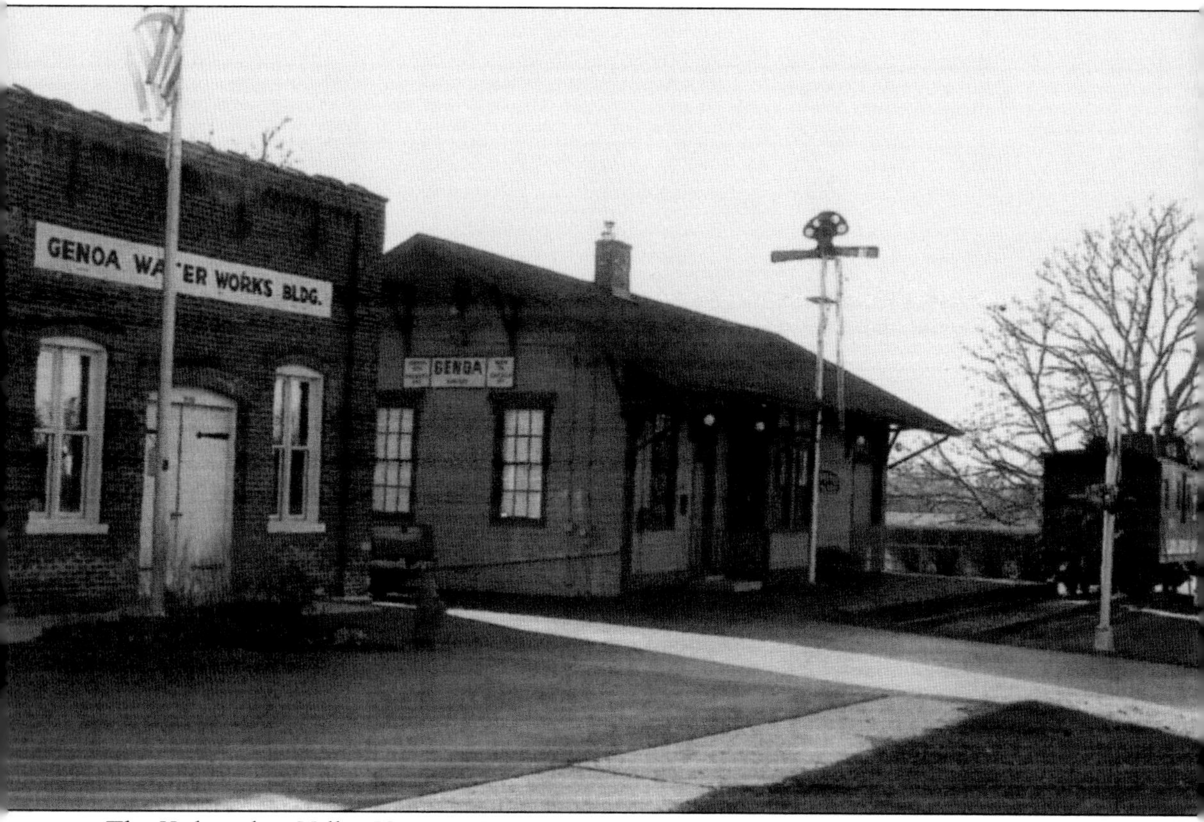

The Kishwaukee Valley Heritage Society, a non-profit 501(c)(3) corporation, was founded in February 1977. Its purpose is to bring together those people living in the Kishwaukee Valley area with an interest in local and regional history and its preservation. The museum includes an 1882 Milwaukee Road depot, a waterworks building from around 1902, a 1950 caboose, Leich Electric memorabilia, model trains, and a 1907 Thompson piano. The passenger-freight depot has a brick platform that was originally installed in 1906. The depot was moved by the society from its original site on North Sycamore Street to its present site at 622 Park Avenue in Genoa in June 1977. The caboose was decommissioned after 32 years in service. It was purchased by the museum in 1983. The museum is open on the second Sunday of every month from 2:00 p.m. to 4:00 p.m. and on every Wednesday from 2:00 p.m. to 4:00 p.m. It is also open on the last Sunday of August from 11:00 a.m. to 5:00 p.m. for the annual Pioneer Day. Volunteer members operate the museum. Contributions to the museum are tax-deductible.

Bibliography

Larson, Sheila Rae Lenihan. *Genoa, Illinois: A History of its Township*. Genoa, IL: Genoa Sesquicentennial Commission, 1986.
Paulson, Alice A. *Fire! Kingston School Destroyed*. Self-published, 2005.
Woodstrup, Thomas E. *Sycamore, Illinois, During World War Two*. Sycamore, IL: self-published, 1991.
Wilson, Marcia Gudmunsen, ed. *Rural School Journeys: A Legacy of Learning*. Evansville, IN: M. T. Publishing Company, Inc., 2006.

Find Your Place in History.

www.arcadiapublishing.com

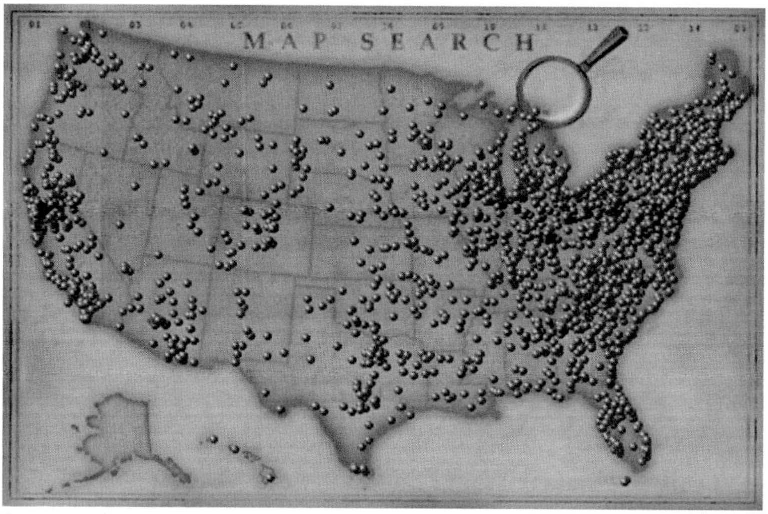

Discover books about the town where you grew up, the cities where your friends and families live, the town where your parents met, or even that retirement spot you've been dreaming about. Our Web site provides history lovers with exclusive deals, advanced notification about new titles, e-mail alerts of author events, and much more.

MADE IN THE USA

Arcadia Publishing, the leading local history publisher in the United States, is committed to making history accessible and meaningful through publishing books that celebrate and preserve the heritage of America's people and places. Consistent with our mission to preserve history on a local level, this book was printed in South Carolina on American-made paper and manufactured entirely in the United States.

This book carries the accredited Forest Stewardship Council (FSC) label and is printed on 100 percent FSC-certified paper. Products carrying the FSC label are independently certified to assure consumers that they come from forests that are managed to meet the social, economic, and ecological needs of present and future generations.

FSC
Mixed Sources
Product group from well-managed forests and other controlled sources

Cert no. SW-COC-001530
www.fsc.org
© 1996 Forest Stewardship Council